Greenhill Books

NAPOLEON IN THE HOLY LAND

'We have committed in the Holy Land enormous sins and great
stupidities; but it is necessary to let the curtain of the
tabernacle fall on all this, and let us beware of ever
raising it again, for fear that the Almighty,
in his wrath, will punish us for our temerity.'

General Kléber, 21 June 1799

NAPOLEON IN THE HOLY LAND

Nathan Schur

Greenhill Books, London
Stackpole Books, Pennsylvania

Dedicated to Naomi

Napoleon in the Holy Land
first published 1999 by Greenhill Books,
Lionel Leventhal Limited, Park House, 1 Russell Gardens,
London NW11 9NN
and
Stackpole Books, 5067 Ritter Road, Mechanicsburg, PA 17055, USA

British Library Cataloguing in Publication Data
Schur, Nathan
Napoleon in the Holy Land
1. Napoleon, I, Emperor of the French, 1769–1821 – Military leadership
2. Napoleonic Wars, 1800–1815 – Campaigns – Palestine
I. Title
940.2'7

ISBN 1–85367–345–5

Library of Congress Cataloging-in-Publication Data
Schur, Nathan.
Napoleon in the Holy Land / by Nathan Schur.
p.   cm.
Includes index.
ISBN 1-85367-345-5
1. Napoleon I, Emperor of the French, 1769–1821. 2. Second Coalition, War of the,
1798–1801—Campaigns—Middle East. 3. Acre (Israel)—History—Siege, 1799.
4. Palestine—History—1799–1917.
I. Title.
DC226.A15838   1999
940.2'7—dc21   98–43920
                                                              CIP

Typeset by DP Photosetting, Aylesbury, Bucks
Printed and bound in Great Britain by Creative Print and Design (Wales), Ebbw Vale

CONTENTS

LIST OF ILLUSTRATIONS

Illustrations (pages 129–144)

Maps

FOREWORD

No other figure in history has inspired so many books as Napoleon. The number of major articles and complete works is estimated at a quarter million, a truly staggering figure. Some of his campaigns and battles – and certainly his entanglements with the fair sex – have been covered in such detail, that one cannot but feel that every leaf of grass at Waterloo, for instance, has been trampled many times over by hordes of eager historians. And yet there still remain a few subjects which have not yet been treated adequately. One of these is Napoleon's activity on the island of Corsica during the years 1792 and 1793. The errors he committed there, and the setbacks he suffered, were of inestimable importance in forming his character. There he was taught the arts of war and politics in the best way possible: by making all the possible mistakes himself.

Another period of his life not yet adequately described is his Holy Land campaign in the spring of 1799. This is the first full length book in English on this subject. Usually this is called his 'Syrian' campaign, though actually he never entered Syria, as we now define it.

Most of his other campaigns come under one of two headings, 'successful' or 'unsuccessful', and can thus be read by Napoleon buffs as tragedies or comedies. Not so his Holy Land campaign. Beside his most severe early setback in the siege of Acre, we have here one of his greatest victories ever, at the battle of Mount Tabor. Never before or after was he to fight an enemy eight times larger than his own army, very rarely, if ever, had chances looked quite as desperate as they did at the beginning of this battle, and very rarely was he able to annihilate an enemy army as completely. And yet, in most descriptions published so far in European languages even the site of this battle has been wrongly identified, and without detailed knowledge of the terrain what actually happened becomes quite unintelligible.

Nor has the theatre of war in which this campaign took place, had the attention due to it. The part played by the near-independent district of Samaria in keeping Napoleon from controlling all of Palestine has never been properly

9

elucidated. The pivotal figure of Ahmed Djezzar is usually described as a quaint old pasha with a penchant for cutting his subjects' noses off, while actually he was probably one of the most formidable adversaries Napoleon was ever to meet.

While the names of the main actions are reasonably well known, even specialists might never have heard of the Battles of Gaza, Kakoon, Sedjera, Nazareth and that of the Bridge of Jacob's Daughters, nor of the siege of Safet, the capture of Tiberias or the sack of Jenin. And yet Napoleon's campaign in the Holy Land was not some exotic interlude without much bearing on the main themes of his life. He surely learned more from his defeat at Acre than from many of his victories. The meaning of sea power was demonstrated to him here more forcibly than in most of his other campaigns.

The worst stains on his good name are connected with events during his two short stays at Jaffa. His life was more often endangered during this campaign than in any of the others. Furthermore, this is one of the most colourful chapters in his life: extreme changes of fortune abound; there is a high incidence of military activity of all types – from pursuit of a beaten enemy, to retreat from a victorious one, from easy capture of one town to utter failure in front of another, with one sea battle, three major sieges and eight full scale land engagements fought in the short span of little more than three months.

Moreover, he engaged in a superabundance of administrative activity and political intrigue, creating a modern day equivalent to the Crusader Principality of Galilee, as well as managing far-flung diplomatic contacts reaching all the way to Persia and India. His relations with the local Jews have been taken to foreshadow the Balfour Declaration and the establishment of the state of Israel.

Therefore it is high time to give serious attention to Napoleon's Holy Land campaign, and this is what is attempted in the following pages.

This has become possible mainly by specialized research carried out chiefly in Israel in recent years. The background of 18th century Palestine has been clarified especially by Professor Amnon Cohen in his *Palestine in the 18th Century*. Over the last thirty years Professor Mordechai Gichon has published a series of articles which throw much new light on various phases of Napoleon's campaign and reinterpret the meaning of his main battles and sieges. But as most of them are in Hebrew, even European specialists in this field are not yet fully aware of how different Napoleon's campaign actually was from the descriptions published so far in the languages accessible to them. Further material can be found in other Hebrew and Arabic publications of recent years.

Some of the main works consulted here will be found in the bibliography at the end of the volume. The present author has had the opportunity to deal with this subject in separate chapters in three books: *History of Safet* (1983), *History of Acre* (1990) and 'History of Jaffa' (ms). Here the sieges of Acre and Jaffa and the battles in Upper Galilee are treated at some length, and full details of sources have been given for each statement made.

In the present book several terms have been used that warrant explanation. The hero of the story is called throughout 'Napoleon' and not General Bonaparte, as he still was in 1799, or 'Buonaparte' as he was called by his British antagonists who apparently believed that there was something derogatory in spelling his name the Italian way.

His enemies are here termed 'Turks' throughout, though actually he was opposed by Albanians, Arabs, Bosnians, Mameluks, Moroccans and Sudanese. These terms are of more consequence today, however, than they were then, before nationalism reached its later popularity. When our sources speak of 'Arabs', for instance, they usually mean 'Beduins'. Arabs as a term for a national unit, is much more recent than 1799 and has therefore not been used.

The central district of Palestine has usually been termed 'Samaria', though to its inhabitants it was then 'Jebel Nablus'. But 'Samaria' means perhaps more to the English speaking reader. Also other geographical names have usually been given in the form best known to present day Europeans.

ACKNOWLEDGEMENTS

I am grateful to my wife for typing the manuscript of this book; to Mr J. Segall for having manfully tried to correct my English; to Professor Mordechai Gichon for his help on various Napoleonic subjects; to Dr Ben Weider, President of the International Napoleonic Society, for his help in getting this book published; to Colonel John Elting for his advice; to the editor, Gerald Napier; and to Jonathan North at Greenhill Books.

Nathan Schur, 1999

Chronological Table

1775–1804	Djezzar rules in Acre
19 May 1798	Napoleon leaves Toulon for Egypt
23 December 1798	General Lagrange is sent to reconnoitre the northern coast of the Sinai Peninsula
17 January 1799	The fortifications of Katia are completed
6 February	General Reynier's division leaves Katia for El-Arish
14–15 February	Battle of El-Arish (Reynier)
20 February	Capture of El-Arish
22 February	The French enter the Holy Land
24 February	Battle of Gaza
1 March	The French reach Ramle
2 March	Some French troops come within three miles of Jerusalem
3–7 March	Siege of Jaffa
7/8 March	Pillage of Jaffa and massacre of many of its inhabitants
8 March	General Damas is repulsed near Kalkilia
8 March	800 prisoners of war massacred
9 March	600 prisoners of war massacred
10 March	1041 prisoners of war massacred
11 March	Napoleon visits the plague-sufferers in the Armenian monastery of Jaffa
15 March	Battle of Kakoon
15 March	Sir Sidney Smith reaches Acre
17 March	The French reach Haifa
18 March	Captain Standelet defeated by British and six of his ships captured
19 March – 21 May	Siege of Acre
28 March	First French assault repulsed
31 March	Junot occupies Nazareth
31 March	Murat captures Safet

1 April	Murat reaches the River Jordan
3 April	Vial reaches Tyre
6 April	Sheikh Abbas occupies Safet (but not the citadel)
8 April	Battle of Lubya (Junot) (Napleon's 'Battle of Nazareth')
15 April	Murat defeats Sheikh Abbas at the Bridge of Jacob's Daughters
16 April	Murat occupies Tiberias
16 April	Battle of Mount Tabor
17 April	Napoleon in Nazareth
27 April	Death of Caffarelli
1 May	Death of Phelipeaux
7 May	Turkish relief force approaches Acre
8–10 May	Second French main assault at Acre repulsed
20/21 May	French retreat from Acre
24–28 May	Back in Jaffa
30 May	Back in Gaza
1 June	The French leave the Holy Land
2 June	They reach El-Arish
14 June	Return to Cairo
23 August	Napoleon leaves Egypt
9 November	Napoleon becomes master of France
27 June 1801	The French army in Egypt capitulates

BIOGRAPHIES OF LEADING PERSONALITIES

Ahmed 'Djezzar' (died 1804)
He was born in Bosnia and sold by an Istanbul slave trader to Ali Bey, the ruler of Egypt, in whose service he served as executioner (hence his by-name, which means 'butcher'). He served later as Turkish aga, defended (unsuccessfully) the port of Beirut, and in 1775 was appointed governor of the province of Saida, with his seat in Acre. Though all other governors were exchanged after one year, he held on to this appointment for nearly 30 years, with the aid of threats, bribes and intrigues. He organized an armed force of his own and suppressed its revolt in 1789. He was famed for his cruelty. Several times he also served as governor of the Damascene province. He reached his full stature as a military commander in 1799, in his epic defence of Acre against Napoleon. Though an old man by then, he made the young Napoleon look like a rank amateur in siege warfare several times, while he himself came up with such revolutionary concepts as letting the French into Acre on purpose, in order to annihilate their forces there piecemeal. After Napoleon's withdrawal, Djezzar's position was much strengthened, he captured Jaffa by force and the Turkish government could no longer remove him, even when it wanted to. Apart from his military abilities, he was also a gifted architect.

Beauharnais, Eugène de (1781–1824)
The son of Josephine by her previous husband, he served as adjutant to Napoleon in Palestine. In Jaffa he accepted the surrender of the prisoners who were later executed. He suffered a head-injury during the siege of Acre, and returned with Napoleon to France. He became an imperial prince in 1804 and Viceroy of Italy in 1805, married a Bavarian princess, and served quite successfully as Commander in Chief in Italy in 1809 and 1813–14. He did not join Napoleon in the '100 days'. He became Duke of Leuchtenberg (in Bavaria) and of Eichstadt, and died in 1824. His sons, daughters and grandchildren married,

17

throughout the 19th century various Swedish, Portuguese, Russian and Brazilian kings, queens and emperors.

Berthier, Louis Alexandre (1753–1815)
He served in the royal French Army as an officer, participated in the American War of Independence, and was chief staff officer of various units from 1794 onward. He was Napoleon's chief of staff throughout his career, including the Holy Land campaign. Many of the orders quoted in the appendix to this book are signed by him. Later he was appointed a marshal and became Duke of Neufchâtel and Prince of Wagram. He committed suicide in 1815, apparently out of remorse for not joining Napoleon in the '100 days'.

Louis André Bon (died 1799)
A general of division who was born in the Dauphinée, he served in the Army of the Eastern Pyrenees and, later, in the Army of Italy. In the Holy Land campaign he served throughout as a divisional commander. He was rather fat and somewhat slow, and Napoleon often preferred to keep his division in reserve. Still, his men entered Jaffa from the north, when they were not even required to do so. He was mortally wounded during the final assault on Acre.

Caffarelli du Falga, Louis Maria Joseph Maximilien (1756–1799)
A general of brigade who commanded the sappers in the French force. He had been wounded in 1795 and lost his leg, which was replaced by a wooden stump. He was a member of the 'Institut d'Egypte'. He played an important part in the siege of Acre, but had his right arm smashed by a bullet on 9 April and died on 27 April. His body was recovered by modern Israeli archaeologists and returned to France for burial.

Daher al-Umar (1688–1755)
A Beduin sheikh who ruled Galilee during much of the 18th century and rebuilt Acre. After he was driven out and killed, Djezzar fought some of his descendants and had his son Ali killed, but others survived and were immediately ready to cooperate with Napoleon against Djezzar. His son Sheikh Abbas al-Daher was appointed by Napoleon to serve as governor of Tiberias.

Desgenettes, René Nicolas Dufiche (1762–1837)
Originally he was Baron Des Genettes, but changed his name as a tribute to the egalitarian spirit of the time. He was the chief physician of the expedition.

18

His great moment came when he inoculated himself with bubonic contagion in Jaffa, in order to demonstrate to the soldiers that this was not the plague. Later he fell out with Napoleon, as he refused to help kill some of the plague cases, and his career was, as a result, cut short. His book *Histoire Médicale de l'Armée d'Orient*, Paris 1835, is still of great interest.

Dommartin, Elzéar Auguste Cousin de (1768–1799)
A general of division who commanded the French artillery. At the siege of Acre he was severely handicapped by most of his cannon having been captured by the British navy. He headed the group of French officers who opposed Napoleon's plans for an 'Eastern Adventure'. He was wounded in a local uprising in Egypt, and died of tetanus poisoning on 9 July 1799.

Farhi, Haim (died 1820)
Djezzar's Jewish secretary and banker, Farhi was a scion of the Jewish banking family in Damascus, who each year had to finance the *hadj* to Mecca. He was brought to Acre when Djezzar served also as governor of Damascus. He looked after Djezzar's finances and wrote his diplomatic letters to Istanbul. This did not save him from Djezzar's cruelty and because of unfounded suspicions he had his nose and one ear cut off and an eye gouged out. Still, he continued to serve his master and was of great help as administrative assistant throughout Napoleon's siege of Acre. After Djezzar's death (1804) Farhi helped Soliman Pasha to wrest the governorship of Acre from a competitor. Soliman was peaceful and not very active, and Farhi ran most of the aspects of the government in Palestine from 1805 to 1818 – the first Jew to hold such a position of power in the Holy Land for 1500 years. After 1818 he helped young Abdalla to power in Acre, but was murdered on Abdalla's orders in 1820.

Ganteaume, Captain Honoré Joseph Antoine (1755–1818)
He commanded the French navy in the eastern Mediterranean, after Rear Admiral Perrée had left for France (against Napoleon's wishes). Napoleon advanced him to rear admiral (7 November 1798), and in August 1799 he commanded the vessel which returned Napoleon to France.

Junot, Andoche (1771–1813)
Born in Strasbourg. He became a personal friend of Napoleon, when still a sergeant at the siege of Toulon, and was advanced by him in rank in Italy

and Egypt (where he served as his adjutant) up to general of brigade. In Palestine he captured Nazareth on 31 March, and defeated a large Turkish force near Lubya on 8 April (Napoleon referred to this as the 'Battle of Nazareth'). He commanded a brigade at the Battle of Mount Tabor, 16 April. Later he was advanced further in rank, but when he was defeated in 1807 in Portugal, he failed to get his marshal's baton. Still, he became Duc d'Abrantes (Napoleon originally wanted to make him 'Duke of Nazareth'), participated in the Russian campaign, and served as governor of Illyria. He committed suicide in 1813. His wife, the Duchess of Abrantes, published many volumes of memoirs, which are some of the least reliable of the Napoleonic era.

Kléber, Jean-Baptiste (1753–1800)
Born in Strasbourg. He commanded forces in the Vendée and in the Army of the Sambre and Meuse. He was the senior divisional commander in Palestine, and participated in the battles of El-Arish, Gaza and Kakoon and the sieges of El-Arish, Jaffa and Acre, but is mainly famous for his part in the battle of Mount Tabor. When Napoleon left for France, he nominated Kléber as his successor in the command. Kléber negotiated an armistice with Sir Sidney Smith, but when it was not ratified by the British, he defeated, with his 10,000 men, the Turkish army of 70,000 at the battle of Heliopolis on 20 May 1800, and recaptured Egypt. He was assassinated by an Arab fanatic from Jerusalem on 14 June 1800.

Lannes, Jean (1769–1809)
He commanded a brigade in Italy and was advanced to the command of a division with the commencement of the Holy Land campaign. He participated in the various battles (except for Mount Tabor), headed the decisive assault on Jaffa and was severely wounded at the last attack on Acre. Later on he was one of Napoleon's most successful battle commanders, became a marshal and was appointed Duke of Montebello. He was killed at the battle of Essling, in Austria, in 1809. His widow became the main confidante of Empress Maria Louise.

Larrey, Dominique Jean (1766–1842)
Surgeon-in-chief of Napoleon's numerous campaigns, including the one to the Holy Land. He was a member of the 'Institut d'Egypte'. He was later created a baron and continued to serve as chief surgeon at the battle of Waterloo. In

1842 he was sent on a mission of inspection of the medical services during the French occupation of Algiers.

Murat, Joachim (1767–1815)

Murat helped Napoleon decisively in the suppression of the Vendémiaire revolt in Paris in 1795, by obtaining the essential artillery. He commanded the cavalry in the Holy Land campaign, captured Safet twice and Tiberias once, and won the battle of the Bridge of Jacob's Daughters. Later he commanded the cavalry in Napoleon's great campaigns, married Napoleon's sister Caroline, became a marshal, was appointed Grand Duke of Cleve and Berg, and was later crowned King of Naples. In 1815 he opened the hostilities which led to Waterloo, and was executed by firing squad when he tried to return to Naples.

Napoleon Bonaparte (1769–1821)

As a young man he attended French army schools and specialized in artillery. In 1791–92 he tried unsuccessfully to make his mark in his native island of Corsica, but in 1793 he took a decisive part in the capture of Toulon. He rose to brigadier general and chief of staff of the Army of Italy, and subdued royalist revolt in Paris in Vendémiaire 1795. Under his command (1796–97) the Army of Italy defeated Austria decisively. He came to Egypt mainly in order to remain in the public eye (1798), and organized and commanded the campaign in Palestine in the spring of 1799. After his return to Egypt, he defeated the British–Turkish invasion at Aboukir, before returning to France in August 1799. On 18 Brumaire he took over the rule of France, as First Consul (1799–1804) and as Emperor (1804–1814). In the great campaigns of 1803–06 he conquered most of Europe, although Great Britain continued to rule the ocean. He still won his 1809 campaign against Austria, but was not successful in Spain and was defeated in Russia in 1812, in Germany in 1813 and in France in 1814. On his return from exile in Elba, he was defeated at Waterloo in 1815 and exiled to St Helena, where he spent the last six years of his life.

Phelipeaux, Louis Edmond de Picard de (1768–1799)

He studied with Napoleon at the Ecole Militaire de Brienne, where they are said to have disliked each other. As an aristocrat he left France in 1791, and served in Condé's emigré army. He was arrested, escaped and also helped Sir Sidney Smith to escape, going with him to the Mediterranean. He served in Acre as adviser to Djezzar, and proved his worth especially in the utilization of the French guns which had been captured from Napoleon's ships. He died on 1 May.

Reynier, Jean Louis Ebenézer (1771–1814)
A general of division who hailed from Lausanne, he participated in the conquest of Holland and served as chief of staff to General Moreau. He defeated the Mameluks in Egypt at El-Kanka (5 August 1798), won the battle of El-Arish (20 February 1799) and commanded one of Napoleon's four divisions throughout the campaign in the Holy Land. He was a member of the 'Institut d'Egypte' (for political economy). He was later less successful in Europe, was defeated at Maida in Calabria in 1806, but commanded a corps in 1813 and was captured at the battle of Leipzig.

Selim III (born 1762), Sultan of Turkey 1789–1808
He was helped by the French in building the defences of the Bosporus, but he declared war on France when Napoleon invaded Egypt in 1798. His authority was ultimately involved in Djezzar's defence of Acre, and the attack of the Pasha of Damascus which was defeated at the Battle of Mount Tabor. Another of his armies was defeated by Napoleon at Aboukir and another, after Napoleon had left, by Kléber at the Battle of Heliopolis. In Turkish history Selim is regarded as the first of the reforming sultans.

Smith, Sir William Sidney (1764–1840)
A British naval officer (commodore) who served for some time in Sweden where he obtained his patent of aristocracy. When Toulon fell to the French he was left behind to sink the ships in the harbour. Later he was imprisoned in Paris, but was rescued by Phelipeaux. In 1799 Nelson sent him to help Djezzar, and his arrival on 15 March at Acre may have been what induced Djezzar to stay and fight. Smith's part in the defence of Acre was most important. His marines manned the captured French guns and he intervened on shore when the occasion demanded it. Later he negotiated a settlement with Kléber, which was not, however, ratified by the British government.

Tippoo Sahib (1753–1799)
The Sultan of Mysore who revolted against the British in 1782. He exchanged envoys with Napoleon, with a view to inducing him to extend his expedition to India. This was one of the reasons for the latter's Holy Land campaign. However the British were quicker: they captured Mysore in 1799, and killed Tippoo.

Vial, H. (1766–1813)

A brigade general who commanded the provinces of Damietta and Mansura in Egypt, in 1798. He commanded a brigade in Palestine. He captured the city of Tyre, in present day Lebanon, on 3 April 1799. No French force reached any further north than this during the Holy Land campaign.

1

THE CURTAIN RISES

All through history the Holy Land has been a land of transit. Here passed the route from Africa to Asia and on to Europe. Therefore many great conquerors of the past marched this way during their wars. Thutmosis III, the greatest conqueror of Egyptian history and king of Egypt from 1504 to 1450 BC, occupied the country on his way to Syria and near Meggido won his most famous victory.

Some of the great Assyrian warrior-kings, such as Tiglath Pilesar III (745–727 BC) and Sanherib (Sennacherib) (704–681 BC) conquered great parts of the Land of Canaan in their campaigns.

Alexander the Great, most famous among the conquerors of ancient times, passed through in 332 BC and destroyed the towns of Acre and Gaza. The Roman Pompey occupied Palestine in 63 BC. The greatest of Roman commanders, Julius Caesar, visited Acre in 47 BC. The great leaders of the armies of Islam conquered Palestine between 634 and 640 AD. The Christians reacted when Tancred and the other leaders of the First Crusade conquered Jerusalem in 1099. One of the greatest Turkish captains, Sultan Selim I, took Palestine from the Mameluks in 1516. And in 1799, the greatest of the conquerors of modern times, Napoleon Bonaparte, campaigned here.

He was then just 30 years old, fresh from the triumphs of his Italian campaign of 1796–97. After years of desperate struggles it was he who finally brought peace, and a victorious peace at that, to war weary France. As a result, no other French commander could compete with his popularity. Some of his intimates suggested that he should grasp the reins of government in his own hands. While not averse to the idea itself, Napoleon – or, as he still was then, General Bonaparte – thought that the time was not yet ripe for this. His problem was, however, that he dared not rest on his laurels, as otherwise he might be quickly forgotten by the fickle public. To stay in the limelight he had to find another triumphal campaign to fight.

First he considered the possibility of leading an invasion to England, which was now the only country still at war with France. But after he had inspected the preparations already made, he decided that the chances of success were too slim in view of the absolute supremacy of the British fleet in the Atlantic Ocean and the adjacent seas.

Next he considered the possibility of an invasion of Egypt. This, too, was a naval operation, but at that stage the struggle for supremacy in the Mediterranean had not yet been decided. A strong and, for the time being, unopposed, French fleet was based on Toulon. The idea of occupying Egypt was not a new one. In the 18th century France enjoyed a privileged position in the Levant trade. French merchants were stationed in the main areas of the Middle East and almost monopolised the trade with Europe. But at the end of that century their standing was badly shaken because of the spreading anarchy in Egypt in one hand, and because of conflicts with the Governor of Acre, Ahmed Djezzar, on the other. Therefore several secret projects were discussed in French government circles during the last quarter of the 18th century, concerning the possibility of a military occupation of Egypt. It was feared that if France would not act, her great rival, England, would. But, at this late stage of its existence, the Bourbon regime lacked the willpower and the financial means to carry out such projects. With the advent of the French Revolution this situation changed completely. The French Consul in Cairo, Magallon, visited Paris in 1797–98 and described Egypt to the members of the Directory as a fruit ready to be plucked. Again, he stressed the danger that if France would not undertake such an operation, England might. To her Egypt would be a station on her way to India. The new French Minister of foreign affairs, Talleyrand, was ready to accept these arguments and Napoleon, too, now supported the idea of an invasion of Egypt to be led by himself. Objectively regarded, there seemed little reason to rush immediately from one long and difficult war, which had just been successfully ended, into a new armed conflict, which can hardly be described as really essential. But the real motive behind this new venture had little to do with foreign policy. To Napoleon, as pointed out already, it was essential to head a new military campaign, in order to rivet the eyes of the public on his progress. The romantic East seemed just the place where easy success could be gained at no great cost. The Directory, too, had its own political reasons for embarking on this adventure: the young and all too ambitious Napoleon should best be employed as far away from France as possible, so that he would not be able to take part in any move to overthrow the regime. Thus the invasion of Egypt was decided upon, perhaps mainly because of French internal politics.[1]

Egypt was then under Turkish rule and France was not in a state of war with

Turkey. However neither Talleyrand, nor Napoleon, thought this to be very important, as the Ottoman rule in Egypt was only nominal. The real rulers of the country were a few Mameluk Emirs. Mameluk means 'white slave' in Arabic. The Mameluks were indeed in their youth purchased as such, mainly in the Caucasus and in the Balkans, and brought to Egypt, where they were raised in the army and at the court of the local rulers, who were Mameluks themselves. The most gifted and ruthless among them rose to positions of influence, both in the army and, at the same time, in the administration. The Mameluks had been the rulers of the country after the Crusades, but had to accept the Ottoman rule in 1516. Only in the 18th century were they able to get the reins of power into their hands again. In the last third of that century there were periods when they no longer recognised Turkey's suzerainty over Egypt, even nominally. Thus Napoleon intended to legitimize his conquest by representing it as an effort to return the Land of the Nile to its proper ruler, the Turkish Sultan.

In actual fact the operation was intended to further France's interests in her struggle with Great Britain. The occupation of Egypt was to put into French hands a shorter way to India than the long English one, around the Cape of Good Hope.

During the 18th century the British had defeated the French in both main areas of colonial expansion, in North America and in India. Napoleon hoped now to revoke this verdict of history by occupying Egypt and turning it into a French colony, thus threatening the long British imperial supply lines to India.

British policy was not usually dictated from London. Local leaders were expected to reach their own decisions. This policy had proved very successful under Clive and Hastings in India and under Wolfe in Canada. In Napoleon's day it was commanders like Nelson and Sidney Smith who crossed his path and eventually defeated his plans without any detailed plans from the British government.

In France matters were handled differently. The central government, both before and after the Revolution, decided on policy and initiated campaigns. Thus Talleyrand was supposed to leave for Istanbul in an effort to convince the Porte that the French invasion of Egypt was in her own best interest. But in the end he decided that prudence would be the better part of valour and stayed in Paris, without even advising Napoleon of his change of plan.

In the meantime, Napoleon had sailed in May 1798 from Toulon with his squadron of some 400 ships and his expeditionary force of more than 30,000 men. On the way Malta was occupied, and about a tenth of the troops were left there as a garrison. The rest of the force sailed on to Egypt and landed near Alexandria, which was captured on 2 July 1798. Napoleon continued southward and occupied Cairo, after having decisively defeated the Mameluk army. But the Mameluks were not completely annihilated and continued to control large parts of Upper (i.e. southern) Egypt, while the French army was in control of the great centres of Lower (i.e. northern) Egypt.

A decisive blow was dealt Napoleon's great scheme when Nelson destroyed the French fleet at anchor in Aboukir Bay, near Alexandria, on 1 August. This battle had the gravest of consequences for France: at one stroke the Mediterranean was turned into an English lake. This influenced the Porte as well and in the absence of any diplomatic effort from Talleyrand, Turkey declared war on France and started to concentrate forces for a counter invasion of Egypt.

Napoleon's high hopes for the creation of a new French colonial empire were thus dashed on the hard rock of British naval supremacy. The fate of the French expeditionary force was actually decided at the very beginning, as it was now cut off from its homeland and had no hope of receiving supplies or reinforcements from there.

But Napoleon disregarded these facts. He organised the French rule in those parts of Egypt which were under his control, completely changed the administrative system and tried to introduce western ideas, management and techniques. In the end his effort was to fail and the French were to be evicted from Egypt after three years, but the short-lived French rule was to influence future developments greatly. The ease of the conquest of Egypt demonstrated the superiority of European arms and the western ways of administration introduced the inhabitants of the Levant to a new world. Thus his conquest opened the door to the rapid Europeanisation of the Middle East in the 19th and 20th centuries.

But to our story it is perhaps more important that Napoleon managed to create a secure base in Egypt, which served as a springboard for his Holy Land campaign early in 1799.

2

THE HOLY LAND IN 1799[1]

The Holy Land – or Palestine – had seen 282 years of Ottoman rule by 1799. In the 16th century there had been an Indian summer of firm Government and economic prosperity, but for the last two hundred years it had been a downward road, leading to political dissolution and economic ruin. Strong, active, rulers in Istanbul were followed by weak sultans, controlled by harem favourites and eunuchs. The janissary army, which had previously defeated the best forces of Christendom, was now routed by all its adversaries and its strength was felt only in Court intrigues. The efficient tax structure which had previously supplied all the empire's financial needs, passed increasingly into the hands of tax farmers, who managed to line their own pockets with most of the money collected. The Ottoman system of government had been geared to constant expansion. It functioned less and less well when conquest first ground to a standstill and was later replaced by retreat from the frontiers and crisis at home. Security of roads and property, which had been the mainstay of a healthy economy in the 16th century, disappeared and was replaced by universal lawlessness, brigandage, economic decline and dissolution.

The strong government of the 16th century became weak and impotent. Local chieftains gathered into their hands the reins of government in their provinces. They still recognised the Sultan as their nominal superior, but ran matters increasingly without any regard to his wishes. The Porte was less and less able to impose its will and had to rule by intrigue and by inciting one local ruler against the other. Its main effort was directed not to more efficient rule, but to preventing the local strongmen from developing any firm and efficient rule themselves, which might have turned them into adversaries too powerful to cope with and thus endanger the balance of power within the empire.

The first such near-independent local ruler in Southern Lebanon and northern Palestine was the Druse Emir Fakhr-e-Din II, at the beginning of the 17th century. During the same century the rulers of Gaza and Samaria and the Terebei beduins on Mount Carmel and in the Valley of Jezreel also enjoyed an increasing measure of local independence. The situation became even more pronounced in the 18th century. By the end of that century, in the mountainous district of Samaria real authority was in the hands of the Tukan family, in Nablus (ancient Sichem), and of the Gerar family to the north, in Jenin. The heads of these families were to lead their men against Napoleon during his invasion. Similar families lorded it over the districts of Jerusalem, Hebron and Gaza.

The very concept of 'Palestine' as an administrative unit and a geographical entity existed neither in the Ottoman administration nor in the consciousness of the local Muslim population. Only the few Jews and some of the Christians, residents in the country, still regarded it as one unit and as the Holy Land of their religion. But even in the West, Palestine was regarded as part of Syria, and Napoleon's campaign there was (and still is) generally called his 'Syrian' campaign – though he never got beyond the limits of Palestine, or entered what we now term 'Syria'.

The most important near-independent ruler in Palestine in the 18th century was the beduin, Sheikh Daher al-Umar, who controlled the district of Galilee[2]. His family first ruled in the Tiberias area, (on the shores of Lake Genezareth), but he steadily extended his dominion westward and finally made Acre his seat of government. Before his time both Tiberias and Acre had been little more than heaps of rubble, having been destroyed by the Mameluks at the end of the Crusades. Daher rebuilt and fortified them. Saphet, the capital of central Galilee was also strengthened by him. As we shall see, all these little towns had a role to play in Napoleon's forthcoming campaign. Daher's closest allies were the French traders, who had their seat in Acre and could now, under his strong rule, buy up more easily the cotton grown in Galilee, which constituted their main export to Marseille and to all of Europe. In return they supplied him with money and arms, which enabled him to successfully fight his many enemies. Under his rule northern Palestine prospered again, agriculture was extended and trade was renewed. New inhabitants moved to his dominions: Jews from Smyrna settled in Tiberias, which had been an important Jewish centre both in the times of the Talmud and again in the 16th century. A further wave of Jewish immigration, this time from Eastern Europe, started arriving in 1777 and settled both in Saphet and Tiberias.

However Ottoman authorities did not regard Sheikh Daher's activities, however beneficial to the areas under his rule, with any degree of goodwill. Between 1770 and 1775 repeated efforts were made by the Turks to oust the old Sheikh and to restore direct rule over his dominions. Two expeditions were mounted from semi-independent Egypt, one by Daher's ally, Ali Bey, and the

The Holy Land in 1799

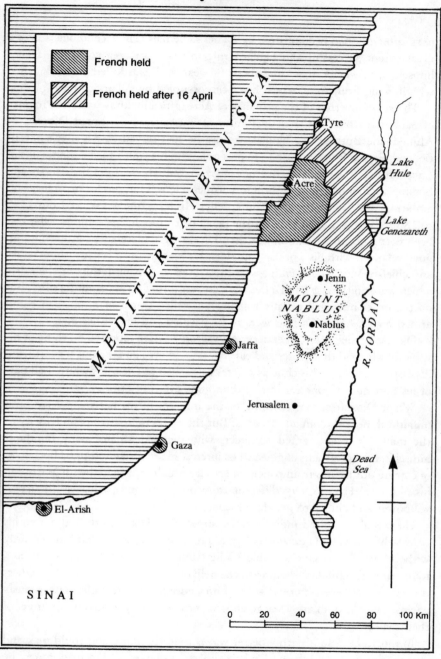

French held

French held after 16 April

MEDITERRANEAN SEA

Tyre

Lake Hule

Acre

Lake Genezareth

Jenin

MOUNT NABLUS

Nablus

R. JORDAN

Jaffa

Jerusalem

Gaza

Dead Sea

El-Arish

SINAI

0   20   40   60   80   100 Km

next, after Aly had been ousted, by Daher's enemies. The second one was to a great extent successful and Daher's rule in the coast area collapsed. Daher himself, who was by that time about 87 years old, was killed in 1775, when withdrawing from Acre, which had been occupied by a Turkish fleet.

The new Governor of the province of Acre (officially known as the Province of Saida) was one of the main figures of our narrative, Ahmed Djezzar, or Ahmed 'the Butcher', so named because he had served as Aly Bey's executioner.[3] He was born in Bosnia, sold as a slave in his youth to the Mameluks of Egypt, rose to the office of governor of Cairo, but left the Egyptian service and became a senior officer in the Sultan's armies. He was famous for his ability and ambition, and even more so for his cruelty. His long rule in Galilee from 1775 to 1804 was less outstanding for the benefits it brought his subjects, who had been better off under Daher, but then Djezzar was more adept at keeping up good relations with his Turkish superiors. He was aided by his Jewish secretary and chief banker, Haim Farhi, who specialised in writing letters to the Porte which were on the one hand a model of correct form and apparent servility, but on the other managed usually to convey a veiled threat of disobedience and armed revolt, unless Djezzar were to be pacified and his wishes met.

Djezzar's cruelty was legendary. All visitors of Acre reported on those of his subjects who had their noses and ears cut off and eyes gouged out for incurring his displeasure. Even his close associate, Farhi, had at Djezzar's whim, had part of his nose cut off, one ear removed and one eye torn out.

When Djezzar suspected some of the inmates of his harem to have been unfaithful, he had them all executed. But there was more than plain ferocity to the man. He was a gifted architect, who planned all his many buildings himself, and a proficient engineer. His interest in art is attested to by his hobby of cutting out figures from paper, an activity usually associated with Matisse in his old age.[4] He was very different from other oriental pashas in his strong willpower and ability to get things done.

He was also a gifted military tactician, as Napoleon was to find out to his cost. When in 1789 Djezzar's bodyguard revolted and he was left momentarily without armed forces, he was able, by his cunning and power of quick decision, to defeat and annihilate them with the help of the citizens of Acre. His soldiers thereafter were even more afraid of him and preferred to fight courageously against Napoleon, in order not to endanger their lives by incurring the anger of their master.

In return he paid his army better wages than the Porte and could pick and choose the best soldiers and commanders available. The armed forces he controlled were thus of higher quality than those usually met with in the Middle East.

Above all he valued his independence. Just as ferociously as he fought Napoleon, he fended off any attempt by Turkish authorities to interfere in his domains. He did not allow Turkish levies, who were not under his personal control, to enter his fortress Acre and, as we shall see, kept to this principle even when Napoleon's siege was at its height.

Napoleon had no correct appreciation of his antagonist's ability and power. His first mistake was perhaps in attacking head-on the strongpoint of Acre, as main target of his campaign. But it is true that Napoleon first tried to reach some arrangement Djezzar. In August 1798 he sent an officer with a personal letter to him, in which he suggested a treaty of friendship and closer commercial relations. But Napoleon had no Farhi in his chancery and his letter was too self-confident and not sufficiently polite. Djezzar read the letter but would not talk to the bearer.

A second French officer on a diplomatic mission, a Captain Mailly de Châteaurenaud, was imprisoned by him and later executed at the beginning of the siege of Acre.

Turkish authorities were better able to appreciate Djezzar's importance in the coming struggle. In August 1798 they nominated him as commander in chief (Seraskar) of all the Turkish forces being concentrated against Napoleon in the coastal region of Palestine.

From the moment the French invasion of Egypt became known, there was rising excitement among the Muslim population of Palestine. Evidence of this has survived in the archives of the Court of Law (the Sijil of the Shari'a court) of Jerusalem.[5] In July 1798 the notables of Jerusalem asked the Pasha of Damascus for weapons. The Muslim population did not await his answer but attacked the Christian monasteries in Jerusalem and plundered them. The local authorities apprehended the 52 monks living in the town, partly so as to save them from the mob and partly so that they could serve as hostages on the approach of the French. When it became clear that Napoleon was about to invade Palestine, local inhabitants in Jerusalem were mobilised and attached to the regular forces. A letter was sent by Napoleon to the rulers of Jerusalem, who, apparently, did not report the matter to their superiors in Damascus and were later reprimanded for this. Perhaps they expected a French advance toward Jerusalem and were not altogether averse to negotiations with Napoleon. Had he attacked Jerusalem, he might not have encountered the same unyielding resistance as in Djezzar's Acre. Had he decided in favour of a line of advance northward through the mountainous interior of the country, he would have been able to keep at a safe distance from the British fleet, but, as we shall see, would have met with fierce resistance in the district of Samaria.

3

NAPOLEON'S PLANS AND PREPARATIONS

Two different explanations exist for Napoleon's Holy Land campaign. One was put forward by himself and tries to represent it as a latter day oriental expedition in the style of Alexander the Great, with India as its ultimate goal and the overthrow of British rule there as its object. Throughout his life, and especially in the memoirs he dictated on St Helena, Napoleon claimed this to have been his true aim. But these claims have received rather mixed reviews by later critics, who regarded them as efforts by Napoleon, after the event, to refurbish and romanticize his image, without sufficient foundation in fact.

And yet, already during the siege of Acre, the chief tailor of the expedition, Bernoyer, testified to rumours in the camp, that after the city had been taken, Napoleon intended to continue his conquests and to crown himself 'King of Persia'.[1] Some of the French generals, and especially Dommartin, the artillery commander, were supposed to be opposed to the seizure of Acre for this very reason. Bernoyer reports also that three quarters of the generals were initially opposed to the campaign, but only one of them (General Lagrange) dared to express his opposition in a council of war Napoleon convened before its start: 'In my opinion it is both more prudent and more sure to await the enemy when he comes out of the desert; there all the advantage is on our side.'[2]

Napoleon's old comrade, Marshal Marmont, who in 1814 deserted his cause and became his worst enemy and critic, substantially supports his story.[3] According to him, Napoleon planned to fill up the rather meagre numbers of his expeditionary force by enlisting – in Palestine and Lebanon – members of warlike minorities, like Druses, Maronites, Matuwellis, and at the head of his thus enlarged army he planned to establish a new empire of his own on the ruins of the Ottoman state. According to Marmont he intended to cut loose from the French fatherland and to embark on an Alexander-like expedition eastwards. It does not make sense to claim that Marmont, of all people, was trying to embellish Napoleon's name and it seems more likely that there was, after all, quite a bit of truth in these claims. Fantastic though they may sound, they seem to have been believed by the commanders of the British fleet, who felt that at Acre they were defending British India. There was, indeed, in Napoleon's mental make-up a romantic and slightly fantastic element, which did not flower fully under Europe's pale skies, but stretched its wings under the strong sun of the East. There was in him a tendency toward the irrational and demonic, an urge to overcome seemingly insuperable difficulties, which reminds one of Alexander the Great and his Achilles complex.[4] But his very failure in the Holy Land taught Napoleon to control these tendencies during parts of his later career.

The second explanation as to the reasons for the campaign comes from modern historians, who usually disregard these motives and explain Napoleon's expedition as a preventive strike to knock out the Turkish forces which were massing in order to attack the Egyptian base.[5] Though there is undoubted truth in this argument, it could be claimed that the best way to defend Egypt would have been to do so behind the desert barrier which protects it to the east. Napoleon himself, years later on St Helena, put these arguments very forcibly:[6]

'In all times commanders ... who wanted to invade Egypt had to regard the desert as a formidable obstacle ... In order to overcome it, an army has to advance slowly, while it establishes supplies in El Arish, Katia and Salahya ... These measures take however time and enable the enemy to prepare his defences.

'In the summer the march through the desert is a difficult and exhausting task. The heat of the sand, the lack of water, and the absence of any shade can annihilate a complete army. ... It is clear how important a strongpoint like El Arish can prove to be ... Even after it is captured, many weeks would be needed to bring sufficient supplies forward to enable the enemy to undertake the next siege, that of Katia ... Afterwards the army cannot leave Katia before preparing there great stores, which have to serve the further march to Salahya. This army would be so tired out by the march through the desert from Katia to Salahya that it could be beaten by a much smaller force. If it is beaten before reaching Cairo it has but one route of retreat and will be hindered by the enormous number of camels needed for carrying water. If any army is defeated in the desert it has to retreat all the way to Gaza ...

'Undoubtedly such a desert is the greatest of all obstacles which can serve a country in the defence of its borders.'

Very strong personal motives were needed to override these considerations.

That Napoleon was indeed thinking of a protracted expedition is indicated by the fact that he took with him to Palestine some of the civilian members of the scientific mission which had originally accompanied him to Egypt. Their presence would only be an obstacle if he was thinking solely in terms of a short, preventive military campaign. Further, just two weeks before he left on his Holy Land adventure he tried to establish contact with Tippoo Sahib, one of the few Indian princes who had not yet accepted British suzerainty.

But in a letter to the Directory Napoleon did indeed explain the reasons for his campaign in much more moderate terms. Three causes were spelled out there:[7]

- To safeguard French rule in Egypt by striking down the gathering forces beyond her borders.
- To force the Porte to peace negotiations with France.
- To prevent the British fleet from utilizing the ports of Palestine.

Compared with Napoleon's later claims these goals sound common sense, if rather prosaic, and have gained wide acceptance among historians. However perhaps we should regard them as his minimum aims, whilst secretly he hoped to do much better than that.

It is, however, possible to explain his aims also in a different way, stemming from his personality and experience. Ever since his invasion of Egypt there had been talks going on between the British and the Turks as to how to evict Napoleon from the Land of the Nile. Two Turkish task forces were being formed, one on the island of Rhodes, from where it was to be transferred to Egypt with the help of an English fleet and the second around Damascus, from where it was to proceed by land to Egypt. Together this amounted to a giant pincer movement, which probably was much too ambitious for the level of planning and staff work the Ottoman armies had attained (or reverted to) at that time. The correct response would probably have been to await both attacks in Egypt, where Napoleon, in possession of interior lines, could probably have defeated them without great effort. The later battles of Mount Tabor and of Aboukir, in which he did defeat and annihilate both these forces, show that this would have been an easy task for the experienced French army and did not necessitate the perilous and costly Palestinian campaign. However Napoleon's gut-reaction to this threat was apparently different and less cool-headed. In the later stages of his Italian campaign he had experienced a somewhat similar situation. No less than four times was he faced with a strategic Austrian offensive, every time split into two forces, which usually advanced southward on both sides of Lake Garda. In every case Napoleon took the tactical offensive and each time defeated one of these pincer arms before it could unite with the other against him. His sudden and not very well prepared invasion of Palestine can thus be explained as an identical reaction to a situation, though on a much vaster scale than that which he had faced several times before. He intended instinctively to destroy one of the arms of the pincer before both could close on him, perhaps without taking into account sufficiently the vast difference both in performance between the Turkish and Austrian armies and in the nature of the two theatres of operation.

It can be argued that none of these reasons separately should have caused Napoleon to embark on what was basically an unnecessary, wasteful and highly dangerous campaign, for which he did not have sufficient forces and which very effectively enabled his British enemies to use their superior naval strength against him. Only the combined pressures and allures of these reasons and hopes can explain Napoleon's undertaking such an insufficiently thought out expedition. For many years the lesson learnt here kept Napoleon from embarking on similarly ill-considered adventures. But it was forgotten after the fantastic successes of his middle years and he committed similar mistakes of poor judgement: in embarking in 1808 on his Spanish adventure and in 1812 on his Russian campaign. It was to have fatal results for him.

Whatever his open or hidden reasons, by December 1798 Napoleon had decided on his Holy Land campaign. The necessary preparations were started right away. He estimated that the weather would prevent the British from carrying out the naval attack on Egypt from Rhodes before June 1799. Thus if a decisive victory which might topple the Ottoman empire eluded him, he had to be back in Egypt in good time to oppose this threat. Very accelerated staff work was needed in order to start the advance into Palestine in time. It was necessary to concentrate not only the soldiers, which was relatively easy, but also the required beasts of burden, which was much more difficult. Rations also had to be prepared, and this, in Napoleon's financial situation, was a very difficult task. Throughout the campaign the time factor was to remain a limiting element and resulted several times in hasty decisions which Napoleon lived to regret and which go a long way in explaining why the campaign ended in failure.

Napoleon divided his forces into three parts:

- The garrisons in the main cities of Egypt and especially in Cairo, Alexandria and Rosetta, altogether about 10,000 men.

- An expeditionary force of 5000 men approximately to conquer Upper Egypt and hunt down the Mameluk forces still holding out there.
- About 13,000 men concentrated for the Holy Land campaign.

We are concerned here with this last force only. It was composed of 800 cavalry, 370 engineers, 1385 artillerymen (and 52 cannon), 88 camel riders, 400 scouts and 9932 infantry. The latter were organised into four divisions, which were commanded by the generals Jean Baptiste Kléber, Louis André Bon, Jean Louis Ebenézer Reynier and Jean Lannes,[8] the latter serving now, for the first time, as divisional commander and heading for a distinguished career as one of Napoleon's most important marshals. The divisions were undermanned, as, in each, the third battalion of every brigade was left behind in Egypt to form the garrisons. Napoleon hoped to fill the establishment by local recruiting in Galilee and Lebanon. Joachim Murat commanded the cavalry, Louis Maria Joseph Maximilien de Caffarelli the engineers. The latter had a wooden leg from a previous campaign in Germany. He and General Bon were to perish before Acre.

The expeditionary force was also joined by servants, camel conductors, translators, Egyptian pioneers and French civilians serving as quartermasters, paymasters and physicians. There were also a few members of the scientific delegations. Some of the officers took their wives with them. Many of the soldiers were joined by their common law local wives, or female slaves, purchased in Egypt, all of whom were by now dressed according to French fashion. In order to ensure the loyalty of the citizens of Cairo, Napoleon also took with him a group of hostages from among the local notables.[9]

At the end of January 1799 Napoleon was still without the necessary beasts of burden: camels, donkeys and horses. As he did not have the money to pay for them, he organized three raids on beduin encampments in order to get hold of them cheaply – by force. As these were not operations to boast about publicly, Napoleon tried to carry them out as quietly as possible. One was commanded by his close associate, Murat, the second by one of Napoleon's adjutants, and the third by Napoleon himself. The necessary beasts were indeed thus obtained and the beduins' reaction to this act of brigandage is not recorded. Altogether some 3000 camels and 3000 asses participated initially in the campaign. They carried supplies, cannon and above all, water. About 3000 horses were also used.

Supplies were laid in at Katia in the eastern desert: about 80,000 rations of biscuits, 6 tons of rice and 2000 drums of barley. Additional food stuff was sent out from Damietta on board ship, to be landed at suitable ports along the advance route of the expeditionary force: 50,000 rations of biscuits, $2\frac{1}{2}$ tons of flour, $2\frac{1}{2}$ tons of grain and also some rice.

One important necessity was lacking, however: money. Throughout the campaign the French soldiers were to receive no regular pay.

As in so many other armies, corruption raised its ugly head in the French expeditionary force. One case became public. The chief pharmacist, Royer, did not load the camels he received with bandages and the various medicines needed by the wounded and sick, but with wine and other luxuries, which he intended to sell to the soldiers at inflated prices. He was caught, brought to trial and found guilty, but as there was nobody suitable to take his place, he had to be released and was to play a certain role in the alleged poisoning of the plague-stricken soldiers in Jaffa.[10]

4

EL-ARISH[1]

Early in January 1799 the French occupied Katia, on the way through
northern Sinai and fortified it. The French expeditionary force concentrated
here and used Katia as point of departure on its way through the desert and
towards the Holy Land. The march through the desert from Salahya was an
unexpectedly difficult one, Jacques Miot, a civilian quartermaster, describes it
as follows:[2]

'What a voyage was the one from Salahya to Katia! The soldiers, weighed down
by their baggage, their arms, water and food, moved but with difficulty through
burning sands, which gave way under each of their steps and yet seemed, so to
say, to repulse them with each step. When they rested this was in terrain which
the hand could barely touch and without shade to defend their rifles from the
ardour of the sun: to quench their thirst they had but brackish water about
which they often quarrelled and which their horses refused to drink. The
civilians attached to the army were loath to approach its marching columns,
they were mounted on horses and naturally excited the bad humour of the
soldiers who would curse when they saw beings suffering less than themselves.
Extraordinary privations and sufferings bring out the worst in all armies and
cause insubordination and selfishness. Our soldiers, depressed by fatigue and
lack of supplies, did not respect anybody any longer. They cut open the con-
tainers made of animal skins in which water was carried on the backs even of the
generals' camels and it would have been dangerous and pointless to try and stop
them from satisfying their strong desires.'

The first to arrive at Katia was Reynier's division, the weakest as far as
numbers were concerned. Reynier left Katia on 6 February and this can be
taken as the date on which Napoleon's Holy Land campaign commenced. Thus
Reynier's division formed the advance guard of the expedition.

Napoleon regarded the passage through the desert as highly critical. He
attached a unit of engineers to each brigade, with the dual mission of looking
for water holes and of helping to clear routes for the troops over the sandy and
stony ground. Each unit was supplied with tools to dig for water and pails to
draw the water from the wells. Light cannon were taken apart and the pieces

loaded on camels. The heavy siege cannon, however, and also other items of equipment needed for siege warfare were loaded on small ships and rafts and sent by sea, keeping parallel to the advancing army. This disregard by Napoleon of the British control of the sea was to cost him dear.

Reynier's division, reinforced by 300 engineers and by a battery of field guns, advanced through Romani, Bir el-Abd, south of the bay of Bardawil, named propitiously after the crusader king Baldwin III, through Bir el-Mazar, and arrived on 8 February at the outskirts of El-Arish. Reynier was supposed to take El-Arish as quickly as possible and thus enable the rest of the expeditionary force to pass through. Time was short and it was essential to get into Palestine as quickly as possible and thus to surprise both Djezzar in Acre and the pasha of Damascus by the very speed of the manoeuvre.

However, things immediately started to go wrong. Though El-Arish was part of Egypt, Djezzar had it occupied with some of his troops. He had sizeable stores transferred there in preparation for an invasion of Egypt. The French hoped to get hold of these and thus to assure themselves of a plentiful supply of food for the next stage of their campaign. Further, they also hoped to find there ample reserves of water, to enable them to continue on their way through the desert.

However the French preparations had been too rushed and turned out not to have been thorough enough. They had thought El-Arish to be an undefended place. But, in fact, they found that a sturdy fortress had been erected southwest of the village, with four strong towers, which jutted out and enabled the defenders to cover all approaches with enfilading fire. About a dozen cannon were placed on its walls and a force of about 1000 of Djezzar's best Albanian and Moroccan troops held the citadel, commanded by one of his lieutenants, Hassan Aga.

Reynier's men had spent the night of 8/9 February in the date-palm groves north of El-Arish. When they approached El-Arish itself on the morning of 9 February, they were faced, much to their surprise, by an enemy determined to resist. The first phase was easy: without any preparations Reynier's men attacked the weak wall around the village and forced their way in. The inhabitants and some of the soldiers tried to put up some resistance, but were killed by the French.

One of Reynier's men describes the village of El-Arish the morning after:

'Our eyes fell on an awful spectacle. The streets were choked by a layer of corpses. Nobody dared to bury them, because the defenders of the fort fired

The battle of El-Arish, 14—15 February 1799

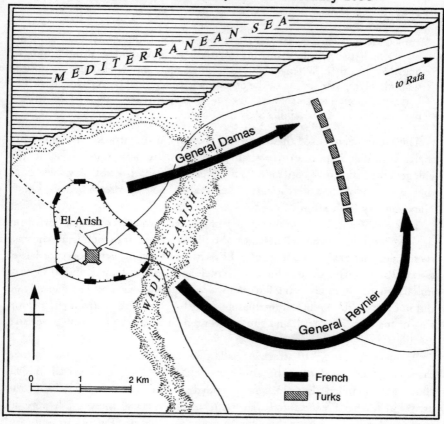

immediately when they saw a Frenchman. I do not know how my friend and myself managed to evade this fire. Actually we advanced stealthily from one house to the other. When we entered a small room in one of them, we noticed six bodies lying one on top of the other – all of them had been bayonetted. The body of a single French soldier, killed by sudden fire, lay across the doorstep. I have never seen so dreadful a sight.'

The French now based themselves on the village and attacked the fort from there. Of great importance to them were the abundant water wells in the village which they now controlled. However in the absence of heavy siege guns they were unable to take the fort. Their efforts took up precious days, which Napoleon could ill afford.

This delay enabled reinforcements of Djezzar's men, commanded by his deputy for all of southern Palestine, Abdalla Pasha, to approach from the east to succour the besieged garrison of El-Arish. His forces were not very large: 600 of Ibrahim Bey's Mameluk cavalrymen and 1200 Albanian and Moroccan infantrymen, together with a few Arabs – a total of about 2000 soldiers. They did not attack the French immediately, but threatened them from their camp east of the Wadi El-Arish and thus prevented them from mounting a decisive assault against the fortress.

Reynier decided not to attack Abdalla's force as long as he had only his own division, which did not number much above 2000 men, at his disposal. But he thoroughly planned the attack he intended to carry out immediately on the arrival of further French forces. Several reconnaissances of the possible approaches to Abdalla's camp on the high ground above the wadi were carried out.

General Kléber's division had been due to join Reynier's men only twelve hours after their arrival, but because of various delays it was unable to leave Katia until 12 February, reaching El-Arish two days later, at noon. Reynier immediately acquainted Kléber with his operational plan and it was agreed to carry it out the same night. Kléber undertook to neutralize Hassan Aga's men in the fortress. One of his brigades, under command of General Damas, was allocated the task of carrying out a diversionary attack on Abdalla's camp from the west. Reynier concentrated his whole division for the main attack. At 23.00 hours on 14 February he left for a wide outflanking march to the south. No artillery preparation was made in order to utilize the element of surprise to the fullest. Each soldier wore a white band over his shoulder as identification. Some of the officers carried dimmed lanterns. Since many of them had participated in the preparatory patrols, the ground was by now well known to them and there were none of the usual mistakes in finding their targets.

Reynier organised his men in three combat teams, each composed of a first echelon of grenadiers (the elite infantry of Napoleon's time), together with assault engineers, and of a second echelon of fusiliers. The deep silence of the approach enabled the French to approach quite near to Abdalla's camp before their presence was revealed by the barking of a dog in the camp. The first echelon immediately commenced to attack the camp from the south and east. Most of Abdalla's soldiers were surprised in their tents by this attack from a completely unexpected direction and most of his cavalrymen were even unable to mount their horses.

The second echelon also had time to take part in the attack. The Turkish force had no chance to fight and was completely defeated and dispersed. Many of the cavalrymen were killed when they tried to negotiate the steep western bank of the wadi El-Arish on their horses. One of the participants wrote in his memoirs that without the warning it had received from the barking of the dog, Abdalla's force would have been annihilated completely. As it was, quite a few of his men escaped to fight another day. The complete battle took less than an hour.

The diversionary force of General Damas arrived late, in spite of its much shorter approach, probably because the terrain was unfamiliar to his men. When they approached their target, they found Reynier's men, who were advancing westward, there already. In the darkness both forces opened fire on each other, assuming the other side to be Turks. Only by sheer luck were casualties avoided. However the operation itself was completely successful and was highly praised by Napoleon in his memoirs. He especially singled out Reynier's thorough preparations for praise and compared them, to his advantage, with Kléber's lack of preparations in the night approach at the beginning of the battle of Mount Tabor[3]. Napoleon estimated that 400 of Abdalla's men had been killed and 900 were taken prisoners[4]. This would have amounted to nearly the complete annihilation of his force. As only a few days later Abdalla was able to oppose Napoleon once more near Gaza, it seems probable that his losses must have been smaller. On St Helena, while dictating his memoirs, Napoleon could use almost no original documents and many of his figures are based on his memory, which was remarkably good for figures, but not infallible. Fifty Frenchmen were killed and wounded. Many of the Mameluks' horses were captured by the French, who now also obtained camels and other draught animals, tents and additional materials of war.

Napoleon himself, with the rest of the expeditionary force, now made the passage through the desert. Years later, on St Helena, he was to say that the desert had always held a special fascination for him. He had never crossed it without a certain emotion. To him it was the symbol of immensity, it showed no limits, and had neither beginning nor end: it was a motionless ocean.

The fortress of El-Arish, however, still held out, though it was now completely cut off. On 17 February Napoleon and the rest of the expeditionary force joined the French in front of it and its close investment from all sides was now organised. On 19 February the French artillery concentrated its fire on one of the four towers, partially destroying it. However the garrison continued to hold out and repaired some of the damage. Napoleon offered the garrison terms if they would surrender. They were to be allowed to withdraw to Baghdad and would not be otherwise harmed. First Hassan Aga rejected these terms, but a further bombardment on 20 February opened a breach which was regarded as 'practicable' by the French, i.e. suitable for an attempted break in. By the law of war then customary, if the garrison continued to hold out, they were liable to be massacred if the attack succeeded. Hassan Aga therefore agreed that day to the French terms. His men lay down their arms and evacuated their fortress.

The French themselves were apparently the first not to adhere to the conditions agreed upon. Instead of allowing the garrison to withdraw unharmed, they incorporated some of its soldiers in their own ranks, against their will. As soon as possible these men deserted again and regarded themselves now free to regain their comrades fighting for Djezzar – which they might possibly have done anyway. However, when they were soon recaptured by the French and treated most barbarously as we shall see, some of the French excuses had rather a hollow ring.

In the meantime the French wounded were in rather a piteous stage, as medical services were as yet very primitive. The French physicians were not yet commissioned officers and were attached to the army only as civilians. Most of them had learned their profession from outdated textbooks. Outstanding, however, were two chief physicians of the expeditionary force. René Nicolas Dufriche Desgenettes was in charge of hygiene and headed the fight against sickness and epidemics, while Dominique Jean Larrey was the chief surgeon, in charge of treating the wounded. Larrey was among the pioneers in caring for the wounded in matters such as the importance of cleanliness, of quick evacuation and of speedy operation – all principles which are valid still, but in 1799 were quite new. On arrival at El-Arish Larrey found that most of the wounded had not yet been attended to. He immediately got the physicians of all the divisions to help operate on the many wounded of Reynier's division. In his memoirs he claims that though there were a few difficult cases, nearly all the operations were successful.[5]

The siege of El-Arish was, however, an unmitigated disaster for Napoleon and his plans. Twelve irreplaceable days had been lost there. All the armed forces in Palestine and Damascus had by now received ample warning. Worse, Napoleon's tight time schedule had become even tighter. The chance to bring about, in the short period left, the collapse of the Ottoman empire, now looked rather chimerical. The mounting pressure of the time factor, under which Napoleon had to operate from now on, explains some of his mistakes and lack of success during the siege of Acre, and thus the failure of the campaign itself.

The garrison fired a parting shot at their French conquerors. On entering the fortress some cases of the bubonic plague were found and an epidemic of this terrifying disease started to spread in the French ranks. It is true that some earlier cases had already occurred, mostly in the garrison of Damietta, but those had been of a much less virulent type and the number of fatalities had been small. The plague which Djezzar's men had brought with them from Palestine was of a much deadlier variety as the French were soon to find out.

5

THE BATTLE OF GAZA

Part of the expeditionary force set out from El-Arish on 21 February, with Murat's cavalry and Kléber's division serving now as advance guard. The next day Lannes' division left also together with Napoleon's headquarters and bodyguard. At first Reynier's division was left at El-Arish to recuperate. Kléber's division lost its way and had to march and counter march for 18 hours. His men were so tired that Lannes' division took over the duties of advance guard the next day.[1]

In those days when as yet no Suez Canal divided Sinai from Egypt, Rafa was regarded as the point where Asia met Africa. That the entrance into Asia was by the two old pillars, which were all that was left of ancient Rafa, is mentioned in several of the diaries kept by members of the French army.[2] The expeditionary force left the desert of northern Sinai and started to advance into the Holy Land proper. Slowly the ground became less sandy and the going improved. On the 23rd the French were approaching Khan Yunis, when Napoleon and some of his staff officers advanced too fast and only barely avoided capture.

His aide-de-camp, La Vallette, recounts that they were accompanied only by a bodyguard of 50 men, two of whom served as scouts. Suddenly these two stopped and returned with great haste, firing their pistols as sign of warning. They reported to have seen Abdalla's main camp beyond the next rise of ground. Napoleon was in a difficult position: his army was some two miles behind and he found himself facing an enemy force of about 600 men. He could neither withdraw nor engage them. With great presence of mind he organised, however, his few men in a single line, giving the impression that they were but the advance guard of a much bigger force. Abdalla did not wait to find out if this was indeed so, struck camp and withdrew.

That evening the French reached Khan Yunis and found here for the first time since leaving Egypt sizeable plantations and abundant water.[3] Here the expeditionary force had a long night's rest after its passage through the desert. Napoleon dictated identical letters to the inhabitants of Gaza, Ramle and Jaffa, in his best flowery Eastern style:

The battle of Gaza, 24 February 1799

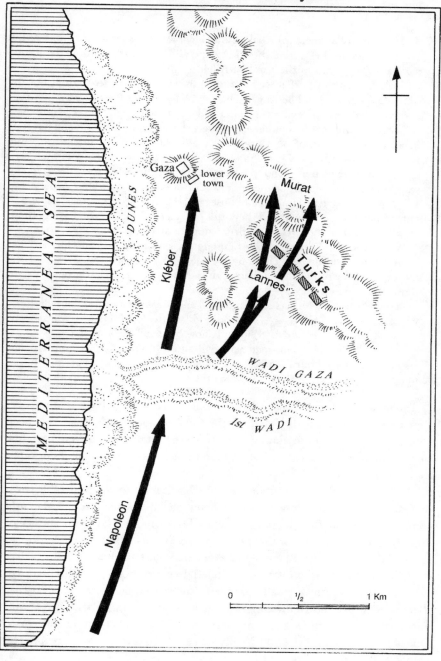

MEDITERRANEAN SEA

DUNES

Gaza

lower town

Murat

Kléber

Lannes

Turks

WADI GAZA

1st WADI

Napoleon

0   ½   1 Km

'In the name of all merciful Allah, from General Bonaparte, commander of the French forces, to the Muftis, the Ulema and all the inhabitants of Gaza, Ramle and Jaffa. Greetings in the name of Allah!

'Be it known to you that we have come to this area in order to drive out the Mamelukes and the soldiers of El-Djezzar. Why should Djezzar's soldiers stay here and maltreat the districts of Jaffa and Gaza which have never before been subject to his rule? Why has he sent soldiers to the fort of El Arish, and has thus invaded the territory of Egypt without any justification? He intends to wage war against us. We have come in order to direct this war against himself.

'However we do not intend to hurt you, the inhabitants of these areas, in any way. Stay in your homes and in your district peacefully and without anxiety, and ask those who have fled from their houses and their country to come back and to remain here. We offer you and them full safety and defence. You have nothing to worry, neither about your property, nor about your income.

'We expect the Kadis to go on fulfilling their functions as henceforward and the religion of Islam will continue to rule with all its prerogatives, and the mosques will be full of men adhering to their religion. Let God give victory to those who deserve it!

'You will see that all acts against us will end in defeat and will not help those who initiate them. All we do is intended only for the good. He who will show us goodwill will prosper and he who will show hate will be annihilated.

'After all that has happened you will surely know that we torment our enemies but defend our friends, and this especially so as we are naturally full of mercy and bear only goodwill towards the weak and the downtrodden.'

The inhabitants of Jaffa, to whom among others, this letter was addressed, were to witness the fact that rarely in the annals of man has a declaration been penned which stood in so glaring contrast to the actions which were to follow it. Yet Napoleon later took a similar line in his letters to the nobles of other towns in Palestine.

On 24 February the expeditionary force was nearing the more sizeable town of Gaza and was met there around noon by an enemy force, apparently commanded again by Abdalla Pasha. In his memoirs Napoleon speaks of 10,000 infantrymen, 700 or 800 cavalrymen and two cannon.[4] In his report to the Directory immediately after the event he mentions 3000–4000 cavalrymen, but this too seems grossly exaggerated. In the contemporaneous diaries of other participants much smaller numbers are spoken of. Some mention that there were in the hills to the east of the main route to Gaza about 400 or 500 infantrymen, and further on, slightly to the north-west, about 800 cavalrymen. One of the diaries speaks of 400 cavalrymen only and 'a few infantrymen'.[5] The French had to traverse two wadis. The second one was the deep Wadi Gaza, which at this time of the year carried some water, as a result of rare winter rains in the desert. Kléber's division advanced northwards on the left side of the French force, along the main route to Gaza. To his right the cavalry and part of Lannes' division fanned out, opening up the French array. Napoleon received information indicating that further enemy forces were due to arrive on the battlefield, including the troops of the Aga of Jerusalem and cannon from Jaffa. He therefore decided to attack immediately so as to forestall their intervention. Kléber's division forded the Wadi Gaza and advanced northwards, without meeting opposition. Murat's cavalry and Lannes' infantry advanced towards the enemy on the hills opposite them. Bon's division stayed in reserve in the centre. Bon was rather a corpulent man and thus perhaps no match for lean and active commanders like Reynier, Lannes and Murat. Thus his division was often deployed as reserve, or on diversions, while other were given the more important missions. Napoleon claims in his memoirs that he hoped to encircle the enemy opposite.[6] But most other accounts show the enemy not in the centre, where this might perhaps have been feasible, but in front of Murat's and Lannes' force only. However one of the participants corroborates Napoleon's statement that Abdalla's forces were supported by cannon. He mentions that one of their balls landed near Napoleon and threw up stones from the ground, one of which struck Napoleon's head. The wound was not severe, but after the battle Napoleon consulted Dr Desgenettes, who suggested that Dr Larrey, the chief surgeon, might be better able to help him. Napoleon however remarked that Larrey was much too quick to operate for his taste and that he would prefer Desgenettes' advice.[7] The wound was, however, apparently a light one and in his memoirs Napoleon does not mention it at all.

Murat's and Lannes' men opened fire on the enemy. According to Napoleon the Mameluk cavalrymen tried at this stage to attack the French and showed good fighting spirit, but the other sources mention only the quick retreat of both the cavalry and the infantry. They stress the good quality of the horses used by the Mameluks, which enabled them easily to evade the pursuit of the Frenchmen, whose horses were tired out. Thus the Mameluks managed to make good their getaway and the French had to fight them all over again at the battles of Kakoon and of Mount Tabor. The engagement drew to its close near evening. Kléber's division had in the meantime reached Gaza and camped for the night in the vast olive groves to its north. The rest of the French force rested slightly to the east of Kléber. In his memoirs Napoleon analyses the qualities of the soldiers opposing him that day. While he had a good opinion of the Mameluk cavalry, he had rather a low one of the Arab soldiers.[8]

On the outcome of the battle becoming evident a deputation of the notables of Gaza called on Napoleon and officially surrendered their city. Bernoyer describes their meeting thus:[9] 'Some distance from the town a group of Turks without arms approached us: this was a delegation sent out to offer us all we could ask for. Bonaparte appreciated this prudent step and gave them presents. He told them that he had come only as their friend; that his intentions were only to punish the oppressors of the people but to grant the inhabitants complete independence. Such words would have electrified all other nations except for the Syrians as they, throughout the centuries, have become accustomed to the most abject slavery. The words Liberty and Independence are completely unknown and mean nothing to them.'

In the citadel of Gaza a Turkish force, commanded by an aga, still held out, but surrendered the next morning. Much military equipment was found there, as well as foodstuffs. In his report to the Directory Napoleon mentions 200,000 rations of biscuits, six cannon, 150 hundredweight of powder, further ammunition and bombs.[10]

Gaza, though a town of some antiquity mentioned in the Bible, did not impress Napoleon very much. In his memoirs he describes it as being formed by three wretched villages, having together some 3000 to 4000 inhabitants.[11] However, the vicinity was fertile and pleasant looking, with sizeable olive groves. During the night a thunderstorm came up, lightning flashed and rain poured down. This aroused noisy enthusiasm in the French camp, as the soldiers had not experienced rain for nearly a year.

However in the days to come the soldiers were to suffer from the wet winter climate of Palestine. According to Miot, 'The army, clad in the simple blue cloth, which was so suitable to the hot climate of Egypt, suffered astonishingly from the abundant rains which poured down right from the first step into Syria. The freshness of the wet ground and the humidity of the nights rendered sleep dangerous; insects further troubled the repose of our fighters; often they had to pass part of the night in warming themselves and did not fall asleep until the undeniable need for slumber had closed their eyes.'[12]

The expeditionary force relaxed here for four complete days in order to rest thoroughly. Napoleon used this period to write further letters to the notables of such towns as Jerusalem and Nazareth and also to the various tribal heads of southern Lebanon. The army carried with it a mobile printing shop and proclamations to the civil population of the country were now printed and sent out by messengers and agents.

The French engineers started immediately to strengthen the old citadel of Gaza. A garrison was left behind. Reynier's division had in the meantime left El-Arish – leaving a garrison there as well – and had caught up with the main body.

On 28 February the whole force started moving northward again. Kléber's division formed the advance guard. The next night Napoleon slept near the village of Isdud (Biblical and present day Ashdod) and the night after in the Franciscan monastery of Ramle, where the room he used is still shown.

The French found in Ramle 100,000 rations of biscuits, much barley, and about 1500 goatskins for carrying water, all of which Napoleon claims in a letter to the Directory to have been prepared by Djezzar for his planned march through the desert to Egypt.[13] Reynier's division was to stay in Ramle when the rest of the army moved on and he was instructed by Napoleon to set up a new city council there.[14]

Bernoyer remarks:[15]
'On the 21st we passed the night at Lydda[16], a small village (near Ramle), where we found an immense store of provisions. The Turks are so arrogant that they never plan for a retreat and when they do have to retreat they do not have the time left to evacuate their stores. This tactical mistake is of the greatest advantage to their enemies. Bonaparte doubtless knew of this oriental practice as he neglected to have food stores follow immediately behind the army.'

Some of the French troops approached Ramle later than the others. The paymaster André Peyrusse, who was in charge of Napoleon's war chest, did not reach it until 8 March. In a letter to his mother he reports:

'On the early morning of the 16th (Ventôse) we noticed a great assembly of beduin and fellahin; they had been informed that the treasury of the army was there and all the villages had risen; they emitted terrible shouts, some of them were armed, all the others were without arms, and had no other resources than their voices. Some detachments were despatched against them, but they kept prudently out of the way. The wagon of the general in chief, Bonaparte, which had traversed the whole desert, got stuck in the mud, which gave the Arabs time enough to reassemble, and after three hours they covered the hills. They speeded up their advance, and reaching a height in front of us, they believed that they had intimidated us and that we would halt; but our convoy closed up, the troops formed up for battle, the drummers sounded the charge, and in a moment all the mass of men had fled; as they did not dare to sustain the first assault. At that moment a boar pursued by four dogs passed along our convoy, several shots were fired, but none stopped it. We continued on our way and arrived at Ramle without further incident.'[17]

On 2 March some of the French troops approached Jersusalem, within three miles. Eugène de Beauharnais claims in his memoirs to have approached with five companions within sight of Jerusalem and to have been kept from entering it only by a concentration of beduin. Napoleon stopped all excursions towards the Holy City, as he started concentrating all of his forces against Jaffa. His secretary, Bourienne claims in his memoirs – which are not always very trustworthy – to have asked Napoleon why he did not want to occupy so famous a city. Napoleon is supposed to have answered – 'Oh, no! Jerusalem is not in my line of operation. I do not wish to be annoyed by mountain people in difficult roads. And, besides, on the other side of the mountains, I should be assailed by swarms of cavalry.'[18]

6

THE CAPTURE OF JAFFA[1]

During his Holy Land campaign Napoleon conducted three siege operations. That of Acre was a complete debacle. In that of El-Arish the French had been surprised and its long duration contributed towards the ultimate failure of their campaign. Only the third one, that of Jaffa, was a typical Napoleonic operation: forceful, speedy, ruthless and successful.

The city was defended by about 6000 soldiers commanded by an aga, also named Abdalla, who was a native of Jaffa. He did not try to meet the French in the open field – perhaps as a result of the battles of El-Arish and Gaza – and preferred to take cover behind the walls of his town. His soldiers were mercenaries from many countries: Albanians, Moroccans, Anatolians, Egyptians, Syrians and even Sudanese. Also a few of the Mameluks had retired to Jaffa. A large force of about 1200 artillerymen (trained near Istanbul by French instructors, as part of the programme to modernise the Ottoman forces) was also stationed in Jaffa, equipped with 30 cannon. Forty additional cannon of older types were placed on the ramparts of the town. Jaffa was situated on a hill and thus most of the houses which were built on its slopes, jutted out above the town walls and their flat roofs could be used by her defenders as positions to fire from.

Napoleon describes the city thus:

'Jaffa is about 400 kilometres distant from the port of Damietta, with which she keeps up strong commercial ties. The port installations are quite good. The town had about 7000–8000 inhabitants and among them a few hundred Greeks. Several monasteries were placed here, one of which belonged to the so called Fathers of the Holy Land (i.e. the Franciscans). The towns stands on a hill and has two very rich springs of water. On the land side it was contained by walls forming a half-hexagon, strengthened by turrets. The walls were very high, but without moats; there were, however, cannon placed on the towers. The sea coast, which constituted the diameter of the hexagon, formed a shallow bay. Around the town there was a valley filled with orchards and vegetable gardens. The ground is broken, so that it is possible to approach the fortress within half a pistol shot's distance, without being seen. Within range of a good cannon shot there is a ridge which commands the area. This would have been the correct position for the army to erect its camp. As it was quite bare however, waterless and without any cover against the heat of the sun, it was decided to place the camp between the town and the ridge and to occupy the latter with sentries only.'[2]

Another member of the French force describes the town thus:

'Jaffa is situated on the shore of the Mediterranean on a hill which looks like a sugar loaf. It is surrounded at half the height of this loaf by a wall, strengthened by towers, so that the interior of the town is clearly visible, like the seats of an amphitheatre, from outside the ramparts. The height is connected on the left to the chain of hills which border on the Mediterranean and is separated from it only by a ravine of little depth. This is the best place for an attack against this place. There is good cover on the left side and at the centre, formed mainly by a veritable forest of tightly packed orange trees, reinforced by sweet lemon trees, almond trees etc. The right side is less covered; there is nothing to fear from that side, except from two isolated and not very elevated heights.

'The interior of the town is poorly served by through routes. The roads are narrow, the houses badly built, except for some soap factories and the buildings around the port. The port is formed by a line of rocks. The entrance is to the right when you face the sea. Only boats of up to 100 tons can enter it; the quay is not large.

'The surrounding fortifications are formed by a single line of walls, crowned by battlements, but without bastions. In order to give it some strength it would be necessary to construct two bastions, one at the point of our attack and the other at the other end, opposite the cemetery.'[3]

The French force appeared in front of Jaffa on 3 March 1799. The plan of attack was worked out by Caffarelli, the general in command of the engineers, and by Elzéar Auguste Cousin de Dommartin, the commander of the artillery.[4] Dommartin took an active part in the proceedings here, very different to his attitude during the siege of Acre, which bordered on insubordination.

Kléber's division was to hold a defensive line to the north, along the Yarkon river; Reynier's division was left at Ramle to defend the area of the siege towards the south-east and especially against intervention by forces coming from Jerusalem. Bon's division was to create a diversion by staging a demonstration against the northern side of Jaffa, while Lannes' division was to carry out the main attack on Jaffa from the south. Most of the artillery of the expeditionary force was put at Lannes' disposal.

There was an ample supply of food, both from the warehouses of Gaza and Ramle and fresh vegetables and fruit from the local gardens. The diaries of the participants mention oranges, lemons, almonds, pomegranates, peaches and figs growing in the orchards of Jaffa. Most of the army was camped within these orchards and, after their long stay in the desert, the French soldiers were glad to find themselves in such pleasant and fertile surroundings.

Immediately on arrival at Jaffa Napoleon led a reconnaissance around its fortifications, sometimes as near as 100 metres from the walls. A sniper's bullet missed him by inches.

Regular siege warfare at that time meant opening trenches for approaching a town gradually and putting up fortifications also for purposes of defence. Napoleon decided to dispense with all this in order to rush the operation along. This cost the French dear, as on 6 March, at noon, the garrison mounted a major assault and overran the new gun positions the French were preparing south of the town. Napoleon describes in his memoirs the defenders' attack as 'a spectacle of much charm' because of the variegated and multi-coloured dress of the various national groups taking part in the rush. Some of the Frenchmen were killed however, the positions were damaged and only by a timely counter-attack were the French able to force the men of Aga Abdalla back behind their walls.

By now Lannes' men had completed their preparations for an attack from the south and the artillerymen placed their cannon in position. Before the attack a French officer and trumpeter were sent to the Aga with Napoleon's proposal that he surrender. Abdalla, however, preferred to demonstrate his will to hold out by having both Frenchmen killed and their heads shown to their countrymen from the ramparts. This proved to be a gesture which was to become very costly to the defenders and inhabitants of Jaffa. The French regarded it as a severe breach of the conventions of war and took their revenge after their town had been captured.

The bombardment of the town started right away. The French artillery operated at a rate of ten rounds per hour per gun, except for one battery which had to open the breach in the wall and operated at twenty rounds. At 14.00 hours on 7 March a sizeable breach had been made in the southern wall and Napoleon decided to start the attack. First a small force of assault engineers and two companies of grenadiers forced their way into the breach and prepared it for the passage of larger forces. Napoleon stood nearby and the moment he gave the signal to one of the colonels next to him to start the main assault, a musket shot passed so close to his head that his hat was knocked off and the same bullet instantaneously killed the much taller colonel. Later Napoleon mentioned that this was the second time that his short stature had saved his life.[5]

In order not to hold up the assault General Lannes himself took over its direction. One of the brigade commanders, General Rambaud, forced his way into the town and with the help of grenadiers and assault engineers occupied the first building to the right of the breach. The French had to fight their way from room to room in order to capture it. The defenders' fire was so strong however that Rambaud did not manage to widen his lodgement. In the meantime Lannes had managed to get a small three-pounder gun into the breach and so could shoot into the streets of the town, but was still unable to beat down the fierce resistance of the defenders. The centre of the enemy resistance was the building immediately left of the breach, which was the highest structure in the vicinity. A French captain of engineers, Aymé, managed to force his way into the cellar of this high building as there was no connection to the storeys higher up. More soldiers followed him and managed from there, underneath the feet of the defenders, to continue into the town itself. There were quite a few casualties among the French, but they now started to force their way into the narrow alleys of Jaffa. The defenders of the high building were attacked from behind and finally liquidated.

To the north of the town General Bon was only supposed to demonstrate, in order to create a diversion. However things developed differently. Some of his soldiers found that near the shore there was a breach in the town wall and they managed to infiltrate into northern Jaffa. However most of them were killed by the inhabitants. The survivors returned to their camp and demanded of their commander that he renew the attack to avenge their fallen comrades. Bon went to inspect the wall and the breach and decided that it was quite feasible to break into the town from here. He gave the necessary orders and his soldiers renewed their infiltration both through the breach and with the help of ladders, over the walls. They found but weak resistance; as the defenders were by now all fighting Lannes' men to the south. Bon's men first gained a foothold in the northern harbour quarter and from here fanned out southwards.[6]

When Lannes' men heard that Bon's men were already in the town, they redoubled their efforts. The morale of the defenders, attacked from both sides, was badly shaken, and after a short while the defence collapsed and the actual fighting stopped.[7]

The French soldiers did not stop killing at this stage, however. Fired by the thought of their slain comrades, Bon's men started killing and looting.[8] Lannes' men, still in the heat of the battle, did not lag behind and had also the murder of the envoys to avenge. The French went beserk in the streets of Jaffa, in the afternoon of 7 March, throughout the night and in the morning of 8

March. The local inhabitants were massacred, their wives and daughters were violated. The descriptions of what happened border on the unbelievable.

Miot, a civilian quartermaster, was supposed to collect the French wounded. However all the soldiers allocated to him for this purpose deserted him and joined the looters. When he tried to get a soldier passing by with a looted horse to allow him to load on it a badly wounded French soldier, he not only refused but passed over dead and still living wounded Frenchmen with the horse, stepping on them without any regard for their suffering. Once within the city Miot reports:

'What a sight! The paleness and terror of the inhabitants, the loud shouts of our soldiers! The women wandering around with torn veils, having to step over dead and dying and seeking their parents and friends among the mutilated corpses, the pieces of furniture and torn pieces of cloth strewn around on the ground; our soldiers picking out among the debris the richest dresses ... this will convince anybody who has seen war from nearby, as I had now a chance to see it, that its sight is hideous.[9] [About the conduct of the French soldiers Miot has the following to say:] The soldiers excited by the noise and the powder, gave vent to all the ferocity which is the outcome of a forcible entrance into a town: they wounded, they killed. Nothing could stop them, and in spite of all their love of glory, what really drove them on was love of plunder, which caused them to withstand all the dangers and even to disregard the fact that they had been wounded. Disorder was everywhere. All the horrors which accompany the sack of a town were repeated in every street and in every hour. Here you could hear the cries of a girl being violated, appealing in vain for the help of her mother who had herself been raped, or of a father whose throat had been cut. The soldiers showed respect for no place of refuge. Blood flowed everywhere. With every step one met a human being dead or dying.'

Another description was given by the chief tailor of the expedition, Bernoyer: 'Everything was destroyed by fire and blood. All deeds which should not be done, were done on this calamitous day. Our soldiers did not stop killing, neither age nor sex stopped them till fatigue forced them to desist from the massacre.'[10]

And, finally, the words of a member of the scientific mission, Malus:

'The soldiers hacked to pieces men and women, the old and the young, Christians, and Turks. All human beings fell victim to their ferocity. The sights which met the eye [were terrible] – the noise of the massacre, broken doors, ruined houses, the sounds of shots and of the cleaning of swords, the shrieks of women, father and son one on top of the other (on the same pile of bodies), a daughter being raped on the cadaver of her mother, the smoke from the burnt clothes of the dead, the smell of blood, the groans of the wounded, the shouts of the victors who were quarrelling about the loot taken from a dying victim, angry soldiers who redoubled their blows the more their victim cried out in order to finally sink, satiated by blood and gold, without further feeling, on top of a heap of dead.'[11]

Napoleon who knew his soldiers only too well, did not even try to interfere and so let them find their release from weeks of toil and danger in a sea of blood. It is also possible that he wanted to show the inhabitants of the other towns of the country what their fate would be unless they surrendered in good time. But, if so, he did not succeed and the atrocities of Jaffa only served to strengthen the resolve of the defenders of Acre.

There were, however, Frenchmen who tried to help. Dr Larrey reports that he gave first aid to twenty of the women of Jaffa who were wounded during the massacre. One of the mosques of the town was turned into a first aid station and there the wounded were collected.[12]

In spite of the bitter fight the number of Frenchmen killed appears to have been only 30, and 200 were wounded. [13] About 2000 of Aga Abdalla's soldiers were killed and 3240 were taken prisoners. In the next chapter we shall report on the fate of the latter. The number of civilians killed has not been reported. However, after the capture of the town many of the survivors fled the city and Jaffa turned into a half empty ghost town. It was only after Napoleon's retreat to Egypt that its citizens returned to their houses.

The French captured a very sizeable amount of booty in Jaffa: 50 cannon, in good condition, 30 of which were field guns with their carriages; 15 boats were captured in the harbour; 400,000 rations of biscuits (i.e. five times the amount the expeditionary force set out with from Egypt), 100 tons of rice, 13,000 bales of barley; many drums of vinegar and of olive oil, much soap and also some tobacco.

7

THE MASSACRE OF THE PRISONERS

Europe was not shocked by the atrocities committed by Napoleon's soldiers during the sack of Jaffa. During the wars of the Revolution worse had been seen in Europe itself. Nor was Napoleon criticized by his contemporaries for the hundreds and thousands of men killed during his wars. War was still regarded as an integral part of life and everybody admitted its necessity. To be a great captain meant to be a great killer of men and this was not only not held against a general, but was indeed his main avenue to power and glory. But not everything was allowed. Napoleon's good name was stained mainly by three events in his long career. One was the kidnapping and execution of the Bourbon prince, the Duc d'Enghien. Of all places the two others happened in Jaffa, where Napoleon spent but a few days out of his long and active life. The matter of the poisoning of the French soldiers, sick of the bubonic plague, will be dealt with in a later chapter. The third we shall now discuss at some length, because of its importance in Napoleon's life: the alleged massacre of the prisoners taken at Jaffa.

The main question is: did it indeed take place? The world was to hear about it first in 1803. The peace of Amiens between France and Great Britain had collapsed (mainly over the question of another one of the conquests of Napoleon's expedition: the island of Malta) and the mood in England was very hostile to Napoleon personally. In that year a second edition of a book by Robert Thomas Wilson was published, named *History of the British Expedition to Egypt*, in which the matter of the massacre – though in no way connected to the subject of the book – was raised at great length. We shall quote here only one passage:

'Buonaparte having carried the town of Jaffa by assault, many of the garrison were put to the sword; but the greater part flying into the mosques and imploring mercy from their pursuers were granted their lives; and let it be well remembered that an exasperated army in the moment of revenge, when the laws of war justified the rage, yet heard the voice of pity, received its impression and proudly refused to be any longer the executioners of an unresisting enemy.

Soldiers of the Italian [sic] army, this is the laurel wreath worthy of your fame, a trophy of which the subsequent treason of an individual shall not deprive you.

'Three days afterwards, Buonaparte who had expressed much resentment at the compassion manifested by his troops and determined to relieve himself from the maintenance and care of three thousand eight hundred prisoners, ordered them to be marched to a rising ground near Jaffa, where a division of French infantry formed against them. When the Turks had entered into their fatal alignment and the mournful preparations were completed, the signal gun fired. Vollies of musquetry and grape instantly played against them and Buonaparte, who had been regarding this scene through a telescope, when he saw the smoke ascending, could not restrain his joy, but broke out into exclamations of approval . . . '[1]

The massacre of the prisoners became part of the British war propaganda against Napoleon and as the war went on for eleven years, it was given the widest of play and became an integral part of Napoleon's generally accepted life story and perhaps the darkest stain on his good name.

During Napoleon's rule, for obvious reasons, nothing was published in France itself on this subject. But after his abdication in 1814 the situation changed rapidly. Miot, the quartermaster, whose book of memoirs we have mentioned before, did not breathe a word on this subject in the first edition of his work which came out in 1804. However in the second edition, which was published in 1814, there appears a long and partly highly melodramatic account of the massacre:

'Ventôse 20th [10 March] in the afternoon the prisoners of Jaffa were made to walk into the centre of a vast square formed by the troops of General Bon's division. A dull noise emanated from the preparations and caused me, like many other people, to mount a horse and to follow this silent column of victims in order to make sure that there was truth in what I had been told. The Turks walked without order, guessing already their destiny. There were no tears shed nor did they cry out, they were resigned to their fate. Some were wounded and could not follow quickly enough and they were killed by bayonet along the way . . . The Turks did not try to escape. When they reached the sand dunes south of Jaffa, they were stopped near a pond of yellowish water. The officer in charge of the troops divided the mass into small groups, and these platoons were conducted to different points and shot there. This horrible operation necessitated much time, in spite of the great number of troops allocated to this sinister sacrifice, who participated with great repugnance in this abominable mission. Near the pond there was a group of prisoners amongst whom there were some elderly chiefs of noble appearance and great self assurance, and one young man, who was badly shocked. At so tender an age he felt himself to be innocent and because of this he acted in a way which shocked those who surrounded him. He threw himself among the hooves of the horse which carried the commander of the French troops and implored him to spare his life. He cried out "Of what am I guilty? What wrong have I done?" The tears which he shed and his cries were of no avail; he could not arrest the fate awaiting him. Except for this young man, all the other Turks calmly made their ablutions in the stagnant water, and afterwards put their hand on their heart and their mouth, in the way Moslems salute each other and thus gave and received a farewell for eternity. Their courageous souls seemed to defy death, their tranquility, in these their last moments was inspired by their religion, and their hope for a happier future in the hereafter . . .

'This spectacle made my heart tremble . . . Finally there remained no prisoners except those near the water. Our soldiers saved their cartridges and killed those left with the bayonet. I did not stay to watch this horrible spectacle . . .'[2]

The question in this case is: should we regard Miot's description as an eyewitness report, or as a piece of anti-Napoleonic propaganda in the first flush of the Bourbon restoration?

A further witness is Bourienne, Napoleon's secretary. According to his narrative, two of Napoleon's aides-de-camp – one of them was Eugène de Beauharnais, the son of Josephine by her previous marriage – accepted, during the massacre of the civilian population, the surrender of a great group of soldiers holding out in a local khan, who surrendered on condition that no harm would come to them. They were brought safely to headquarters, where Bourienne reports Napoleon's reaction to have been 'What do they wish me to do with these men? Have I food for them? – ships to convey them to Egypt or France? Why in the devil's name have they served me thus?'[3] Bourienne claims that Napoleon convened a council of war in which it was decided to have the prisoners executed.

Bourienne claims to have been present during the execution, which he says, took place on 10 March. He ends with the words: 'I have related the truth, the whole truth'. If nothing else has roused our doubts about his narrative, this protestation of truthfulness certainly should. Bourienne on closer inspection turns out to be a poor witness. He was later dismissed by Napoleon for shady deals, managed to get an appointment in the trading centre of Hamburg, occupied at that time by the French, was dismissed once more because of improper conduct, joined the Bourbons on Napoleon's fall and was appointed a cabinet minister, but was speedily dismissed once again. In difficult circumstances he produced, with the help of some journalist friends, his four-volume memoirs, which are so full of inexactitudes and downright lies that a complete book was published just enumerating them. Thus, though his story has found its way into all history books, it should be treated with extreme caution.

A witness of very different calibre is the English clergyman and later professor of mineralogy at Cambridge, E.D. Clarke. He was the first scientist to recognise the importance of the Rosetta Stone and on his insistence it was transferred to the British Museum.

He visited Jaffa in 1801 and tells about meeting the English Consul there:[4]

'He had just ventured again to hoist the British flag upon the roof of his dwelling and he told us, with tears in his eyes, that it was the only proof of welcome he could offer to us, as the French officers under Buonaparte had stripped him of everything he possessed. However in the midst of all his complaints against the French, not a single syllable ever escaped his lips respecting the enormities supposed to have been committed by means of Buonaparte's orders or connivance, in the town and neighbourhood of Jaffa. As there are so many living witnesses to attest the truth of this representation and the character of no ordinary individual is so much implicated in its result, the utmost attention will be here paid to every particular likely to illustrate the fact; and for this special reason, because that individual is our enemy. At the time we were in Jaffa, so soon after the supposed transactions are said to have occurred, the indignation of our Consul, and of the inhabitants in general, against the French was of so deep a nature that there is nothing they would not have said to vilify Buonaparte, or his officers: but this accusation they never even hinted.'

When Clarke and his friends found a mass grave of bodies along the shore, which by others is identified as the grave of the massacred prisoners, the Consul 'told us that these were the remains of bodies carried thither during the late plague, for interment, but that the sea, frequently removing the sand which covered them, caused them to be thus exposed.' This testimony is doubly important as coming, not from an admirer of Napoleon's but, on the contrary from one opposed to him in every way.

In corroboration of his own statement Clarke quotes other visitors to Palestine and especially a naval captain named Culverhouse. 'Captain Culverhouse then, before the whole company present, expressed his astonishment at the industrious propagation of a story concerning the murder of the prisoners of war, of which the inhabitants of Jaffa were ignorant and whereof he had never heard a syllable until his arrival in England.'[5]

We are thus faced with the difficult choice of whom to believe. While the story of the massacre of the prisoners has been part of every Life of Napoleon in the past, it is only fair to point out that the second half of the 20th century a general revision of his life story is under way, partly as a result of additional sources, but mainly by the increasing readiness not to use many of the books of memoirs such as those of Bourienne, or of Napoleon's valet, or of the duchess of Abrantes, which obviously were mainly concoctions compiled by hacks. The question we shall have to decide here is whether the story of the massacre of the prisoners has to be discarded together with so many others (mostly derogatory to Napoleon, though he himself originated quite a few of the favourable stories which have no more basis in fact, when he was on St Helena).

Napoleon himself is quoted by O'Meara on St Helena to have reacted to O'Meara's assertion that Miot had claimed in the 1814 edition of his book that Napoleon had caused between 3000–4000 Turks to be shot after the capture of Jaffa:

' "It is not true that there were that many. I ordered about a thousand or twelve hundred to be shot, which was done. The reason was, that amongst the garrison of Jaffa a number of Turkish troops were discovered, whom I had taken a short time before at El-Arish and sent to Bagdat upon their parole not to serve again, or to be found in arms against me for a year. I had caused them to be escorted twelve leagues on their way to Bagdat, by a division of my army. But those Turks, instead of proceeding to Bagdat, threw themselves into Jaffa, defended it to the last, and cost me a number of brave men to take it, whose lives would have been spared, if the others had not reinforced the garrison of Jaffa. Moreover, before I attacked the town, I sent them a flag of truce. Immediately afterwards we saw the head of the bearer elevated on a pole over the wall. Now if I had spared them again, and sent them away upon their parole, they would directly have gone to St Jean d'Acre, where they would have played over again the same scene that they had done at Jaffa. In justice to the lives of my soldiers, as every general ought to consider himself as their father, and them as his children, I could not allow this. To leave as a guard a portion of my army, already small and reduced in number, in consequence of the breach of faith of those wretches, was impossible. Indeed, to have acted otherwise than as I did, would probably have caused the destruction of my whole army. I therefore, availing myself of the rights of war, which authorize the putting to death of prisoners taken under such circumstances; independent of the right given to me by having taken the city by assault, and that of retaliation on the Turks, ordered that the prisoners taken at El-Arish, who, in defiance of their capitulation, had been found bearing arms against me, should be selected and shot. The rest, amounting to a considerable number, were spared. I would . . . do the same again tomorrow, and so would Wellington, or any general commanding an army under similar circumstances." '[6]

But O'Meara is not always a reliable witness. By the time he published his memoirs the emperor was safely dead and he could put into his mouth any words he wanted on this controversial subject, without fear of being contradicted.

However Napoleon in his memoirs does not deny the story either.[7] He says that among the 2500 prisoners there were 800 of the soldiers released by him after El-Arish on parole, who had broken their parole and hence his order to have them executed. These memoirs were dictated nearly twenty years after the event. Is Napoleon's own evidence thus reliable? Can he be expected, after more than 60 battles and sieges to remember the minor siege of Jaffa in detail? Is there no chance that he himself has been influenced by the publications of others? It is perhaps possible, but not very likely.

The real evidence that the massacre of the prisoners did actually occur comes, however, from the contemporaneous accounts of eyewitnesses which were published, not during the Bourbon period, but later in the 19th and 20th century, and should thus not be biased one way or the other. The account of the chief tailor, Bernoyer, for instance, was published as late as 1976. He puts the blame squarely on Napoleon:

'In order to escape the massacre, a part of the garrison, numbering 1500 men, had escaped into a mosque where they defended themselves full of despair ... Our soldiers tried to dislodge them from this strong position, but in vain. Bonaparte, forseeing the losses which would result from attacking this formidable position invited the survivors to capitulate; these were glad to accept the proposition of General Bonaparte. He promised them that if they would lay down their arms he would have them conducted to the frontiers of Syria. They left their retreat fully confident in the word of Bonaparte; he had them taken to the sea shore, and there six thousand men in battle order, were massacred or thrown into the sea. During this barbaric execution I withdrew into my tent in order to reduce the noise of the weapons and the sad shouts of the dying who were killed without mercy.'[8]

Thus even the story of the two aides-de-camp is not confirmed here, and the responsibility is placed on Napoleon's shoulders. Substantially the same story is told by other French eyewitnesses: by General Doguereau, by the chief map maker of the expedition, Colonel Jacotin, by the assistant paymaster Peyrusse, by Dr Desgenettes, by Captain Gerbaud, by Major Detroye and also in an anonymous account.[9] There are too many of them for the verdict to be in doubt any longer: the massacre of the prisoners is fact, not fiction. Dr Clarke and his friends, who, after all, were not eyewitnesses were misinformed for reasons we can no longer ascertain.

From the above sources, and additional ones mentioned by the historian of the expedition, de la Jonquière, we can form a fairly clear picture of what happened. Bernoyer's version as to how Napoleon tricked the remainder of the garrison to surrender comes from a more reliable source than Bourienne's story about the two aides-de-camp. Eugène de Beauharnais himself, in his memoirs does not mention the part he was supposed to have played, according to Bourienne. He does mention that a Colonel Boyer refused to undertake the execution and it was carried out by Colonel d'Armagnac and his 32nd Regiment, of Bon's division. Also Bourienne's story of a war council does not sound likely. Napoleon usually made up his own mind. The reasons mentioned for the massacre, such as lack of food and lack of men to guard them might have been the ones which decided their fate. But food was actually found in such sizeable quantities in Jaffa that some could surely have been spared for the prisoners. Napoleon's claim, that many of the soldiers had broken the parole given them at El-Arish might have had some weight with him, but does not hold water objectively: the French were apparently the first to break the terms of the convention there. What was Napoleon's real motive? Perhaps to influence, by a show of frightfulness the garrisons of other towns to surrender more quickly. If so, he failed. The garrison of Acre, seeing what befell those who had surrendered to Napoleon, held out against all odds.

Perhaps the pressure of events, and the ever present pressure of time, forced upon Napoleon not only an inhumane, but also a rash and ill-considered decision. The massacres at Jaffa are an exception in Napoleon's annals. Usually he was a humane commander. Therein lies perhaps their special interest as we here see him acting out of character under the pressure of occurrences which he could no longer control, though he himself had initiated the chain of events leading up to them.

Let us now return to the fate of the prisoners. They were divided by Napoleon's order into two groups. One was composed of Egyptians – about 800 of them. Napoleon regarded them as citizens of a French colony. Hundreds of them were kept in the camp in order to serve as workers, and pioneer labour to help the engineers. The other Egyptians were sent back to their country, where they arrived on 31 March.

The other group was composed of all the other prisoners, all of whom were to share the same fate. Their execution took place on three consecutive days.[10] On 8 March about 800 of the Moroccan prisoners were taken to the beaches about one mile south of Jaffa and there they were shot to death by the men of two of Bon's battalions. Some tried to escape by jumping into the sea and swimming out to the rocks which jut out of the water at some distance from the shore. The French shot some of them while still swimming and followed the others on improvised rafts and killed them too.

The next day (9 March) a further 600 prisoners were killed, this time among the non-Moroccans. The last day (10 March) the largest number were executed: 1041. These had not received any food for the last two days. Again Bon's division was in charge of the execution. Altogether in the three days of the massacre 2440 prisoners were dispatched.

The recently published memoirs of Bernoyer bring another, even more extreme charge against Napoleon:

> 'Bonaparte had been informed about the trouble which reigned in the camp as a result of the women captured by the soldiers, and he issued an order that those who held them were to conduct them at noon to the court of the hospital; any disobedience was to have been severely punished. This order was carried out punctually, as the men expected that these poor creatures would be returned to the ruins of the town, where an asylum would be found for them. However in reality a company of Chasseurs was assembled to shoot them.'[11]

This episode, more revolting even than the shooting of the prisoners, has not been mentioned by any other source. A somewhat different fate awaited Abdalla Aga, the garrison commander. He was taken prisoner, but kept alive, apparently again as a figure in Napoleon's game of psychological warfare, in order to show Djezzar what his fate would be if he were to submit. However when the expeditionary force returned to Egypt, there was no longer any need for the Aga, and Napoleon had him quietly killed.[12] His daughter was among the prisoners of Jaffa. Bernoyer reports that she was stabbed to death in his presence by the brother of the French envoy whose head had been cut off by order of her father.

The remaining inhabitants of Jaffa were required to collect the rotting bodies of the dead in the streets of the town and bury them outside. They had also to help in repairing the fortifications of the city. A very sizeable monetary contribution of 175,000 livres was levied on Jaffa by Napoleon and this slightly improved his financial situation.[13] The inhabitants had also to help tend the sick and wounded whom the French left behind, together with a garrison of some 150 men. The wounded were lodged in the Greek Orthodox monastery, next to the harbour, and the Greek inhabitants were required to look after them; the sick – about 200 of them – were placed in the Armenian monastery nearby, and were to be nursed by the Armenian and Roman

Catholic inhabitants.

The latter was a task of no little danger, as now the bubonic plague was making its rounds in the ranks of the French army. Most historical accounts have not failed to point to the curious coincidence of the outbreak of this dreadful epidemic occurring immediately after the massacres which took place in Jaffa. Quite a few of them have regarded it outright as a heaven-sent retribution. Be this at it may, from now on and until the end of the campaign, Napoleon had another severe problem to deal with. Dr Desgenettes tried to hide the real nature of the plague from the soldiers and did not use its real name, in order to keep up their morale. Desgenettes himself tried to show the soldiers that the sickness was not contagious, by publicly inoculating himself with it. In his memoirs he relates the episode. 'It was in order to calm the fears and restore the spirit of the army that one day, in the middle of the plague wards I plunged my lancet into the pus of the bubo of a convalescent ... and made slight incisions with it in my groin and near one of my armpits, without taking any other precaution than to wash myself with water and soap.'[14] He was as lucky as he was brave and did not catch the disease.

On 11 March Napoleon himself, with some staff officers, visited the Armenian monastery, also in order to show his soldiers that he was not afraid of the plague. He knew that if its true nature became known, this would cause a panic, which might ruin the campaign. Thus extreme measures were needed. Therefore he personally helped to carry one of the cadavers from the plague ward. He too was lucky and did not catch the plague.[15] Later on this episode was depicted by his court painter Gros, but for reasons of composition, Napoleon is seen to touch a living patient; however Gros had tried the true scene out in a preliminary sketch, which survives too, but shows why it was less suitable for full scale treatment. Throughout the 19th century visitors to Jaffa went to see the scene of this painting and were somewhat disappointed by the much more modest size of the Armenian Convent than Gros' picture would lead one to expect. The building survives to this day, but no longer as a convent.

It is interesting to ponder the character of a man who one day was prepared to order the execution of thousands of innocent men and the day after to endanger his life, in order to set an example of sang froid, by courting contagion of one of the most deadly diseases known to man. The key to his conduct in both cases was probably that he regarded it as necessary to the success of his campaign. In order to assure this success, he was prepared to go further in both directions – that of cruel execution and that of self-sacrifice –

than most men and this surely is one of the reasons why he was usually so successful a commander.

Another reason is that he fully understood the importance of psychological factors and always included them in his calculations. If he was often wrong about the reaction of Djezzar and his soldiers, this was caused by his unfamiliarity with conditions in Palestine. However with regard to his own soldiers he made almost no mistakes and thus he was able to extract from them wonders of performance, often way beyond other commanders' capabilities. We shall see in a later chapter, however, that even this had limits and in his Holy Land campaign there occurred one of the very rare cases in which he overstepped the limit.

8

THE BATTLE OF KAKOON AND THE CAPTURE OF HAIFA

A hmed Djezzar and his court at Acre did not constitute the only centre of resistance to Napoleon in the Holy Land. A secondary centre came into being in the mountains of Samaria. None of our sources reports that the mountain people of Hebron, to the south of Jerusalem, participated in the struggle against Napoleon. However in the mountains to the north of Jerusalem, in Samaria, with its capital in Nablus, Istanbul's exhortations for an all out war against the infidel invasion found a ready audience and Djezzar's sizeable presents to the local notables, found eager takers. The local mountain people were experienced fighters, who usually followed one local faction against another, but were even better at defending their mountain passes against outside interference. They were fanatical Muslims who hated all foreigners and Christians. The heads of their two main factions, Ahmed Bei el-Tukkān and Jussef Gerar, now united to face the common danger, and led their men against the French.[1]

The first encounter was with a unit from Kléber's division. While the massacre of the prisoners, to the south of Jaffa, was still running its course, on 8 March, Kléber — whose division was placed to the north of it, in the area of the Audja (Yarkon) river — sent a force eastwards, to the Kalkilia region, in order to advance into the mountains of Samaria. The commander was General Damas, who had not been very successful in the battle of El-Arish and was to be no more so this time. The French command hoped to clear its right flank and take control of Samaria without much of a struggle. However immediately Damas' men started to ascend the narrow paths up the mountains, they were ambushed by local fighters.[2] In the ensuing encounter a company of Moroccan soldiers in French service distinguished itself by its coolness under fire, in spite of the fact that eight of its men were killed and five wounded. Possibly they were used to this type of fighting in the mountains of their homeland. Their commander was advanced in rank immediately afterwards.

71

However the bravery of these men did not prevail. The fight was decided when a bullet shattered General Damas' arm. The French were forced to withdraw. Local tradition in the Kalkilia area has not forgotten this encounter and has embellished it as its story passed from generation to generation. The fight is supposed to have taken place near the village of Azun, east of Kalkilia. The version still current there about a generation ago was that a local chieftain, 'Abd 'Azzuni, had first spotted the approaching Frenchmen, and later led the local levies against them, personally firing the shot that hit General Damas.[3]

Damas was evacuated to Egypt and his force rejoined Kléber's division, which had in the meantime advanced northwards into the forests of Maski. Though Palestine, after centuries of Muslim misrule, was no longer a densely wooded country, it was not yet as bare of trees as it was to become a century later, after the remaining copses had been cut down by local charcoal burners. The forest of Maski was probably the biggest forest remaining west of the Jordan.

From here Kléber sent reconnaissances out to the north, in preparation of the new advance of the expeditionary force. On 11 March one of these was attacked by about a hundred beduin near the village of Kallansawa and had to beat a hasty retreat. Another one was completely annihilated, with only its commander, a second lieutenant Delesalle, surviving. The following is his report about his harrowing experiences:

'I am aboard the English ship, the *Tigre*. During the reconnaissance made Ventôse the 24th [14 March] I was taken prisoner by beduins who numbered about 250 men. After a lively defence we had to retreat, and the enemy, with his superior numbers, surrounded us from all sides and tore us to pieces. I fought on for more than ten minutes ... and received five thrusts by lances and one cut by a sabre ... I remained alone and had four Arabs after me. I was stripped completely and they left me only my shirt and drawers. We arrived the same evening at a spot nearly three miles into the mountains and after I had experienced a thousand horrors, they showed me the heads of my poor dragoons, who numbered eight to ten ...

'I stayed some eleven hours among these scoundrels, who threatened a hundred times to cut my throat. I ran a terrible fever and was bathed in my blood. Still, when one of the Arabs near me had gone to sleep and four others attended to the fire, I escaped from this place and made my way into the mountains and took off my shirt so as not to be seen by the Arabs near whose villages I was forced to pass ... I did not know where I was and had no strength left to continue and was recaptured by Arab farmers who conducted me to their

The battle of Kakoon, 15 March 1799

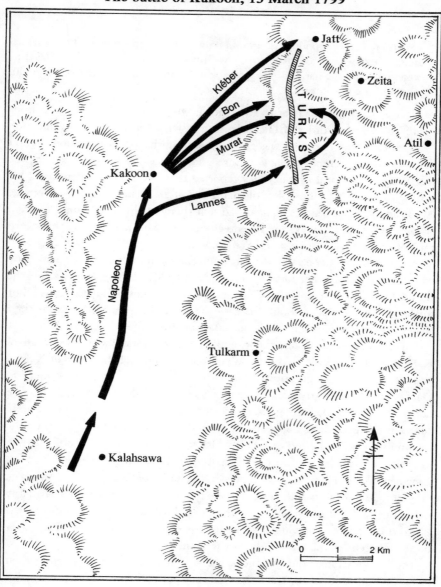

pasha. He had me conducted, around midnight, by three men on horseback to Acre, where we arrived after three days' march. On my arrival a mob tried to wrest me from the hands of the Arabs who led me. I was brought to the pasha who had me put in prison.'[4]

He was later handed over to the British, who managed to keep him from being killed by the order of Djezzar and transfered him to their flagship.

In order to find out what was going on among the local population beyond his lines, Kléber employed not only reconnaissances by his own troops, but made use also of local agents. They reported that Djezzar was intensifying his activity among the notables of Samaria, after General Damas' retreat. According to these reports Djezzar had sent them one hundred purses (quite a sizeable amount of money) and seventeen rich fur coats, in order to get them to take offensive action against the French.[5]

After spending some rainy days in Jaffa, the main body of the French army was resuming its movement to the north.[6] On 14 March Napoleon reached the Maski forest. The main line of advance was now not along the coast, but further inland so that it would be easier to cross the local wadis nearer their sources, since some of them still carried water from the winter rains.

On 15 March, at noon, the vanguard made contact with the Khan of Kakoon with a sizeable force. It was composed mainly of the levies of Nablus and all of Samaria, who hoped now, after their easy success against General Damas, to be able to bar the further advance of the whole French force northwards. Also Djezzar's presents to the notables of Samaria had certainly contributed towards the appearance of this force beyond the borders of the mountains of Samaria, and on a task which was more in Djezzar's interest than in their own. Their number was estimated at 4000 men and they had been joined by about 1000 Mameluk cavalrymen of Abdalla Pasha. This was the biggest field force to face the French since the start of their invasion of the Holy Land, but was still not much more than one third of the total number of the expeditionary force, showing that the leaders of the Nablus district had as yet no real concept of the real might of the French.[7]

The Turkish forces did not block the way northward, by deploying their forces on both sides of the track. Instead they placed them parallel to the path and eastward of it; thus, on the one hand, threatening the flank of the French, but on the other, keeping an easy route of retreat open, to the mountains in their rear.

The French first stopped the advance of Lannes' division which was to form their right wing, and then that of Kléber's division, which was to form their left, and had thus furthest to go. Their centre was formed by Murat's cavalry, and General Bon was, as usual, in reserve.

The horsemen of Abdalla (the commander of the Mameluk cavalry), on the right flank of the Turkish line, opened the action by charging Kléber's division, but were stopped by the fire of the French artillery. Their advance turned into retreat, and finally into headlong flight. The French now attacked the mountain people of Nablus further south, and forced them to abandon their positions and withdraw eastwards. The Mameluk cavalry was in the meantime making good its withdrawal to the north. Kléber's men followed in the squares adopted by Napoleon in Egypt and Palestine, especially in order to counter the Mameluk cavalry, which, however, did not allow them to move quickly enough to catch up with the enemy. According to one estimate, the total loss of the Turkish force was about 400 killed and wounded.

The levies of Samaria withdrew into their mountains, followed by General Lannes' division, which tried to move through the mountain passes, towards Nablus. This was the second French advance into the mountain fastness of Samaria and ended in failure, just as had that of General Damas. Lannes' men were repulsed with considerable losses, and one of their colonels was among those killed. Altogether about 60 of them were wounded or killed. They had to withdraw to the main French camp, which had been erected near the village of Zeita. Napoleon rebuked Lannes sharply for this unnecessary action, and for the losses incurred. Lannes' excuse was 'that he had wanted to teach the canaille a lesson', but Napoleon pointed out to him that the French army was not in a position to indulge in such adventures.[8] Thus the men of the district of Nablus failed in their effort to stop the French advance northwards and were defeated in the battle of Kakoon, but managed to repulse two French attempts to penetrate into their mountains. They continued to hold on to these throughout the French campaign. Having now embarked on offensive action against the French, we shall see them making several further attempts against Napoleon's men later on.

The strong stand of the district of Samaria had a negative influence on the strategic position of the French expeditionary force. Its avenue of advance was limited now to a narrow corridor between the sea, which was controlled by the British fleet and the mountains which were in enemy hands as well. When the French established themselves later on, as we shall see, in an enclave in Western Galilee, this corridor was closed behind them and Napoleon was forced to rely mainly on the insecure sea communication between the tiny port of Tantura and Jaffa and Egypt. Only with a sizeable force was it possible to travel overland back to Jaffa to bring supplies up from there. When Napoleon sent an officer with despatches to Egypt he had to instruct the commander of Jaffa to provide him with an escort of 100 men.[9] The French garrisons of El-Arish, Gaza and Jaffa were thus turned into islands in a hostile sea. As a result Napoleon's attempt to add all of Palestine to the French colony of Egypt failed, because of the resistance of strategically central Samaria.

Not foreseeing this development, on 10 March Napoleon had nominated General Jacques François Menou as commander of conquered Palestine, with Jaffa as his seat. However, this man who had shown his incompetence already during the 1795 Vendémiaire uprising in Paris, and was to do so again in 1801 when he lost Egypt to the British, preferred to stay on in Rosetta. This was partly in order to prepare the area against a possible English landing and partly, after his conversion to Islam (upon which he added the name Abdallah to his first names), in order to complete the arrangements for his forthcoming marriage to a Muslim lady.[10]

In the meantime, on 16 March, the French expeditionary force rested from the previous day's battle and tried to stay under cover because of a downpour (in Palestine the rainy season ends about the end of March, though there are also a few rainy days in April). A small force under General Junot (who had been only a sergeant when Napoleon first met him at Toulon six short years before), reconnoitred the seashore, in spite of the weather. In particular he examined the ruins of the ancient port of Caesarea – from where Pontius Pilate had ruled the country 1770 years earlier – but did not find it suitable for the needs of the French army. Junot rejoined the main force on the 17th and the whole army resumed its march northwards. However it soon turned north-eastwards and traversed the easy passes of Mount Carmel, until it reach Yokneam, on the south western border of the Valley of Jezreel. The army camped there on the left bank of the small river Kishon.

On the afternoon of 17 March Kléber's division was despatched to the port of Haifa, beneath the eastern slope of Mount Carmel, but found its gates locked. Djezzar did not believe that he could hold Haifa at the same time as Acre, and as the latter was then by far the bigger and the more important, he had his cannon evacuated from Haifa. However he had to leave his stores behind in the local citadel, in which the French were to find 50,000 rations of biscuits and also rice. Kléber encountered a member of the European colony of the little township waiting for him outside the walls with the keys to the city gate and which were handed over to the Frenchman with a request to treat the inhabitants humanely. As a result, no looting was allowed, and some of the diaries kept by the French mention the friendly attitude of the inhabitants.[11]

Napoleon joined Kléber at Haifa and in his memoirs he describes it as a small town of about 2000 or 3000 inhabitants, with a small port.[12] The town was encircled by an old wall, but Napoleon stressed that it could be completely dominated from Mount Carmel. Much to his surprise he espied two large English warships at anchor in the bay which separates Haifa from Acre. These ships had arrived two days previously from Istanbul, and were commanded by Commodore Sir Sidney Smith, the third main actor on the stage of our story, besides Napoleon and Djezzar. He was born in 1764 and had seen service in both the British and Swedish navies. In 1793 he had met Napoleon for the first time in action, in the French port of Toulon. The British had been forced to evacuate this harbour, previously held by them, mainly as a result of Napoleon's tactics and artillery fire, and Sir Sidney Smith volunteered to burn the French ships which had to be left behind.[13]

Napoleon, from his position on the slope of Mount Carmel, sent messengers posthaste to the port of Tantura, to warn the commander of his naval squadron, not to continue northwards towards the bay of Haifa. However the warning did not reach Captain Standelet, who commanded the squadron of nine small ships, carrying the siege train. 18 March was a foggy day and Standelet did not notice the two British war ships (*Tigre* and *Theseus*) until it was too late. Six of his ships were captured, and only three got away. One of these, the *Cerf*, with Standelet on board, returned all the way to Toulon, not exactly a sign that he had much stomach to continue the fight.

The following is Standelet's report on this action:

'On the 28th (Nivôse), at 6.00 hours in the morning, we noticed a vessel windward from us, about four to five miles distant. The weather was very foggy, and this did not enable me to identify it; it turned out to be an English man-of-war of 74 cannon, named the *Theseus*, as I found out afterwards. At 7 o'clock we noticed another vessel, which was somewhat down wind from us; I chased it and signalled the rest of the squadron to follow my lead, at 9.00 hours we were very close, and it struck its flag. It turned out to be the *Torride* which the English captured from us at Béquiers. I had it taken over by our men in whose charge it sailed on. I had the Captain, the second in command and four of its crew put under guard. At 11.00 hours we turned towards the cape of Mount Carmel. I had the sails of the *Cerf* reinforced, as she was our fastest ship so that she could reconnoitre the cape and find out if there were any of our vessels at anchor there; the weather was very foggy which enabled me to see the cape only from a very short distance. At 3 o'clock I saw ships in the roadstead, which I could not identify; they signalled that the enemy had superior forces there. I followed suit and signalled my squadron to reinforce its sails and to hold closely into the wind, so as to have it fill the sails from port, as we were very much to windward of the enemy. It followed suit but the [British] vessel *Tigre* gained on us and the frigate *Cheval Marin* ['Seahorse'] advanced speedily.

'As I saw that their vessel had overtaken our squadron, I had the sails [of the *Cerf*] rigged up so as to create a diversion in the chase; she chased me but as night was falling it appeared that if she continued doing so most of the others would escape and she abandoned the chase when the distance was still that of a short cannon shot. The weather was calm throughout the night, I navigated so as to be at a maximum distance from the pursuers at daylight. At 10.00 hours in the morning I saw a ship which I identified as the [French] *Pluvier*; I talked to her and was told that she had not been captured as [the enemy] had not sufficient small vessels, and thus she had escaped in the mêlée.'[14]

This sea battle was as fateful as any of the land battles of the campaign, as the French lost all their heavy siege guns, and their other siege equipment. This was indeed a severe blow to them. Napoleon was to claim later that if this naval engagement had not taken place, he would have captured Acre by 1 April and Damascus and Aleppo soon after.

The French could not now use the port of Haifa, because the British fleet was too near, and had to make do with the tiny port of Tantura. However the French kept Haifa and the Carmelite monastery on nearby Mount Carmel served as their base hospital throughout most of the siege of Acre.

The battle off the Cape of Mount Carmel, 18 March 1799

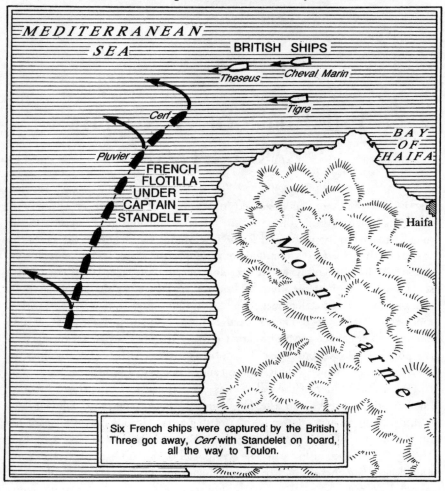

MEDITERRANEAN
SEA

BRITISH SHIPS

Theseus *Cheval Marin*

Tigre

Cerf

Pluvier

FRENCH
FLOTILLA
UNDER
CAPTAIN
STANDELET

BAY
OF
HAIFA

Haifa

Mount Carmel

Six French ships were captured by the British.
Three got away, *Cerf* with Standelet on board,
all the way to Toulon.

9

THE SIEGE OF ACRE: THE EARLY STAGE[1]

The town of Acre was described in 1799 by a French officer as follows:[2] 'The town is built on a tongue of land, jutting into the sea at the (northern) extremity of the gulf formed by Mount Carmel. Two sides face the sea; its further side forms an angle pointing into the plain. Its circumference is no more than 1000 toises[3] and it does not contain more than 10,000 to 12,000 souls. Its fortifications are anything but modern; there is a single wall without bastions, but with battlements, flanked by round and square towers, with a moat 16 to 18 feet deep. Djezzar's palace forms a square fort with a moat, one of its sides adjoins the town ramparts (to the north). In the part facing the gulf is a port defended against the sea by a breakwater constructed of masonry, at the extremity of which stands, as a means of defence, a lighthouse.'

The absolute ruler of the palace was the Pasha Ahmed, aptly nicknamed Djezzar, the 'butcher'. In the beginning Napoleon despised Djezzar and regarded him as just another old Turkish pasha. He did not appreciate his toughness, his willpower and his resourcefulness. In a letter he sent him during the advance of his army, he wrote, full of disdain: 'In a few days time I shall approach Acre, but why should I shorten the lifespan of an old man, whom I do not know? What is the importance of a few miles more, compared to the area I have already conquered? Since God gives me victory, I wish to follow His example and be merciful and compassionate, not only towards the people, but also towards their rulers.'[4] Such hubris could only end in disaster.

Why did Napoleon regard Acre as his main target? First of all, because, being the seat of Djezzar, it was the de facto capital of Palestine. Further, it was the most important harbour in the whole area, and Napoleon wanted to keep the British from using it. History had endowed Acre with great importance, especially in the eyes of the French as the capital, during the last hundred years, of the mainly French speaking Latin kingdom of Jerusalem. Napoleon and his

The siege of Acre, 14 March – 20 May 1799

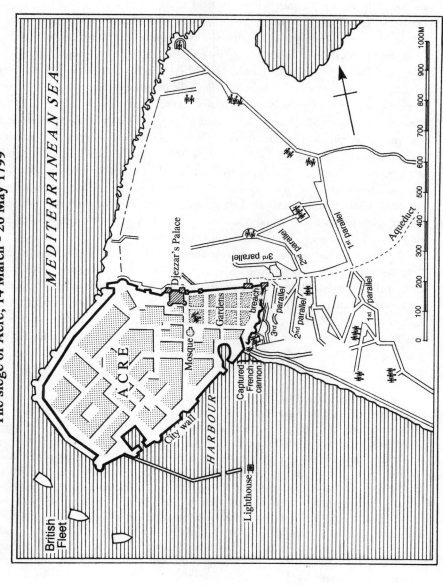

MEDITERRANEAN SEA

British Fleet

HARBOUR

Lighthouse

City wall

ACRE

Mosque

Gardens

Djezzar's Palace

Captured French cannon

breach

3rd parallel

2nd parallel

1st parallel

3rd parallel

2nd parallel

1st parallel

Aqueduct

0   100   200   300   400   500   600   700   800   900   1000M

men regarded themselves sometimes as the heirs of the crusaders, who had preceded them to these shores by some 600 years. Further, Acre was the key to further advance into Southern Lebanon, with its minorities – Druses, Matu-wellis, Maronites and various Christian sects – who might be turned into allies. Here he hoped to establish a secure base for his far-reaching plans, among a friendly people, whose young men could be enticed to enlist in his expeditionary force, and with their help its size could be enlarged considerably. Even during the siege of Acre he was vouchsafed a certain amount of assistance from some of these national groups, in the area of supply, of help with his wounded and mainly in the area of intelligence. Their reports about enemy movements were essential to Napoleon. However, to start with, only the Matuwellis came out openly on Napoleon's side, as well as the descendants of Daher al-Umar, who had been removed from power in Galilee by Djezzar. The other sects and tribes of Galilee and Southern Lebanon regarded the siege of Acre as the supreme test: if Napoleon succeeded they intended to join him, and if he failed they would remain loyal to Djezzar and the Ottoman Sultan.

In Acre itself the situation was near chaotic when there was no doubt left that Napoleon was approaching. We have only one report from the town in those final days before the siege started, and it was penned by Rabbi Nah-man from Breslau, one of the major figures in the Hassidic movement. He had visited the Holy Land, and now wished to return to his home in Eastern Europe. In Acre he was trying desperately to book passage on a ship of the neutral trading republic of Ragusa. Here are some of his impressions of Acre:

'And in the city itself there was great fear, because of the great concentration of Moslem soldiers and because the city gates had been closed. And on Saturday in the morning the dragoman came and reported that passage on no ship from Ragusa could be obtained any more, and the only ships left were those owned by Moslems and sailing to Istanbul. And though it is dangerous (for a Jew) to sail with them, it is less dangerous than staying here, as it had been ordered that the war here was to start in two days time ... And the dragoman booked passage for us and during that time ships with soldiers from England arrived and the terror mounted. The town was badly overcrowded, there were too many people to contain. We who had already booked passage were content, however had not prepared any provisions for the journey, as everything was so sudden, that nothing could be obtained. On Sunday ... suddenly there was great commotion and it was ordered by the pasha (Djezzar) that there were only two hours left for whoever could not bear arms, to get away out to the sea, as the gates had been closed and the only exit left was seawards, and whoever could not get away would be slaughtered by the Moslems, as they wanted to prepare the town for defence and therefore they intended to massacre all [noncombatants] left behind. There was awful noise, and fright and great terror...'[5]

However, Rabbi Nahman managed to get away in the nick of time on one of the remaining ships. We have here a vivid description of the utter confusion reigning in Acre, and of Djezzar's draconian measures to inject into it some sort of order and coherence.

The English ships mentioned by Rabbi Nahman belonged to the squadron commanded by Sir Sidney Smith which arrived in Acre on 15 March. Besides the English commodore, there arrived with it a French royalist colonel named Louis Edmond de Picard de Phelipeaux (1767–99). Though only 4 feet 10 inches in height, he was strongly build, and was to play an important part during the siege.[6] He, like Napoleon, was a specialist in artillery and had actually studied together with Napoleon at the War Academy in Paris. Phelipeaux was usually the first in their class, while Napoleon was generally only the third. Though they shared a desk in class, they seem to have disliked each other intensely. Now chance placed them on opposing sides before Acre. Phelipeaux, being an aristocrat, had emigrated from revolutionary France and had won Sir Sidney Smith's friendship and gratitude when he saved him from a French jail. He had joined his friend on his eastern cruise, and was put ashore in Acre in order to help Djezzar organise his defences. In Acre, before his death during the siege, he proved that his success at the Ecole Militaire had been no fluke. He placed the guns captured from Napoleon in position, however, British marines were used as gun crews, ensuring all through the siege a standard of precision and ability not to be met with elsewhere in the forces opposing Napoleon in the East. Napoleon, the artillerist, was defeated at Acre, to a certain degree, by artillery. Beyond this was the combination of European know-how and Djezzar's fierce determination, which forged Acre's surprising power of resistance.

Napoleon certainly did not expect anything beyond what he had experienced at Jaffa. The walls of Acre looked unimpressive – only a single line, erected originally by Daher al-Umar, out of the debris of the crusader edifices still lying around in mid-18th century. The second line of walls, still standing today, was erected by Djezzar only after the end of the French siege.[7] Nor did Napoleon regard the garrison as being any different from the Levantine levies he had been up against in the past. It was not to be expected that these eastern soldiers, inexperienced in modern European warfare, would be able to stand up to the greatest captain of the age and his war-hardened veterans. However there were several points which evened the score:

- Djezzar's soldiers were better trained, more disciplined and better paid than those of other Ottoman formations.
- Their determination to fight was greater than usual, as Napoleon's massacre of the garrison of Jaffa had showed them that they had no choice but to fight to the death. Also Djezzar's fame for cruelty served as an extra incitement.
- What they lacked in technical know how was supplied by their Western allies, by Colonel Phelipeaux and his helpers, who personally placed and laid the guns. The British gave Djezzar mortars which proved highly efficient against the shallow trenches the French were to dig. The British navy passed on to the defenders 1300 bombs, 4000 cannon balls and an ample supply of good and reliable powder. The British landed about 800 marines who were to work the guns captured from the French and did so sometimes from two redoubts they raised beyond the moat, outside the walls, from where they were able to lay down enfilading fire against the French trenches and the French assaults. In addition the naval guns on the British warships were able to give fire support to the garrison.
- Djezzar had some 250 cannon of his own, though mostly of rather anti-quated design and make.
- The fortifications of the town were stronger than they looked. The dry moat outside the walls had been deepened and had been properly walled also on the side away from the city. This was to decide the fate of the first great French assault.

However the unexpected points of strength of the defence are not sufficient to explain this first great defeat of Napoleon. There were additional points of weakness on the French side:

- A besieging force was expected to be superior in numbers to the defenders who had their walls to add strength to their position. Djezzar's regular forces were about 7000 strong and they were strengthened by irregulars and by the inhabitants of Acre, where even women and children had to help in constructing defences whenever necessary. Further there were the British marines on shore and sailors afloat, who would intervene in moments of supreme crisis. The French forces numbered by now about 12,000 men which was insufficient for their manifold tasks: to besiege Acre, to acquire

Galilee and hold it against enemy forces, to renew from time to time contact with the garrison of Jaffa and to fight outside forces such as those of the pasha of Damascus and the levies of Samaria.

- To effectively besiege a town like Acre, two thirds of the length of the walls of which were facing the sea, it is usually necessary to possess control of the sea. However in this case the British squadron controlled the nearby sea and kept its supply routes open.
- Heavy siege artillery is needed against a fortress of Acre's strength. Napoleon had not only lost his siege guns, but had them actually used against his own forces. He ordered his commanders in Egypt to send the siege guns still remaining there out to Acre, but this, inevitably, entailed some delay.
- The French lacked ammunition and could not quickly get sufficient from their base in Egypt either. Thus they could not fully use the limited number of cannon at their disposal. They had to collect the balls shot at them by the British along the sea shore and reuse them.
- More serious than anything else were, perhaps, the mistakes made by Napoleon himself. His disdain for his enemy and the pressure of the time factor caused him to make hasty decisions which, in the end, defeated all the French efforts. Before the walls of Acre we meet a different Napoleon from the great captain who blazed a chain of unequalled victories all through Europe.

And in spite of all this, the siege of Acre was two months of bloody and hard fought struggle of nearly equal forces. Napoleon's soldiers, so used to constant victory, did not believe that this small eastern fortress could hold them up or stop them.

The French reached the vicinity of Acre on 19 March. Here they found a town of about 10,000 inhabitants, jutting out into the sea and surrounded by little gardens and orchards, divided by high cactus hedges. Behind these some of Djezzar's soldiers offered stubborn resistance and had first to be evicted before the army could settle down to the serious business of the siege.

Napoleon's headquarters were set up near an ancient water conduit raised on pillars, which bisected the whole area. To its right, opposite Acre's northern wall, Kléber's division was in charge. To its left, opposite Acre's eastern wall, it was Reynier's sector. Bon's and Lannes' divisions remained in reserve in the centre. A small force held nearby Tel el-Fukhar, which ever since the Crusades had been called 'King Richard's Hill', after Richard Coeur de Lion who had from here guided the siege of Acre during the Third Crusade. But ever since 1799 this hill was to be called 'Napoleon's Hill' and is thus known to this very day.

Reynier's division engaged the garrison by gun fire. Djezzar's men did not interfere in the beginning with the French dispositions. General Caffarelli, the French chief engineer, suggested that Acre should best be attacked at its north eastern corner, from the east. Here the walls formed sharp angles which could be bombarded from both sides and were difficult to defend. This was also the point furthest from the sea and thus it would be difficult for the British naval guns to interfere effectively. This, too, was where the ancient conduit (recently restored by Daher al-Umar) entered the town, and by advancing alongside, the French soldiers would be less exposed to enemy fire. Unfortunately for the French, however, this was also where the town wall had been strengthened by the strongest tower, which throughout the siege proved a tough nut to crack for the enfeebled French siege artillery.[8]

Napoleon and his officers reconnoitred the walls several times, and especially the sector chosen for the assault. However, because of the defenders' fire, they did not approach near enough to find out that the moat had been deepened and strengthened. One of their officers, Major Sanson, tried to reach the edge of the moat at night, by crawling forward on his belly, in order to inspect its depth and the construction of the counterscarp, but he was detected by the defenders, who opened fire, wounded him and forced him to retire.[9] The failure of his reconnaissance had grievous and perhaps decisive results.

Orthodox siege warfare was supposed to necessitate the opening of trenches which would enable attackers to concentrate before the assault. Further it was regarded as desirable to mine the point of assault in the walls and blow it up at the proper time, thus opening a breach in the walls which would enable the attackers to gain entrance into the town. Usually the final artillery preparations, to help opening up this breach, were started only when other arrangements were complete. The defenders could, of course, hinder these preparations by sudden sallies of their own, with a view to destroying the engineering works, sabotaging the mines, blowing up the siege cannon and so on. During the siege of Acre the defenders were actually to mount more assaults in defence of their city than the French in their attempts to gain control of it.

However, Napoleon decided to dispense with most of the preparations, just as he had done at Jaffa. There were initially no large scale mining operations undertaken. Further he decided not to await the arrival of the heavy siege guns from Egypt. Also the trenches dug by the French were only shallow. When Napoleon, who was short, inspected them with Kléber, who was tall, Kléber is reported to have remarked: 'Damned funny trenches they had made here; they may be alright for you, General, but as for me they hardly reach up to my belly.'[10]

Napoleon, however, was not prepared to wait, to improve on his preparations. Instead of advancing his cannon step by step, meanwhile preparing positions further forward, he had them open fire at their maximum range. But when it became apparent that their effectiveness was minimal at that distance, he decided to concentrate all the cannon at his disposal, at the planned point of breach, and to advance them in only one forward movement. An open water reservoir, next to the conduit, half the distance between his camp and the walls, gave him the chance to do so. The reservoir was emptied of water by his engineers and prepared as a forward gun position and a concentration point for the assault force.

The great attack was to take place on 28 March. But now the weak points in Napoleon's plans became only too apparent. As he had concentrated all his guns in one place, it was quite clear where he intended to break in and thus the defenders were able to concentrate all their forces and take counter-measures, in the same area as well. Colonel Phelipeaux concentrated his fire against the French guns in the dried-out water reservoir and thereby hindered the preparations and interfered with the French efforts to make a breach in the corner tower of the wall. As a result their fire was much less effective than it would have been otherwise and the French failed during the morning hours of 28 March to effect the breach. Not until noon had part of the tower collapsed and a narrow breach appeared, but so high up that it would be difficult to reach. Napoleon, impatient as ever, gave the sign for the onslaught to commence. The French army was organized for this purpose in several columns:

- The Forlorn Hope, composed of assault engineers and grenadiers, commanded by Captain Mailly de Châteaurenaud. They had to storm the breach first and to prepare it for the passage of the main forces.
- The main assault force, of 800 men, which was to wait behind the raised conduit for the sign that the breach was ready.
- Kléber's division, to the right of the conduit and Reynier's division, to its left, were to serve first as covering forces and later to pass through the breach into the town.
- Lannes' and Bon's divisions, which had borne most of the fighting during

the capture of Jaffa, were now in reserve and were to join the assault later on. Napoleon's disdain of his enemy is evident from his not using these ample reserves for any diversionary effort.

- Murat's cavalry was in charge of safeguarding the area of operations against outside interference.

When the smoke had cleared and the breach in the wall was seen by all, a great shout went up in the French camp. On the other hand it had the opposite effect on the morale of the defenders.

The French now blew up a mine, in order to connect their system of trenches with the town moat. This was necessary to enable the assault party to reach the breach. But here the French were faced by a great surprise: the wall of the moat had not been, as expected, constructed of earth, which would have collapsed and settled at an easy angle into it, thus enabling the assault force access to the fosse. Actually the outside wall of the moat had been revetted solidly with stones to the height of eight metres, a fact which had escaped the French in spite of their reconnoitring near the city walls. Thus the wall did not collapse, as expected, as a result of the explosion of the mine and the assault party was left with ladders five metres in height to negotiate the eight metres descent into the moat. Composed of picked men, as it was, the assault party somehow achieved the descent into the fosse, in spite of their short ladders. The defenders were at first in a state of shock, and thus their fire was not too heavy. Mailley and several of his men managed to cross the ditch and to ascend into the breach in the main tower. But the men of the break-in force were apparently less athletic and found the eight-metre drop into the moat too much for them. They stopped near the wall of the fosse and created an easy target, into which Djezzar's men poured their concentrated fire.

However in the town of Acre the civilian population began to panic, and believed the town about to fall. Quite a few boarded ships and started to sail away. Some of the soldiers also began to withdraw from their posts. At this crucial moment Djezzar placed himself opposite the breach. He raised the morale of his men, some of whom had been ready to retire, by shooting his pistol at the French and shouting 'What are you afraid of? Look they are retreating!'[11] This was one of the two critical moments of the siege and the fear of Djezzar proved stronger in the breasts of his soldiers than the fear of the attacking French.

And indeed the assault had lost its momentum. Only one platoon of the break-in force managed to descend into the moat, but their commander was killed, the men scattered to look for suitable ladders and were picked off by the fire of the defenders and killed in the fosse. The rest of the break-in force were standing in a dense mass near the outside wall of the moat and provided good targets for the fire of Djezzar's men and also for the artillery handled by the marines and even for the naval guns of the British fleet. Many of them were wounded and some were killed. The spirits of the defenders rose considerably, when they saw the attack thus checked, and they increased their fire. Most of the initial assaulting force had by then been killed in the moat and only ten Frenchmen remained inside the breached tower. Most of these started to retreat as well. Only four stayed on, among them their commander, and these were finished off by Djezzar's Sudanese bodyguards.

Napoleon now stopped the forward movement of the divisions which were to participate in the attack and the assault collapsed. The French returned to their camp. One of the participants claims that only 25 of them had been killed and that 87 had been wounded.

This first French repulse proved fatal. The French artillery did not have sufficient ammunition to renew a full scale bombardment, without which it was impossible to open a new breach. The existing one was quickly repaired by the inhabitants of Acre. Those of them who had set out to sea, now returned to their city. On 30 March Djezzar ordered the execution of about 100 of the leading Christian citizens of Acre, just in case they should feel any sympathy for the Christians outside the walls. Their bodies were thrown into the sea stuffed into boxes of coffee and rice and were carried by the waves to the shore. When the French opened the boxes they were surprised and shocked to find among them the body of the brother of Captain Mailly de Châteaurenaud, who had been sent by Napoleon half a year earlier on a diplomatic mission to Syria, had been arrested on Djezzar's orders, and had now been strangled inside the jail on his order, two days after his brother had fallen in the breach of the tower.

Napoleon was left now with no choice but to postpone the renewal of the assault until after the arrival of his siege guns and further ammunition from Egypt. Instead of the quick capture of the town which he needed so badly, he was left now with a full scale siege. His effort at short cuts had backfired. A slower and more methodical approach might have been the better solution after all.

10

FRENCH RULE IN GALILEE[1]

The siege of Acre did not take place in a vacuum. Potential enemies were concentrating all around the French besieging force. It was necessary for Napoleon to take appropriate steps to seal off the siege area against interference from the outside. This became especially urgent after the failure of the first great assault of 28 March, when there remained no doubt that the siege was going to be a protracted one. In spite of the limited size of forces at his disposal Napoleon had no choice but to allocate a portion of them to the safeguarding of the area of operations. Having done so, he decided to go a step further and to extend his direct rule to all of Western Galilee, and later, even to all of Galilee, from the Mediterranean to the Jordan and Lake Genezareth. One of the reasons was the potential threat from the pasha of Damascus: It will be remembered that the French expedition to the Holy Land was organized, among other reasons, because Turkish forces were being massed around Damascus. By now Napoleon had moved his force much nearer to this town the the local pasha could now attack him with shorter supply lines and fewer preparations.

The army of Damascus was, however, not the only danger threatening the French. The inhabitants of the district of Samaria did not intend to stay within their mountain fastness and were once again massing under the leadership of Jussef Gerar of Jenin, and also intended to come to the aid of Ahmed Djezzar in Acre.[2] Furthermore, there were the remains of the Egyptian Mameluk cavalry units, who had been fighting the French ever since the start of the French invasion of Egypt. They had withdrawn northwards through Palestine and were now in Galilee looking around for allies for a renewed attack on the hated French. Local beduin tribes posed a further threat.

Against all these dangers Napoleon decided to organize a defensive interior area, in Western Galilee, from the mountain ridge of Nakoura in the north to Mount Carmel and beyond, to Tantura, in the south,[3] and from the blue waters of the Mediterranean in the west to the green foothills of the mountains of Galilee in the east. This area encompassed all of Western Galilee, at that

The first advance into Galilee, 30 March—8 April 1799

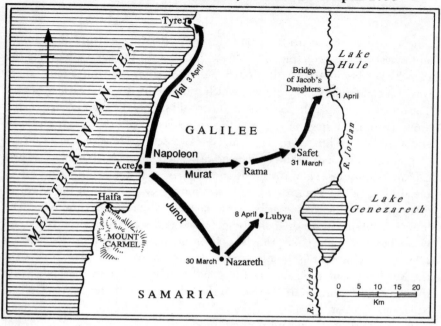

The second advance into Galilee, April 1799

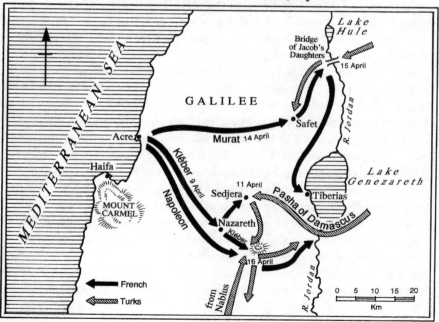

time a country of rich fields, of plentiful fruit orchards, of many olive groves and of varied vegetable plots. It offered thus a valuable supply base for the French expeditionary force. In March and April, after the winter rains, there was also a plentiful supply of grass which could be used by the cavalry horses. The mills along the little Na'aman rivulet could supply the flour needed by the army. During the siege of Acre the French soldiers could thus eat fresh bread and would not be limited to their usual diet of biscuits. However the local type of grain – dura and sesame – which was found in great abundance in the captured stores of Haifa, Nazareth and Tiberias, did not make for a type of bread liked by the French soldier. It was too sticky and felt, in the words of quartermaster Miot, like 'glue between the teeth' and tasted accordingly.[4] The local inhabitants also raised sheep and goats and sometimes even cows and water buffaloes, and could thus supply meat, milk and cheese. The French soldier could also obtain locally grown tobacco. Wine was scarcer, because of the Muslim prejudice against it, but could be obtained from the Jews living mostly in Shafr Amr, Kafr Jasif and in the cities of central and eastern Galilee, Safet and Tiberias.

In order efficiently to utilize these products of Galilee, Napoleon did not confiscate the foodstuffs needed, but made use of the existing local markets. Here his civilian quartermasters effected the purchases on behalf of their units, and officers and men could privately buy additions to their army rations. As payment was in cash, the local inhabitants were glad to bring their products to the markets, the expeditionary force did not lack for fresh food and in addition obtained the goodwill of the population.

In order to safeguard Western Galilee, French units occupied strong points in Ras el-Nakura in the north, in Danun and near the entry of the valley of Madjdal Krum in the east, in Shafr Amr and the entrance into the Valley of Jezreel to the south-east and in Haifa and Tantura to the south.

Haifa was neutralized by the British naval squadron cruising in the bay of Acre and its harbour could thus not be used by the French. On 21 March the British tried to retake Haifa. Its French commander, Lambert, installed only two days previously, decided to trick the British by running up a Turkish flag on a flag pole. The attacking force now believed the place to be in Turkish hands and landed without sufficient precautions, promptly falling into a French ambush. Some of the Royal Marines were killed and others wounded, but, more important, they had to abandon a little gun boat, which carried a heavy piece of artillery – a 32-pounder.[5] A few days later the French at Haifa managed to obtain a 24-pounder gun – by a similar trick – from a Turkish gunboat. These two guns were brought to Acre and during most of the siege were the only two pieces of heavy artillery in the possession of the French.

On 5 April Lambert was ordered to send a reconnaissance to Tantura. He reported afterwards that a small harbour existed there, usually used only by small boats carrying water melons, but still of sufficient size to be utilized by the French. As an alternative he also investigated slightly further to the north, Atlit, the Castellum Peregrinorum of the Crusaders, and their last stronghold in the Holy Land. It was found that the local headman had been a prisoner of Djezzar's, therefore hated him, and was prepared to co-operate with the French. However because of its better harbour, Napoleon decided in favour of Tantura and it became the main naval base of the French expedition. Supplies which could not be sent northwards by land from Jaffa, because of the hostile attitude of the mountain dwellers of the Samaria district, could thus be sent by sea and could be landed south of Mount Carmel, safe from detection by the British squadron, cruising in Haifa bay. Tantura was the ancient Dor, one of the more important harbours of the Holy Land in the second and first millennium BC, until it was superseded by Caesarea, founded by King Herod. For a short instant, during Napoleon's campaign, it returned to the limelight of history.[6]

Lambert was also responsible for the more easterly area of Shafr Amr. This place was attacked by a force from Samaria on 22 March, but the small French garrison there was speedily reinforced by a unit from the central reserve in the camp before Acre, which repulsed the attack. Two of the four French divisions before Acre usually served as central reserve. Every 24 hours the assignments were rotated between the divisions, with one of them manning the trenches surrounding the besieged city, the second covering it by fire support, and the two remaining ones being held in readiness for operations elsewhere in Western Galilee. On 26 March, for instance, a unit from the central reserve operated against a beduin force which was concentrating in the hills of Sekh Abrek, to the south-east, which was promptly dispersed. On 19 April a considerable Arab force concentrating near Mount Carmel, was surprised and destroyed by another unit from the central reserve.

The units of the reserve were used, too, for expanding the French radius of operations beyond Western Galilee. This was sometimes done in conjunction with local elements who were prepared to co-operate with the French. Already on the very day Napoleon appeared before Acre, he was joined by the beduin chieftain Abbās el-Daher (one of the sons of Daher al-Umar, who had controlled all of Galilee in the middle of the 18th century) and who brought with him 400 or 500 horsemen. Later Napoleon appointed Abbās as civil governor of Tiberias, which had been the original stronghold of his family.[7]

The Matuwelli inhabitants of Southern Lebanon, too, were prepared to co-operate with Napoleon. In the past they had been the close allies of Daher al-Umar, but since his downfall they were hard pressed by their enemy Djezzar, and their situation had become a very difficult one. Thus Napoleon, as Djezzar's foe, was their natural ally. In order to strengthen their pro-French attitude, Napoleon sent General Vial on 3 April with 300 soldiers northwards to seize Tyre, in southern Lebanon. In biblical times this had been one of the chief Phoenician towns, but like all other coastal towns had been destroyed by the Mameluks after the end of the Crusades and was now a sleepy and rather dilapidated little port. On the first approach of the French, the inhabitants took flight, but returned when General Vial promised neither to harm them, nor their property. Vial now expanded the French sphere of influence to the mouth of the river Litani. Many of the local Matuwelli inhabitants joined his forces and 200 of them under their Sheikh Maneh, were appointed as garrison of Tyre. Others took over, on behalf of the French, further strong points in the nearby mountains, thus safeguarding the northern flank of the French army before Acre. Still others came to the aid of the French in the final phases of the battle of Mount Tabor. On 5 April, his mission completed, General Vial returned with his men to the French camp before Acre.[8]

However the main danger to the French loomed in the north-east, from the Damascus area. Napoleon despatched General Murat in this direction, at the head of a force of 200 cavalrymen, 500 infantrymen and two light cannon, ordering him to occupy Safet, the mountain capital of central Galilee. Murat had been one of Napoleon's closest associates ever since, as a young captain, he helped him in the month of Vendémiaire 1795 to suppress the uprising of the Parisian sections, by obtaining, in the nick of time, the all important cannon, which provided Napoleon's 'whiff of grapeshot'. On the way to Safet Murat was joined by the Sheikh Mustafa Bashir, who had been governor of this district under Djezzar, but had fallen out with him, had joined the French, and was now appointed by Napoleon to his previous post, much to the vexation of Abbās el-Daheer, who had hoped to become governor of Safet himself. Napoleon however followed a policy of 'divide and rule' and preferred not to give too much power into the hands of either of these as yet unproven allies.

The departure of Murat's little force was delayed by the great attack on Acre on 28 March, and took place only on 30 March. Murat's men passed through the valley of Madjdal Krum, with the high mountain ridges of Upper Galilee to their left. They approached Safet through the broken country to its south, from where they had to send their cannon back, as they could not get them over the deep wadis. Safet was held by a small garrison of soldiers from Morocco, who evacuated it so quickly that their aged commander fell into the hands of the French. In the dilapidated huge citadel, which overlooked the little town, and had originally been constructed by the Crusaders in the 13th century, Murat's soldiers found six ancient cannon, and, more important, sufficient amounts of flour, tobacco and lentils for their immediate needs. From the numerous Jewish inhabitants the soldiers purchased wine and brandy, which comforted them after their forced march. In spite of their plentiful consumption of spirits, the soldiers were sufficiently wide awake to repulse a counter attack during their first night in Safet.[9]

The next morning Murat led a small force down the mountain towards the Jordan and the Bridge of Jacob's Daughters, on the main highway towards Damascus. As no enemy was met, and the supply of grass for their horses was running short, Napoleon ordered the main force to return to the camp before Acre, and only a force of 200 men, under a captain named Simon, was left in Safet. Sheikh Mustafa was left in charge of civilian affairs and was ordered to provide 50 men to hold the Bridge of Jacob's Daughters, similar to the Matuwellis in Tyre. However he proved unable to do so, as he was too unpopular with the local inhabitants, who remembered him as Djezzar's avaricious governor and tax gatherer. They asked Murat to have him replaced by Abbās el-Daher, but Napoleon would not agree to this. During the first days of April, Murat with most of his force returned to the camp before Acre. Thus Upper Galilee, too, became part of the French-controlled area.[10]

A similar force left the camp before Acre on 30 March, to occupy Lower Galilee as well. It was under the command of General Junot, and consisted of 300 infantrymen and 150 cavalrymen. They were to clear the area of unfriendly beduin, and report any offensive movements by the men of Nablus. They first passed through Shafr Amr, where they were joined by several of the relatives of the late Daher al-Umar. On 31 March Junot reached Nazareth, the capital of Lower Galilee. He was received with great enthusiasm by the local population, about half of whom were Christian, as his was the first Christian force since the Crusades, to reach this cradle of Christianity. A deputation of local Christians was sent to call on Napoleon in his camp before Acre, and promised him the active help of the Christians of Lower Galilee. They did indeed live up to their promises, by gathering information and reporting enemy movements beyond the French controlled area.[11]

Junot quartered himself in the Franciscan monastery in Nazareth, and had a company of cavalrymen serve as his bodyguard. The French were attacked by some of the local beduin, but repulsed them easily. One of the French participants[12] reports that Nazareth was only a village, but another puts the number of its inhabitants at 4000 to 5000 souls,[13] which would have been quite a sizeable town for Palestine at that time.

On 1 April Junot sent a reconnaissance southwards, through the valley of Jezreel, towards the town of Jenin, in the foothills of Samaria. This was the capital of Jussef Gerar, the 'Sheikh of the Mountain', and one of the leading personalities in all of the Samaria–Nablus district. From afar the French soldiers noticed military forces milling around there, whom they estimated to number between 2000 and 4000 men. Prudently they did not approach too near Jenin. Lambert, from Haifa, reported to Napoleon on 2 April that there were about 4000 footsoldiers in Jenin and 500 cavalrymen. Further he reported that this force was being raised as a result of Djezzar's propaganda and presents from him to the notables of Samaria.[14] Because of this concentration of enemy forces, Junot was ordered by Napoleon, in contrast to Murat and Vial, not to return to Acre, but to stay on in Nazareth. He was to safeguard the vicinity, watch the Nablus mountain people, and send spies to Tiberias, in the east, to report on any military movements there as well.[15]

The French commanders in the various outlying stations were ordered by Napoleon to move their men around as much as possible, so as to create an impression of much greater forces than those actually employed. In this way Napoleon succeeded in keeping the local population suitably impressed and loyal. As a result Napoleon's headquarters received a steady flow of information on enemy movements from such friendly elements as the Christians of Lower Galilee, the Matuwellis in Southern Lebanon and the beduin followers of the Daher family. In Galilee, the French did not feel as if they were in an enemy country, as had been the case in Egypt and in Southern Palestine, and could move around freely from place to place. The cooler, still rather wet climate reminded them of France, as Napoleon was to point out in his memoirs.[16]

One of the most important long-term achievements of French rule in Galilee was perhaps its being measured and mapped properly for the first time, by the army's engineer-geographers, under Colonel Jacotin. On 2 May Napoleon wrote to Kléber, who was then in charge of Eastern Galilee: 'I send you herewith all the engineer-geographers so that they can sketch the country. You will appreciate how essential it is for them to apportion this work among themselves so that I shall have, as soon as possible, a plan of the land.'[17] Jacotin notes in his journal that he left the camp near Acre for this purpose on 3 May and reported to General Kléber the same day in the afternoon. A better map of Galilee based on actual trigonometrical measurements, was produced only 80 years later, this time by a British Royal Engineers team, headed for most of the time by another distinguished soldier, H.H. Kitchener.

The administration of Galilee was run by Napoleon with the help of his oriental secretary and translator, an aged Frenchman named M. Venture, who had spent all his life in the east, had married a Greek woman and whose daughter had been born in Egypt. He was helped by other men with similar backgrounds, one of whom, M. Jaubert, took over his duties after Venture's death. Napoleon ordered the headmen of all the big villages and little towns – Nazareth, Ez-Zib, Kafr Kanna, Safet, Tiberias, Tyre and so on – to meet at his camp, so as to show their defection from Djezzar's party, and their adherence to the French cause, and to make arrangements for co-operation with the French forces who might operate in their vicinity. Whenever necessary Napoleon passed direct orders to the local authorities, such as demanding of Mustafa Beshir not to treat the felaheen of the Safet district harshly, or instructing the headman of Nazareth to return the property in his area belonging to the al-Umar family to Daher's sons.

Galilee's borders were not, however, the limits of Napoleon's activity. His diplomatic messengers and his undercover agents ranged much further afield. He contacted the Emir of the Lebanon, Beshir II, suggesting much reduced taxes for the port of Beirut, in return for closer co-operation, or, in other words, French suzerainty. Other messengers reached the chief mullah (or religious dignitary) of Damascus, the stronghold of his enemies.[18] Christian, Jewish and Muslim agents of his reached Aleppo, in Northern Syria, Armenia, Asia Minor and Persia.[19] He continued to keep up his contacts with the Persian court right through his reign as emperor of France.

His rule over Galilee was actually one of the points in his early life where Napoleon mastered the craft of running a civilian administration, a craft which stood him in good stead when, only a few months later, he became ruler of all France. There surely were not many 30-year-olds in history who had accumulated such varied experience in this field as he:

- In his native island of Corsica, in 1792 and 1793; but there he failed in the end, and his activity helped bring about the occupation of the island by the British.
- In Italy, in the years 1796–97, where he organized, during his campaign

against the Austrians, a new administration, based on the ideological lines of the French Revolution, setting up new republics in place of the old duchies and princely states, controlled by Austria.

- In Egypt in 1798 and 1799, where he set up, in an eastern country, a western type of administration, which was both new and strange to the local inhabitants.
- In Galilee, as reported here.
- In France, after the 18th of Brumaire, when he took over as First Consul.

His associates in the coup of Brumaire, such as the devious Sieyés, thought they could easily push the rude soldier aside, once he had set them up in power and did not realize that he was more experienced both in civil government and political intrigue than they themselves were.

But let us return to the Holy Land. To summarize here, we see Napoleon, or as we should still call him at this stage of his career, General Bonaparte, in the spring of 1799, in charge of a small state of Galilee – of about the same size as the Crusader 'Principality of Galilee' set up by Tancred – which serves as logistical base for his French forces and as centre of his far-flung military and diplomatic activity.

11

THE OFFENSIVE OF THE PASHA OF DAMASCUS, AND THE BATTLES OF NAZARETH AND THE BRIDGE OF JACOB'S DAUGHTERS[1]

The Porte planned a three-pronged attack against the French before Acre. Part of the force concentrating in Rhodes for an attack on Egypt was now diverted to sail instead to Acre. However, its departure was delayed and it arrived too late to participate in the campaign opening early in April. In the mountains of Samaria some 5000 to 6000 men took up arms, and descended into the Valley of Jezreel in order to attack the French from the south. However, the main force was to be contributed by Ahmed Pasha of Damascus. His army amounted to about 33,000 men, who now advanced to the Jordan. Here he divided it into two forces. The main one stayed with him, east of the river, while his son, Sheikh Abbās, at the head of 8000 men, camped adjacent to the Bridge of Jacob's Daughters over the Jordan (north of Lake Genezareth) and advanced from there to Safet. He arrived there on 6 April and laid siege to the citadel, into which Captain Simon and his 200 Frenchmen had withdrawn on his approach. The Turks attacked the French several times and tried in vain to scale its walls. Safet suffered badly during the siege and was partly burnt down by the Turks.

Another part of Sheikh Abbās' force continued southward and occupied the hills south of the village of Lubya, and west of Tiberias, very near to the historic battlefield of the Horns of Hattin, where the Crusaders had been so decisively defeated by Saladin. When Junot at Nazareth was informed about their advance, he came out in their direction at the head of a force of 125 horsemen and 300 foot soldiers. Only some 25 men were left in Nazareth. Near Kaf Kanna (usually identified – though incorrectly – with the Cana of Galilee of the New Testament) one of Daher's sons joined them, advising them that considerable enemy forces were moving towards Mount Tabor. Further east, in

99

the hills of Lubya, the head of the French column was attacked by about a thousand Turkish cavalrymen, and immediately afterwards, some 500 or 600 Turks attacked the tail of the column. The French mounted a counter attack by their small cavalry unit. At first they were unable to pierce the Turkish line and a face to face struggle took place, which was decided in the end by the well directed fire of the French infantry. The Turks fell back and enabled the French to occupy a stronger position on top of one of the hills. Further Turkish forces came up. One of the French dragoon officers estimated their strength at about 3000, which would mean odds of about 1 to 7.[2] At about 10.00 in the morning (8 April) the Turks launched their main attack. The same dragoon officer describes it as follows:

'The Turkish cavalry attacked us at a gallop, shouting horribly. Their sabres glittered in the sun, their flowing coats revealed their gold bordered dress; their horses jumped full of fury and seemed to share the rage of their riders. On our side profound silence reigned . . . Junot gave the order to open fire. The thunder of the fusillade drowned out the shouting and the clatter of the arms. Through the dense smoke which surrounded us I saw the hideous riders with their dark faces, who shouted like demons; however Major Duvivier had already lifted his sabre and we met the furious Turkish onslaught with firm foot and our blades commenced their terrible work. A richly dressed Mameluke fired his pistol at my head, wounding me lightly: but I had the consolation of stretching him out dead at my feet. At that moment I saw Major Prévot fighting on the ground against two Turks, his horse having been killed under him by a shot, but he had disengaged himself in time, and with astonishing calm was countering the blows aimed at him by his adversaries. The brave Pignard came running to his aid and transfixed the body of one of his enemies with his sabre, while Prévot killed the other with a back handed blow . . . A captain of the 3rd Dragoons fell mortally wounded and some of the men of his company had great difficulty in recovering his body. Somewhat further away an NCO of the same regiment attacked a Mameluke who held a battle banner made out of a long horse tail; both horsemen struggling body against body their mounts participating furiously, until the whole group rolled on the ground. However the Turk, hindered by his flowing robes, could not get up in time and the blade of the NCO pierced his chest, and he died full of rage as he saw his banner in the hand of his enemy. After this the attacks became less pressing.'

The fire of the French infantry line became more effective and the Turks withdrew a bit, leaving the French isolated in an area strewn with corpses. Junot reorganized his men, and the Turks renewed their assault, but this time less resolutely. They looked now for weak spots in the French line and hurled their lances against the French so as to create a passage between the French bayonets, but in vain. Junot was attacked by two Turks, but killed one of them by a pistol shot and the other by a cut of his sabre. A further four battle banners were captured by the French, but were lost again in the mêlée. At 3 o'clock the Turks withdrew.

The French lost eight cavalrymen and three infantrymen killed, and 48 wounded. In Junot's report to Napoleon after the battle he stressed the good quality of the enemy cavalry and pointed out that this had been the hottest fight he had ever been in.[3] Napoleon, who always preferred to name battles after places with historically resonant names, did not call the engagement after the village of Lubya, but named it the 'Battle of Nazareth'. He appreciated the spirit shown there by his old friend Junot to such an extent that, when in 1807 he decided to create him a duke, his first choice was Duke of Nazareth. However he had second thoughts: he believed 'Junot of Nazareth' might sound just a bit too like 'Jesus of Nazareth', and thus Junot was created Duke of Abrantes (in Portugal) instead.[4] Junot died in 1813 and his widow, the Duchess of Abrantes, found herself in strained financial circumstances after the Bourbon restoration. In order to regain some of her affluence she concocted her many-volumed *Memoirs*, which are a mine of misinformation and slander about Napoleon and his court. Had it been published under the more resounding name of 'Duchess of Nazareth' even more copies of that worthless work might have been sold.

In the meantime the main force of Ahmed Pasha first stayed east of the Jordan, entering Western Palestine via Mejami'a bridge, south of Lake Genezareth. His army numbered about 25,000 men. He led them up into Lower Galilee, while his son Abbās withdrew his men apparently from the Lubya area and had them return to Upper Galilee, to Safet and the main camp at the Bridge of Jacob's Daughters. In the meantime Ahmed Pasha decided to descend into the Valley of Jezreel, in order to unite his forces with those of Nablus and Jenin. Part of his army might however have advanced into this valley directly from the Mejami'a bridge. According to the French reports the force of the mountain people of Samaria had swollen in the meantime to 7000 or 8000 men, concentrated around Jenin. According to the same source, they were joined there by 4000 or 5000 armed felaheen from the Jerusalem district. Thus the total was put at 10,000 to 12,000 men, including 600 cavalrymen, the whole commanded by Jussuf Gerar. This force now awaited the 1800 Mameluk horsemen, who had originally joined the army of Ahmed Pasha but was now to reinforce them, so as to better balance the ratio between cavalry and infantry, on their march westwards against the French.[5]

The news about the Turkish concentration reached French headquarters in bits and pieces. However, as the reports accumulated, Napoleon saw more and more clearly the shape of a really threatening move of an army of some 40,000 to 50,000 men, under Ahmed Pasha, moving westwards to relieve Acre. He now took his counter-measures. Here we meet a very different commander from the one whose mistakes brought about the final debacle at Acre. Here the young general, in several campaigns which encompassed all of Galilee effortlessly demonstrated his grasp of strategic detail, his decisiveness, and his ability for sheer hard work, which were so typical of him at his best in hours of crisis.

He sent two forces against the enemy: Murat, at the head of 1000 men, again advanced to Safet, and Kléber, at the head of his division of some 2500 men, advanced to Nazareth to reinforce Junot's small force there. Both commanders were instructed to help each other in case of need, because at Acre Napoleon was not yet quite sure if the main enemy effort would be made against Murat, or against Kléber, who had been sent out at the head of the much bigger force. However in this chapter we shall follow Murat.

The following is the operational order Murat received on 13 April from the chief of staff, Berthier:

'Headquarters, Acre, 24th Germinal, Year VII. The Commander in Chief orders you, Citizen General, to leave tomorrow morning at three with all of the 25th light demi-brigade [after the French Revolution the demi-brigade was created in order to fuse regular and conscript battalions into one formation] ... the second battalion of the 9th demi-brigade, and a company of Grenadiers, the second battalion of the 18th demi-brigade, and Brigade General Rambaud, in order to reach Safet. The quartermaster will issue you with 10,000 rounds.[6] [Berthier then gives detailed administrative instructions. The mission allocated to Murat is spelled out in more detail further on.] The Commander in Chief has been advised that 1200 enemy cavalrymen have crossed the Bridge of Jacob's Daughters, and now besiege the castle of Safet. It is the commander's wish that General Murat will move with all possible speed, with the forces mentioned in this order, to the Bridge of the Daughters of Jacob, in order to cut off these cavalrymen from Damascus. He will utilise his knowledge of this area in order to attack them, and to inflict on them all possible damage, so as to force them to discontinue the siege of Safet and to disperse them. Every six hours General Murat will report to the Commander in Chief and will pass on to him information and keep him posted on his advance.

'The Commander in Chief has instructed the Matuwellis to proceed to the Bridge of the Daughters of Jacob in order there to join General Murat, and it is possible that they will get there, but it is impossible to rely on it. The Commander in Chief has advised General Kléber, that if the enemy forces in front of him should retire to Tiberias, and if there will be but little enemy pressure, he should send to Safet a fairly strong unit. In such a case there will be nothing to fear from a cavalry attack of the enemy, and it will be possible to follow the movements of the enemy besieging Safet, while he will know that General Murat is threatening their rear, and he will manoeuvre accordingly.

'If the enemy should turn towards Acre, while General Murat will be at the Bridge of Jacob's Daughters, though this does not look likely, then the unit designated by General Kléber will move to the enemy's flank, or will follow the enemy if he succeeds in passing him by. If the enemy force will attack General Murat, then the unit designated by General Kléber will move with all speed to his aid . . .

'From the moment the siege of Safet will be lifted, and General Murat will end his pursuit of the enemy, so as to remove him as far as possible, he will return to Acre, and will leave in Safet the 25th demi-brigade, which will come under the command of General Kléber. This general is ordered to manoeuvre according to circumstances [according to the information gathered by] the reconnaissances he will carry out, so as to safeguard Acre by all the routes leading to her, from Safet to Nablus.

'The Commander in Chief expresses his wish that General Murat should return here [to Acre] if possible, by the 30 [19 April], but this depends of course on his completing the mission allocated to him, which has to be carried out.

'General Murat is informed of the orders given to General Kléber, which he would like him to carry out. But General Murat should not rely on it completely, as General Kléber does not have to send a unit to Safet unless the enemy situation enables him to do so. Thus it is possible that General Murat will have to act alone against the enemy in Safet.'

This detailed operation order shows Napoleon trying on one hand to foresee all possible eventualities and on the other hand relying on the initiative of his generals, after he has explained to them, in considerable detail, his thoughts and intentions. And indeed, when Kléber and Murat started their movements they quickly found that the real situation was far different from anything that could have been foreseen at headquarters in Acre.

Murat left, on 13 April, with the force allocated to him. He advanced again through the valley of Madjdal Krum and again could not take his cannon with him when he passed through the deep valleys and over the mountains south of Safet. On approaching this town he sent a local farmer to the fortress commander, Captain Simon, in order to advise him of his movements, and to instruct him to sally out and support him. Murat did not approach Safet himself, but passed south of it, and on the morning of 15 April attacked the Turkish force near the Bridge of Jacob's Daughters. At the same time Captain

Simon sallied forth from the citadel of Safet, and drove before him the force which had been besieging him. When Murat heard the musket fire to his left, he thought these to be Turkish forces, and changed direction, but when he became aware of his mistake, he returned to his original line of attack. He now attached one company of infantry to Simon's force and the remainder he organized into two squares, and in this way his men descended towards the Jordan, first walking and later breaking into a run. On sighting his force, a Damascene cavalry unit fanned out to attack him. But their spirit was not up to it, and before making contact they recoiled and rode off. The rest of the Damascene force, commanded by Sheikh Abbās, followed suit. If the French had possessed an adequate force of cavalry, it would have been possible to overtake and annihilate them, but as it was, they had to be satisfied with the rich booty which fell into their hands in the enemy camp: tents, ammunition, other military equipment and food. The Turks suffered some casualties, while there were none on the French side. The sumptuous tent previously used by Sheikh Abbās was now prepared for Murat's use, though four lances with the cut off heads of French soldiers impaled on them, had to be taken down first.[7]

There was general joy and feasting in the camp that evening. Many of the French soldiers danced and on the bank of the river Jordan sang songs of their far away home. Especially popular were the sticky Damascene sweets of which vast quantities were found in the camp.

The next morning Murat continued southward with his force, and on 17 April he captured – without any resistance – the town of Tiberias on the shores of Lake Genezareth. Much to the surprise of the French the garrison had escaped, in spite of the fact that Tiberias was encircled by strong walls, though not by a moat. The French had no siege guns and thus did not believe that they could have captured the place had it been defended.[8] Tiberias is a good example of what could happen in an eastern town, on the approach of French forces, in the absence of somebody like Djezzar to take command.

Murat lodged in the local citadel. Large magazines were found here, with plenty of food, and especially grain sorghum and sesame in great quantities.

But in the meantime the really decisive battle had taken place further south.

12

THE BATTLE OF MOUNT TABOR[1]

K léber left for Lower Galilee even before Murat had left for Upper Galilee. Lower Galilee seemed, in view of Junot's battle, and the various reports about the massing of enemy forces, to be especially threatened. When Napoleon issued his order to Murat, he was not yet sure where the decision would fall. But his intuition that this would be in Kléber's area, soon proved correct.

Some of Kléber's forces had already reached Nazareth by 10 April, but he himself stayed in Safurie to first ascertain the main areas of concentration of the enemy.

A force belonging to Sheikh Abbās' army was at that time still in Lubya, but its units ranged only as far as Kafr Kanna and did not approach Nazareth. Therefore Kléber felt safe to concentrate all his force, on 11 April, in Nazareth. Later that day he continued eastwards, towards Kafr Kanna and Lubya. As a result a battle developed, which history has not yet graced by a name, but which we can call by the distinctly unnapoleonic name of 'Battle of Sedjera', after a little village, somewhat to the west of the hills of Lubya (and about one kilometre to the south-west of present-day Sedjera).

Junot's unit was now included in Kléber's force. The following is Kléber's account of this engagement:

'Nazaret, le 23 Germinal an VII [12 April 1799]
Yesterday I took the way of Tiberias with about 1500 men, following the plain. The enemy occupied a mountain, apparently at the end of the plain, but in actual fact it only masked another plain which extended to the right and which it was necessary to pass in order to reach Tiberias or Beisan. This mountain dominates the country all around and the Turks were about to observe us from a mile or so further along. We saw them from the same distance. Independently from that height they occupied all the mountain ridges to our right and we therefore moved considerably to the left. We met them about seven miles from Acre in direct line, and three miles from Nazareth along the way we had taken. If one draws a line from Safet to Mount Tabor, it will cross the field of battle,

and both this strongpoint and this mountain can be seen from there quite well. This field of battle was the same where General Junot had given battle on the 19th with such valour.

'My men were divided into two squares: the first was composed of the 75th demi-brigade, and was commanded by General Verdier; it held the left side ... The 100 cavalrymen were at the centre and marched thus between the two squares, which served as their support.

'We had just mounted the cannon, when, with the speed of lightning, about 4000 horsemen and 500 infantrymen rushed us, completely surrounding us, within less than a minute.

'We expected them to engage in hand to hand fighting and hoped thus to gain the upper hand. But either they did not want to engage so strong a force, or they remembered still how dearly the previous engagement had cost them, anyway no movement of ours could induce them to come nearer than the range of a musket or pistol. But the musket fire was lively and General Junot's square and especially its flank guards were heavily engaged. When we had withstood their musket fire for about an hour, I decided to try and put an end to it and ordered General Junot's square to occupy successively the heights to our right, in order to turn the enemy's left flank and to put ourselves between him and Tiberias. General Verdier was to cover General Junot from behind and the cavalry engaged the enemy by fire. But immediately this movement was perceived by the enemy, the Moslems decided to retire and to abandon the field of battle; afterwards they continued their retreat, some towards Jenin and the others towards Kafr e-Sett, and from there probably on to Tiberias. The enemy had with him four small cannon, transported on the backs of camels ...

'The valour and the steadiness under fire of the generals under my command, is too well known to need elaboration. General Junot had his hat pierced by a bullet and received a slight head wound, the sleeve of his uniform too, was pierced and he received another wound on his arm, but he continued to command without any undue excitement. In addition he had two horses wounded under him and his camel was killed.

'I cannot bestow too high praise on the conduct of the officers and men. Their eyes were constantly turned towards the enemy and their ears were listening to the commands; they all marched together and they presented an imposing picture ...

'We had 47 wounded and 6 men killed. The enemy lost perhaps three times as many; he surely had many killed.

'Our men returned by midnight to their positions in Saffuria and in Nazareth.'[3]

The Damascene forces reorganized too. Sheikh Abbās' men withdrew northwards and the vanguard of the main army which was commanded by Ahmed Pasha, advanced from Tiberias and took over the area of the hills of

The battle of Mount Tabor, 16 April 1799

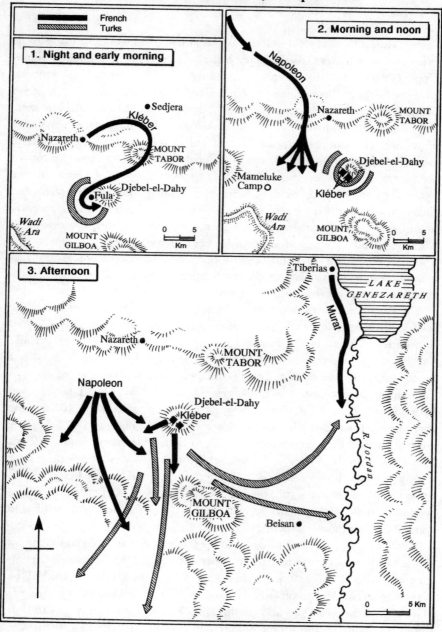

French
Turks

1. Night and early morning

Sedjera

Kléber

Nazareth

MOUNT TABOR

Djebel-el-Dahy

Fula

Wadi Ara

MOUNT GILBOA

0   5
Km

2. Morning and noon

Napoleon

Nazareth

MOUNT TABOR

Mameluke Camp

Djebel-el-Dahy

Kléber

Wadi Ara

MOUNT GILBOA

0   5
Km

3. Afternoon

Tiberias

LAKE GENEZARETH

Nazareth

MOUNT TABOR

Murat

Napoleon

Djebel-el-Dahy

Kléber

R. Jordan

MOUNT GILBOA

Beisan

0   5 Km

Lubya. Thus it became clear that the Turkish main effort would be made in the easier terrain of Lower Galilee and the Valley of Jezreel and not in mountainous Upper Galilee. Ahmed Pasha regarded as his most important task, the junction with the forces of Samaria, now at Jenin. Therefore he did not linger in Lower Galilee, nor did he seek contact with Kléber's division in Nazareth. His army started moving southward, went around Mount Tabor and entered the Valley of Jezreel. The vanguard in the hills of Lubya now became the rearguard, safeguarding the passage of the rest of the army and in the end joined it too. In the centre of the valley, near Jebel Dahy (present day Giv'at Hamoreh) the Damascene army met up with the levies from Jenin, Nablus and Jerusalem and thus formed an armed force of nearly 40,000 men. Ahmed Pasha apparently intended to lead it north-west, through the Valley of Jezreel, towards Acre. Thus he would have passed south of Kléber's division.

Napoleon, in his memoirs, claims that the Damascene force now dis-continued its eastward line of communication to Syria and established new communications southwards, to Samaria.

The French at Nazareth noticed the enemy movements in the centre of the Valley of Jezreel. Kléber received reinforcements from Acre: a cavalry unit and four guns and ammunition. His next movement surprised everybody. It could have been expected that he would have moved parallel to Ahmed's army, but north of it, along the ridge of the hills of Lower Galilee, attacking the enemy's flank from time to time. Alternatively he could have placed his division between the Turks and Acre, withdrawing slowly, and thus falling back on the French main force. But Kléber did neither. During the night of 14/15 April he concentrated all his forces. During the next night, he led them around Mount Tabor and into the Valley of Jezreel, with the intention of attacking a force seventeen times the size of his own. Even given the usual low quality of eastern armies this sounds like a mission impossible. However, Kléber hoped to suc-ceed by surprising the enemy at night in his camp and annihilating him, in spite of his enormously superior numbers.

As such a move sounds foolhardy, to say the least, we are obliged to look for the reasons for such conduct in an otherwise reliable and responsible com-mander. Kléber's biographer claims that Kléber had been instructed by Napoleon to cut Ahmed off from his base in the east and therefore he tried to place himself between him and the Jordan. The biographer thus tries to shift the responsibility for this movement on to Napoleon. As Berthier's instructions to Kléber have survived, we can check up on this: 'If the enemy will dare to encamp near your camp, the Commander in Chief does not doubt that you will attack this enemy with the help of a night attack in which you will attain success equal to that at El Arish.' But the operative word here is 'near'. In fact Kléber had to make an approach march of 25 kilometres, in order to make contact with the enemy and this can hardly be called 'near'. Napoleon severely criticized this move in his memoirs. He stresses that the manoeuvre was pointless, as the pasha had shifted his communications southward and they could thus not be severed by Kléber's move, even if it had succeeded. It is possible, however, that Napoleon had himself inadvertently goaded Kléber to this reckless move, by mentioning in the above order the battle of El-Arish as an example to be followed. Kléber's men had not exactly covered themselves with glory during that engagement, while Reynier, whom Kléber apparently regarded as his main rival (Lannes was still too junior, Bon too fat and indolent) had done all the real work. Now Kléber did not want to hang back and tried by a rather foolhardy manoeuvre to prove his courage and improve his standing with Napoleon.

The latter claims however that the responsibility for this move was all Kléber's and when that general advised Napoleon in writing of his intended attack, Napoleon immediately saw that the results could be catastrophic to Kléber. This was not being wise after the event either, because Napoleon immediately put himself at the head of Bon's division and marched to the aid of Kléber, thus turning defeat into his most important victory in the Holy Land. In his memoirs Napoleon compares the thorough preparations of Reynier at El-Arish with Kléber's irresponsible impulsiveness at the battle of Mount Tabor, much to the latter's disadvantage.[4]

Kléber first wanted to divide his force in two, with himself leading one half in a long approach march through Kafr Kanna and around Mount Tabor, where his force could not be observed by the enemy entering the Valley of Jezreel. The other half, under Junot, was supposed to start later, and descend during the night from Nazareth directly into the same valley. However this second force was scrapped in the final plan, and Junot was attached to Kléber's force, perhaps because it was feared that Junot's men would be discovered too soon, or because it would be too difficult and time-consuming to effect the necessary junction of both forces in unknown terrain, at night. Thus only the long and difficult approach around Mount Tabor was actually carried out by all of Kléber's force. Probably Kléber did not appreciate the actual length of this march in view of the inadequate maps at his disposal. Napoleon might have been better off in this respect, as Colonel Jacotin, the expedition's chief mapmaker, was staying with him.[5] Therefore he was able, perhaps, to appreciate better how impossible Kléber's task was. Kléber and his men needed the complete night from 15 to 16 April for the approach, and instead of attacking the camp of Ahmed Pasha at 02.00, as planned, he did not establish contact with the enemy until 06.00. Kléber failed to surprise the Turks, and his force was discovered by their scouts from Djebel-el-Dahy in the first light of morning. Enemy cavalry started attacking the French when still to the north of this isolated mountain. Some of them might have belonged to the Mameluk force, who had a separate camp further to the south-west, near Leijun, opposite to where Wadi Ara opens into the Valley of Jezreel. Additional units from Damascus and Nablus joined the battle and Kléber's men found themselves under increasing pressure. Around 07.00 they had to halt, to the south-west of Djebel-el-Dahy, and take up defensive positions near the village of Fula (the present-day town of Affule, which perpetuates the old name, lies to the west of the battlefield. Fula itself occupied part of the area which now belongs to Kibbutz Merhavia). At that time there still existed ruins of the Crusader castle of Le-Faba, on the slope of Djebel-el-Dahy which was now occupied by about a hundred Frenchmen. The rest of Kléber's force formed two squares, one commanded by himself, and the other by Junot. In their centre were sheltered the camels and other beasts carrying ammunition and supplies. Kléber also had at his disposal six light cannon, and with their assistance withstood the 20,000 or so enemy cavalrymen who continually attacked him. They made their assaults, sometimes in bigger groups and sometimes in smaller ones. Sometimes they got so near that they made contact with the French bayonets. A few of them spurred their horses to jump over the defenders into the squares, but were killed there. The French veterans held out like a wall and caused the enemy many casualties.

The Turkish force lacked unified command. One of our French sources states that 'It was impossible to assess the number of the enemy; it seemed to be a complete nation; however without order, and apparently without commander. Some were fighting, while others looked after their horses and still others slept.' This was indeed a non-homogenous force: besides the Damascenes there participated the mountain people of Samaria and Jerusalem, who were unused to discipline, and the Mameluk cavalrymen of the aged Ibrahim Bey. These disparate elements had not previously operated together, and most had met up for the first time only the day before. Even their huge numbers might have been a drawback, as it was difficult to concentrate so many men against the small French squares. Ahmed Pasha appears not to have been a strong battle leader, who could bring order out of chaos.

Still, their numbers were so vast, that the French found themselves in a more and more difficult position. Supply ran low and on that hot day they suffered severely from thirst. Most of the casualties were in Junot's square and by noon it could not be sustained any longer and had to be united with Kléber's. The position became so perilous that Kléber was doubtful if he could hold out till evening. He started to consider the alternative of leaving his supplies and wounded, blowing up his guns, and trying to cut his way out through the enemy in the direction of Nazareth. In view of the enormous numbers of cavalry among the Turks, this would have amounted to near certain suicide.

However at this stage he was saved from an unexpected quarter. Kléber did not believe that Napoleon could come to his aid and certainly not that soon. However luckily for him this was one of Napoleon's great days as strategist and commander. In some of his other battles he was to be saved himself by the initiative of others – by Desaix at Marengo, or by Davout at Jena-Auerstedt – but the battle of Mount Tabor was one of his great moments. Without awaiting any news from Kléber's battle, he was so sure that Kléber's plan could not but fail that he immediately set out from the camp at Acre, at the head of Bon's division, and took with him all the cavalry available and eight field guns. He took a severe calculated risk, by leaving only 4000 men (the divisions of Reynier and Lannes) in front of the now vastly superior garrison in Acre, from which Djezzar might now have attacked the French with a force twice their number. However Napoleon was so sure that Kléber's division faced annihilation in view of the foolhardy plan of its commander, that he believed this risk to be fully justified. If Kléber's division was wiped out this might be the end of the whole expeditionary force.

Thus he set out on 15 April at 13.00 hours and reached Saffuria by night, where he rested his men. At first light on 16 April he continued southwards to the ridge of Lower Galilee overlooking the Valley of Jezreel. With his strong telescope he saw, at a distance of some fourteen kilometres, Kléber's small squares, obscured by clouds of powder. Around them milled a vast enemy force, attacking from all sides.

Napoleon ordered his forces to descend into the Valley of Jezreel – well before he had reached Nazareth – and marched now, not towards the battle, but slightly right (i.e. west) of it, with a view to threatening what he regarded as the rear lines of communications of the enemy, those leading southward towards Samaria. He divided his force into four units, keeping a distance of about 800 metres between them. The two most easterly ones were formed by a brigade each, the next one by the Infantry Guides and the most westerly one by the cavalry and the Horse Guides. The very high wild wheat covering most of the valley almost completely shielded his soldiers from view. Still, some of Kléber's soldiers thought they had seen the glitter of bayonets and a great shout of 'Here comes the little Corporal!' went up. Kléber did not believe it possible that a relief force could be that near so soon. He climbed the slope of Djebel-el-Dahy with a spy glass, but did not see anything. He therefore explained to his men the impossibility of Napoleon arriving as yet. The soldiers themselves believed that they must have been mistaken. For quite some time, while Napoleon's men made their way through the man-high wild wheat, there were no further signs of his approach. His men were now moving southward in the general direction of Jenin. Then they slowly changed direction: the 32nd brigade under General Rambaud turned towards the battle, the 18th, under Bon and Vial, continued south-east in the general direction of Nuris on the Mountains of Gilboa, the Foot Guides continued towards Jenin and the cavalry turned right and attacked the camp of the Mameluks near Leijun.

Napoleon recounts in his memoirs that he noticed a change in Kléber's squares, and understood them to form attacking columns, presumably for their break-out.[6] But this is not confirmed by our other sources, and might only have been the unification of the two squares. He decided, however, that no time was to be lost and ordered his cannon to open fire. He also ordered some of his men to ascend a dike, so as to show themselves to Kléber's embattled men. The latter answered with a great shout, stuck their caps on their bayonets as a sign of joy, and opened cannon fire of their own. The Mameluk cavalry approached Napoleon's columns in order to find out who the newcomers were, and they were soon joined by the men of Samaria who saw their escape route threatened. Napoleon now formed three squares of his own and opened fire on the enemy. At the same time, some 300 French cavalrymen broke into the Mameluk camp, looted it, burned its tents and took prisoner the wounded they found there. They also captured some 300 or 400 camels and some biscuits, which one of our sources claims, were of particularly good quality. The sight of the billowing smoke from the captured camp frightened the Turkish force. Some of its battle groups approached Napoleon's squares, but quickly withdrew when fired upon. No decisive engagement actually took place. Napoleon's psychological insight was proved right once again. The fact that he had marched not towards the battle, but had placed his force between the enemy and his base, broke the spirit of the Turks more effectively than a complete day's fighting could have done. Shock and panic spread throughout the vast Turkish army.

Kléber used this moment to open his square and to attack with bayonets the men opposing him. He captured the village of Fula, which up to then had been in the hands of the men from Nablus. Private Millet of this force describes this action thus:

'Remember, reader, what I have told you before, that we were dying of thirst. Well, our thirst for vengeance had put out our thirst for water and kindled our thirst for blood . . . Indeed here we were, wading up to our waists in the water of that same lake of which, only a short while ago, we craved to drink a cup. But we no longer thought of drinking, but only of killing and dyeing the lake red with the blood of those barbarians, who only a moment before had hoped to cut off our heads and drown our bodies in that very lake, where they themselves were drowned and which was filled with their corpses.'[7]

The picture had changed completely. The pursuers had become the pursued. Utter panic spread among the Turkish army. Withdrawal turned into wild flight. Napoleon did not have sufficient cavalry to pursue effectively. The Damascene levies fled eastwards, towards the Jordan, and those of Samaria and Jerusalem dispersed, making their way southward back towards their mountains. According to one source there were only about 300 casualties in the vast Turkish army during the morning's battle, but many more were killed during their flight. Napoleon claims that 2000 drowned when trying to cross the swift flowing Jordan. Other sources mention a total of 5000 casualties. This is probably exaggerated, but however high or low the numbers of casualties, the army of Ahmed Pasha of Damascus, which had been one of the prime causes of Napoleon's Holy Land campaign, ceased to exist. Kléber suffered that day, according to some sources, 60 casualties and according to others 250 or even 300. Napoleon's forces had only three or four casualties. The chief surgeon, Larrey, speaks of about 100 French wounded altogether.

This battle was one of Napoleon's great victories, won against an enemy numbering about eight times the total of Kléber's and Napoleon's united forces. In none of his other battles had Napoleon to face an enemy of such superior numbers to his own, and only very rarely did he manage to turn quite so desperate a situation into quite so decisive a victory.

Napoleon was always very particular about the names he gave his battles. The battle of Omm-Dinar he preferred to call 'The Battle of the Pyramids', though these were far away, and the battle of Fula was called by him 'The Battle of Mount Tabor', though this historic hill could not even be seen, behind Djebel-el-Dahy during most of the engagement. However Mount Tabor was regarded by many as the Mount of Transfiguration of the New Testament, and was actually the scene of the great battle between Barak and Sisra described in the old Testament. Little Fula could not compete with it. In order to give the name a stamp of credibility Napoleon claims in his memoirs to have climbed Mount Tabor after the battle.[8] This is however quite impossible, as it was much too far away. At best he went some way up the slope of Djebel-el-Dahy.

Immediately after the battle Napoleon and Kléber met on the battlefield, and in the excitement of the moment can be excused for having made a rather banal exchange of compliments. Kléber: 'General, you are great as all the world'; Napoleon: 'There is no sight so beautiful as Kléber in the midst of battle!' What Napoleon really thought of Kléber's handling of that particular battle, he kept for his memoirs.

Napoleon had his camp erected near Zar'in, on a ridge south of the Valley of Jezreel, and Kléber was so exhausted that he slept part of the next night in Napoleon's tent.[9] However his division camped further to the east, down in the valley.

Most of the Damascenes tried to reach the Mejami'a bridge and the Bridge of Jacob's Daughters; however the latter was already in Murat's hands and the former was too narrow for the great swarm of men who wanted to cross it. Many who tried to swim across the Jordan drowned. By capturing Tiberias Murat cut off another one of their main escape routes. The Matuwelli force which Napoleon had promised to Murat, materialized now, rather late, when everything had been decided already, near the Mejami'a bridge and attacked the flying Damascenes.

On 17 April the French spread out, all through the Valley of Jezreel. Kléber's division moved eastwards and met up near Mejami'a bridge, with Murat coming from the north and with the Matuwellis. General Rambaud and the 32nd brigade burned down the village of Nuris in the Mountains of Gilboa and the village of Shunem on the slopes of Djebel-el-Dahy. In the latter place they captured a Turkish cannon. The 18th brigade and the Foot Guides penetrated into Jenin, at the foothills of Samaria, found it deserted, looted it and burned down some of its buildings. They burned down another little village nearby and returned northwards.

The men of Nablus were seriously affected by their military defeat and by the looting and burning of one of their main centres and some of their villages, so they now sent a deputation to Napoleon asking for peace. They had to provide hostages and to promise no longer to bear arms against the French – a promise quickly forgotten when the fortunes of war were to change again.[10]

As if touched by a magic wand, Napoleon's situation was totally changed. His men were no longer in any danger of being annihilated by vastly superior forces, the spectre of the Damascene army had been laid for good, all of Galilee and the Valley of Jezreel were now securely in Napoleon's hands. His camp was speedily visited by Druse and Maronite delegations from Lebanon, promising to raise a force of 6000 men – others say of 12,000 men – to fight alongside the French. It seemed as if his most ambitious plans were suddenly about to be realized. However, before the Druses and Maronites were able to carry out their promise, fortune changed sides again, Napoleon was not able to take Acre, and they were free of their obligation.

Napoleon claims in his memoirs that immediately after the battle, he seriously considered despatching Kléber onwards, to occupy Damascus.[11]

'Was it reasonable to send Kléber with 3000 men into that great capital of 100,000 inhabitants, which were the most fanatical in all the Levant? Would the French not be surrounded from all sides the moment their small number was recognized? On the other hand Damascus could have been taken already on the 18th or the morning of the 19th, and this was very seductive. What advantages our army could have achieved thus! There could be found horses, camels and mules, which were badly needed because of the great losses of our animals, furthermore it would be possible to obtain there leather, cloth, linen, apparel, gunpowder, weapons, money. It should have been easy to obtain 7 or 8 million there. For a conquering army, the glory with which such a success would crown French weapons was even more important. The battle of Mount Tabor had already refreshed the fame of the army, which had suffered somewhat as a result of Acre's resistance; but what enormous results were to be expected when it became known in Cairo, Tripoli, Aleppo and Acre that the Tricolour had been raised over old, holy, rich Damascus!'

Here we have one of the rare occasions when Napoleon gave voice in his memoirs to his innermost dreams. However, he decided against it, because of the great distances involved and the smallness of Kléber's force.[12] Thus this division was left spread out along the Jordan. At one time (17/18 April) it held a detachment on the soil of Transjordan, east of Majami'a bridge. Later this detachment was withdrawn to a little fort west of the river, which was now held by 100 infantrymen, 25 cavalrymen and one cannon. Junot, who remained under Kléber's command, took up his station in Tiberias and sent 100 of his men to Safet, which was handed over to him by Murat, and a further 100 to the Bridge of Jacob's Daughters. Another force was sent by Kléber to Nazareth, and his own headquarters were set up on the shores of Lake Genezareth. After the hard days of battle, his men now enjoyed a happy interlude of peace and quiet and of swimming in the water of this lake with which so many stories of the New Testament are connected. However Napoleon's aide-de-camp, La Vallette, claims that the revolution had deeply influenced the French soldiers and most of them showed little interest in religion or biblical associations, in spite of their campaigning in the land of the Bible.

The other forces had, however, to hurry back to Acre. Murat left on 20 April and moved there from Tiberias, to arrive two days later. Napoleon himself was in an even greater hurry to get back, because of the weakness of the force he had left behind. He reached Nazareth in the evening of 17 April, and La Vallette describes his arrival there: 'Before Bonaparte entered the village he stopped near an ancient fountain where a considerable number of cattle were drinking. The elders of the village stood there waiting for the General in Chief. The whole scene recalled to memory the patriarchal times ... The French were received with great demonstrations of joy.'[13] In Nazareth Napoleon's soldiers participated in a service of thanksgiving in the Franciscan church, accompanied by that rarity in Palestine, an organ. Their commander spent the night in the Franciscan monastery, as did the wounded of his force. The next day they were evacuated to the Carmelite monastery near Haifa, and on the 19th Napoleon reached the camp near Acre, after an absence of five days.

13

NAPOLEON AND THE JEWS OF PALESTINE[1]

As we have seen in previous chapters, Napoleon was eager for help from any source, and tried to obtain aid and support from Matuwellis, Christians, Druses, Maronites and even Moslems. However his most lavish promises he might have given to the Jews. Those living in the land of their fathers were not very numerous and mostly did not occupy prominent positions. Still, in nearby Syria, the Pichiotto family had served for several generations as bankers of the pashas of Aleppo, and the Farhi family held the same hereditary office under the pashas of Damascus. The latter was especially important as the Farhis controlled the complicated financial transactions needed to finance the yearly pilgrimage of tens of thousands of devout Muslims to Mecca. In about 1790 the most prominent member of this family, Haim Farhi, had moved to Djezzar's court in Acre and served as his banker and secretary. It has been assumed that Napoleon's propaganda efforts directed towards the Jews were actually meant for Haim Farhi's benefit.[2] However this seems hardly likely. In 1799 his position was not yet as important as it was to become under the next pasha of Acre, Suleiman (1805–1818) and thus it is questionable if it warranted such special attention. However he was certainly in charge of the arrangements which were needed to finance Djezzar's war effort. During the siege of Acre he seems to have played a very active role in organizing the civil population of Acre to build fortifications, repair breaches, look after the wounded, man the supply services, transport ammunition or help in the actual fighting.

It seems impossible that Napoleon's tremendous propaganda effort simply overlooked the Jewish population of Palestine and Syria, any more than it overlooked the Matuwellis or the Christians of Lower Galilee.

We find in the Parisian official *Moniteur* the following passage on 22 May 1799: 'Bonaparte has published an announcement in which he invites the Jews of Asia and Africa to join his army in order to re-establish ancient Jerusalem.

117

He has already equipped many of them with weapons, and their battalions already menace Aleppo.' Some weeks later (27 July) the same paper added, 'Bonaparte has not conquered Syria only in order to return their Jerusalem to the Jews; he had much wider plans ... he intended to advance towards Constantinople, so as to spread confusion in Vienna and in Petersburg.' Here there are some completely inaccurate passages: Napoleon did not organize any Jewish battalions, nor did they threaten Aleppo, nor did Napoleon threaten Austria and Russia via Istanbul. For these and other reasons it has been doubted by some whether he did ever actually issue an invitation to the Jews of the East to join his military efforts so as to regain some sort of official status in Jerusalem. Such a declaration might have seemed far-fetched and unreal in his own time, but became of great topical interest much later when it could be regarded as an early sign of political Zionism, or as a forerunner of the Balfour Declaration. The establishment of the state of Israel gave it further weight and interest, which it did not possess at the time it was issued.

However, in spite of all doubts, some forty years ago a German language version of this declaration did come to light in Vienna.[3] It is headed, 'Headquarters, Jerusalem, First Floréal, 20 April 1799, the seventh year of the French Republic.' It starts by addressing the Jews:

'Bonaparte, Commander in Chief of the armies of the French Republic, in Africa and Asia, to the legitimate heirs of Palestine. Jews, the only nation in the world to whom the lust of conquest and tyranny has for thousands of years denied the lands of your fathers, but has not been able to wipe out your name or your existence as a nation...'

It goes on to promise redress:

'The great nation, which does not trade in human beings and in countries, like those who sold your fathers to the various nations, calls you, not to conquer your inheritance, but to receive what has been conquered already, in order that you will remain there as rulers, and will defend it against all foreigners. [Along the way one incorrect statement follows the other.] The young army, which higher providence has called upon me to serve as its commander ... has fixed its centre in Jerusalem, and in a few days will pass on to Damascus...'

It is a rare piece of bombastic political propaganda. By quite a few scholars it is regarded as an outright forgery,[4] though the reason for perpetrating such a hoax has not been adequately explained. We believe, however, that it might be genuine after all. Its wording is very similar to the 'bogus eastern style' Napoleon used in quite a few of his letters to eastern potentates and heads of towns. The very inaccuracies, such as heading it from Jerusalem, or speaking about Jerusalem as a town already taken by the French, make it unlikely that the latter-day forger would have used them. On the other hand the French original has never been found and it is not included in any of the collection of Napoleon's letters or pronouncements. It might thus have emanated not directly from him, but from his dragomen and oriental secretaries, headed by M. Venture, who tried to copy his style and mode of expression. They might have prepared it, together with other missives to the other small sects, either before leaving Egypt, as part of Napoleon's effort at psychological warfare, or perhaps later, during the halt at Khan Yunis or at Gaza, when quite a blizzard of such missives descended on the heads of the notables of the Holy Land and Lebanon. Most heads of towns received then a personal letter often including promises which were violated even before the ink was dry — such as for example the promise to the inhabitants of Jaffa, that no violence would befall them. Napoleon's secretariat tried to find allies and friends in the cheapest way possible — by an outpouring of ink instead of blood. Djezzar himself received such a letter, as did the mullah of Damascus, on both of whom they certainly seemed rather wasted. Why then skip the Jews of Palestine and Syria? Thus it seems perfectly likely that some sort of missive, as attested to by the *Moniteur*, was indeed issued for their benefit and the extant version might well be the genuine article.

As we hear nothing of its being received by any Jewish community in the Holy Land we have to assume that it was passed on by hand of agents. We do know that Napoleon did use Jewish agents[5] (and also Christian and Muslim ones) and these might have passed this letter on to suitable Jewish notables in Palestine and Syria. Approaching, say, the Pichiottos of Aleppo or the Farhis of Damascus, might have looked more promising to Napoleon than the epistle to the mullah of Damascus, for instance. Obviously such a declaration could not be issued publicly. Only by handing it over clandestinely to men like the heads of the Farhi and Pichiotto clans, might it be hoped that it would have any effect. Napoleon, whose financial position was a very difficult one, might have thought that it would be worth his while to court these two families, who were owners of some of the great fortunes of the East, and also had the best financial connections there, so as to gain their help, for the financing in due time of his further campaigns there. Similar relations were to bind him later to Ouvrard and other French financiers. In the East, however, his financial needs might have become much more desperate and thus the issue of a missive, such as the above, which he certainly did not regard as binding in any way, might seem a cheap price to pay for what he hoped to gain by it.

There are two sides to Napoleon's declaration. On the one hand the accidental connection to later events and developments have given it a standing in history books – as a milestone in the history of Zionism – out of all proportion to its real importance in its own time. On the other hand it could have had the most grievous consequences for the Jews in Palestine, if its existence had become known. On being communicated to any of the leaders of the Jewish communities of Safet, Tiberias, Acre, Shafr Amr, Hebron, Jerusalem, Pki'in or Kafr Jassif, they could have regarded it only a potential calumny, which had to be kept quiet at all cost. If a word had been breathed about it, this could have caused extortions by the Muslim rulers, and anti-Jewish riots and pogroms by the Muslim mob. This perhaps explains, too, why no word has come down to us about it from contemporaneous Palestinian Jewish sources.

The actual effect of the French campaign on the Jewish population was the very opposite of what one would have been led to believe from the contents of this declaration. But there is no difference between it and some of Napoleon's other letters, such as the one to the inhabitants of Jaffa. Here there seems to be no connection between Napoleon's promises and the deeds of his soldiers. Thus it is hinted here and there in our sources (for instance in J. Schwarz)[6] that the soldiers behaved in a most unfriendly way to the Jews of Safet and Tiberias. The old Jewish community of Gaza disappeared during Napoleon's campaign, as did the tiny Samaritan communities of Gaza and Jaffa. On the other hand we do not have any report about the more protracted relations between the French and the Jewish communities of Shafr Amr and Kafr Jassif in Western Galilee.

This does not mean that the Jews were treated any better by the other side. When Sheikh Abbās burnt down a sizeable part of Safet the local Jews certainly suffered, though we lack details. In Jerusalem the Muslim authorities forced the elders of the Jewish community to participate in the work of fortifying their town. The Jews themselves in this city were interested in demonstrating their loyalty to the Muslim authorities, so that they would not serve as targets for the anti-French sentiments of the Muslims, as indeed happened to many of the Christians there and elsewhere.[7] If anything about Napoleon's declaration had become known their situation would have quickly become even more perilous.

In Acre, Haim Farhi, by his strenuous activity in organizing the local population against the French invader, was able to shield the local Jewish community effectively. However Djezzar, who had a hundred Christians executed at the beginning of the siege on the slightest of pretexts, would not have hesitated for a moment to do the same to the local Jews, if there had been the shadow of a suspicion that they might not be completely loyal to him and his cause. After the end of the siege all the minorities were to feel his rage and vindictiveness. Only Sir Sidney Smith's intervention was able to save the Christians and Jews of Galilee from widespread massacres. Further, Djezzar did at least extort as much money as possible from both these communities. The Jews of Tiberias had to pay the enormous sum of 150 purses. The Swiss traveller Burckhardt reported that the Jewish quarter of Safet was looted by Djezzar's soldiers after the French withdrawal.[8] Jewish sources report the execution of two Jewish students by Djezzar's order. There were also widespread outbreaks of mob hatred against Jews and Christians in the districts of Galilee previously occupied by the French. Some of the Franciscan monks of Nazareth had to seek refuge from the persecution of the Muslims among friends at Safet.

And thus there is a vast difference in what was reported in the West about Napoleon's grandiose plans for the restoration of the Jewish nation, and the actual situation of the Jewish communities during his campaign and after. What to the French was another glorious campaign of Napoleon's army, was to the Jews of the Holy Land another tribulation in the long chain of their persecutions, harassments and oppressions.

14

THE SIEGE OF ACRE: HIGH HOPES AND ULTIMATE FAILURE
(1 April to 21 May 1799)[1]

After discussing the battles of Galilee and some of the administrative and political problems of the campaign, we have now to return to its leit-motiv, the siege of Acre.

Most of the time some 8000 Frenchmen were struggling here against some 7000 of Djezzar's soldiers. On both sides, however, additional forces partici-pated as well. These were some local levies and Egyptian pioneers on the French side, and many of the inhabitants of Acre on the Turkish side. Further, as mentioned already, Djezzar was supported by a French royalist team of advisers, and by a sizeable British force: two battleships, the *Tigre* (which had kept its French name after it had been captured by the British in 1795) and the *Theseus*, each of 74 guns, a smaller one, the *Lion* of 64 guns, and several auxiliary vessels; also 800 Royal Marines, manning the cannon captured from the French.

In spite of this external help, if any ordinary Ottoman pasha had com-manded in Acre, there is little doubt that after the news of the outcome of the battle of Mount Tabor, the conquest by the French of all Galilee, and the annihilation of the great army which had set out to succour Acre, he would have found a way to make peace with those formidable Frenchmen, and Acre would have been theirs. However, Djezzar was in command here. In spite of his age, he was still active, irascible, and cruel, with a Balkan temperament which could be both rock hard and as explosive as a volcano, so feared by his soldiers that they stood in greater awe of him than of Napoleon. As far as we know – unlike his adversary he did not dictate several volumes of memoirs – he did not even consider such a step. As a result of British sea power supplies of food and ammunition could be brought into Acre's harbour in adequate quantities. Thus any lengthening of the siege did not necessarily cause, as is usual in siege warfare, a worsening of the situation of the besieged.

The besiegers were also reasonably well off as regards the supply of food-stuffs. They had found an ample supply of biscuits and rice in the stores captured by them in Haifa and Tiberias as well as in the camps of Leijun and the Bridge of Jacob's Daughters. A plentiful supply of fresh food was available in Western Galilee. However ammunition was another story, and they found it very difficult to keep up supplies. In particular for a long period they completely lacked ammunition for their two heavy guns captured at Haifa. The French worked out a highly original method to overcome this deficiency: they reused the cannon balls fired at them by the British fleet. Napoleon paid his soldiers 20 sous for each 33- or 36-pounder ball delivered by them, 15 sous for 12-pounder balls and 10 sous for 8-pounder ones. Some of the French soldiers felt that the British were not shooting a sufficient quantity of projectiles at them to give them a reasonable income (as they did not receive any wages, because of Napoleon's lack of money), and therefore they tried to get them to increase their rate of fire by pretending to put up fortifications along the beach by a simulating martial activity along the white sands of the seashore south of Acre. The increased British fire did them no harm and the cannon balls, conveniently embedded in the soft sand, could be dug out and reused by the French.

But the French lacked heavy guns in sufficient quantity to renew their assault on Acre with any certainty of success. It is possible, too, that the existing guns were not used as efficiently as they should have been. Bernoyer alleges that General Dommartin, the artillery commander, opposed Napoleon's far-flung schemes and tried, together with some similarly minded generals, to sabotage his efforts at capturing Acre.[2] However, immediately the siege began Napoleon had passed on orders to Egypt to send him all siege guns available there. This time, however, they were not sent by sea up to Haifa, because Napoleon had by now acquired a healthy respect for British sea power, and on 19 April three French frigates, under Rear Admiral Perrée, landed nine 24- and 16-pounder guns, 400 balls of heavy shot, 2000 other cannon balls and also a supply of powder at Jaffa. Because of the lack of effective French control of the country between Jaffa and Tantura, it was necessary to send 400 men from Lannes' division to transport them to Acre. This was slow work and the first of the guns arrived in the French camp only on 30 April.

The time lost was crucial for Napoleon's plans, as time was the commodity of which he had the most limited supply. However Djezzar had his problems, too, and one of the most severe was what to do with his many wounded and sick. In the middle of April it was reported that there were 400 wounded in

Acre and the bodies of 200 dead, who could not be buried, since all cemeteries lay outside the walls and were controlled by Napoleon's army.

On the French side many of the wounded were infected by tetanus and died soon after amputation.[3] The increase in the number of cases of plague was an even more severe problem. The sick were transferred to a hospital in Shafr Amr and to the Carmelite monastery near Haifa, so that their presence would not adversely affect the morale of the besiegers. From Dr Desgenette's notes[4] we hear of 269 such cases in the fortnight from 10 to 25 April, that is about three percent of the French force in front of Acre. As two weeks were but one quarter of the period of the siege, we might be tempted to multiply this percentage by four, which would give us twelve percent – a truly enormous number. It seems however not to be correct: apparently the number of new cases dropped off. On the other hand the incidence of the plague was very high, among the besieged in Acre as well as among the isolated French garrisons in Jaffa, Gaza and El-Arish. In Gaza it seems, from Desgenettes' notes[5], that there were periods when the major portion of the garrison (191 men) was hospitalized. But the number of fatal cases mentioned by him was only seventeen during a complete month. In Jaffa the situation was even worse and we shall discuss this in a separate chapter.

However there were others who led rather comfortable lives in front of Acre. Murat's quartermaster, Miot, for instance, reports[6] that the members of Murat's headquarters got up late in the morning, breakfasted around 10.00 a.m. and had their main meal of the day between 4.00 and 5.00 p.m. He stresses the good quality of the meals they had and the abundance of wine they had brought with them from Safet and Tiberias. They spent their many hours of leisure in the sumptuous tent of Sheikh Abbās, which they had brought back with them from the Bridge of Jacob's Daughters. But such a standard of living was surely enjoyed only by a few.

Napoleon led a more strenuous life. For hours he used to stand on the hill which now bears his name and with the help of his spy glass studied the fortress of Acre. On 4 May he attracted the attention of the besieged and they opened fire on him with their cannon. One ball struck a group of soldiers sitting nearby, killing most of them, and another struck only three paces from where Napoleon was standing. Two of his aides-de-camp threw themselves on him, to protect him with their bodies, one of them was lightly wounded and Napoleon was covered by earth. On another occasion a musket ball hit his hat, knocked it to the ground and wounded one of his officers. On still another occasion Napoleon himself is reported to have been lightly wounded. Once a horse he was riding was killed by an enemy bullet. It is interesting that the other instances in which Napoleon was wounded were also during sieges: that of Toulon and that of Ratisbon. However during his Holy Land campaign he seems to have had more near-brushes with death than in any other of the fifteen campaigns in which he participated.

Other important generals such as Caffarelli, the commander of the engineers, spent most of the hours of the day and the night in the trenches around Acre. Caffarelli had a wooden leg, but this did not prevent him from moving up front to direct the trench digging operations. During one night, whilst giving an order, he lifted his arm and it was shattered by a cannon ball. It had to be amputated and for some days he lingered between life and death. When, finally, it became clear that death was near, he had, as a good Republican, some chapters of Voltaire read to him, and expired on 27 April.[7] He was buried on the slopes of what was to be called Napoleon's Hill, where his bones clearly identifiable by the wooden leg, were found by local archaeologists a few years ago.[8]

In the meantime the French attempts at capturing Acre continued. This they tried to effect by local attacks, by bombardments of the walls and especially by exploding mines beneath the corner tower, which had already served as main target of the first assault, on 28 March. The number of these attacks as given by our various sources vary – some mention as few as five, others mention eight, and still others mention twelve or even fourteen attacks during the complete period of the siege. However it seems certain that there were no serious attempts between 1 and 24 April, the reason apparently being the lack of ammunition and the absence of sizeable parts of the army on operations elsewhere. At the end of April, after Napoleon's return from the battle of Mount Tabor, the assaults were resumed.

In the meantime the besieged were not inactive. They seem actually to have carried out more sallies than the French made assaults. Various sources mention different dates for the attacks of both sides, such as: French assaults on 23 March, 1 April, 28 April, 8 and 10 May, and Turkish sallies 7, 25, 28, 29 April and 2 and 16 May (i.e. six Turkish sallies as against five French assaults),[9] while another participant mentions French assaults on 28 March, 1 and 24 April, 1, 4, 6–8 and 10 May, and Turkish sallies on 26 and 30 March, 1 and 7 April and 1, 6, 8, 16 and 21 May) (i.e. nine Turkish sallies against seven French assaults).[10] However the big French attack early in May is counted by most as three or more separate assaults, which according to some sources brings the total up to a dozen and even more. However the difference between our various

125

sources lies in the definition of what constitutes an assault or a sally. Some sort of activity went on almost daily and a few of the operations are borderline cases, which are regarded by some as assaults and sallies and by others as ordinary reconnaissance activity.

Both sides developed various contrivances to confuse the enemy. The French used puppets and scarecrows in order to cause the defenders to reveal the positions of their guns and to squander ammunition. Further, they developed armour to be worn on their backs when creeping towards the walls. Djezzar's men invented incandescent grenades, made by the local potters of Acre, to light up the area of the moat on hearing any suspicious noise. For more prolonged effect they used lanterns and torches, to illuminate areas of the walls, when expecting an assault there. They also put dogs into the moat in order to be warned by their barking of the approach of any French.

Both sides worked hard on various engineering schemes and fortifications. The French prepared additional trenches, and dug tunnels in order to place mines underneath the walls. The besieged strengthened the existing fortifications and repaired those parts of the walls and towers which had been damaged by the explosions of mines. Even the French mention, with some admiration, Djezzar's incessant activity. He could be seen from their side day and night exhorting his labourers and herding men, women and children to work on the fortifications.

Djezzar personally led one of the sallies of the besieged. He was seen, sabre in hand, at the head of his horsemen, assaulting the French working on trenches and tunnels. Napoleon's men suffered some losses, but in the end were able to repulse the attackers.

In other cases the Turks tried to dig counter-tunnels, starting inside the town, but leading towards the French tunnels so as to capture and destroy them and prevent the blowing up of mines.

Once, during the absence of the French army from its camp in mid April, the besieged made their greatest sally. They were organized in three groups, receiving supporting fire from the Royal Marines on the ramparts and from their advanced positions beyond the moat. The Turks who tried to rush the French trenches, came under concentrated fire from the French field guns, which, though ineffective against the fortifications, proved highly efficient against human targets. The attacking groups on the left and on the right were forced to withdraw, and only the central one, commanded by an English officer, Major Oldfield, and composed of Royal Marines from the *Theseus*, reached the entrance of the main tunnel, inside which a big mine was being prepared. But before they could enter, the English major was killed and so were two of his men, and 23 were wounded. This assault also failed.[11]

When the French returned from their battles in Galilee and the Valley of Jezreel, the initiative passed into their hands. Without awaiting the arrival of the cannon from Jaffa, on 24 April Napoleon launched an assault, during which at 0900 a mine was exploded under the same north-eastern corner tower as had been attacked on 28 March. One of the eyewitnesses, paymaster Peyrusse, described the scene thus:[12]

> 'Its only effect was to blow up a corner of the tower ... The grenadiers boldly charged the breach, although it was clear that it was impossible to penetrate it. The enemy, installed at the top of the tower and hidden behind the battlements, knocked down our troops with rocks, shells and hand grenades. However, since nothing could turn them back, the Turks resorted to two or three powder kegs which they dropped on them. All our men were suffocated [by the explosion] although a few managed to run away half-burned.'

This did not stop Napoleon from ordering another assault for the next day. This time some one hundred grenadiers succeeded in penetrating the lower gallery of the tower. However the Turks poured musket fire on them through an opening in the ceiling, and threw bombs and shells on them, thus, after most of them had been wounded or killed, forcing the remainder to withdraw.

These repulses caused morale on the French side, which had been so high after the battle of Mount Tabor, to drop considerably. It was undoubtedly another one of the series of Napoleon's mistakes committed during the siege. The heavy siege guns were already on their way from Jaffa. Why did he not wait the few remaining days for their arrival? His lack of patience, understandable though it is, as he saw valuable days slipping by one after the other, caused him to make the cardinal mistake of warfare: piecemeal attacks, each insufficient in itself, whilst, if they had been undertaken together, there would have been a good chance of success. Had he exploded the mines at a time when he could follow this up by bombarding the walls and towers with sufficiently heavy siege guns, and plenty of ammunition, and before squandering the high morale which was an outcome of his recent successes, his chances of capturing Acre were decidedly good. Here again we see Napoleon being his own worst enemy during the siege of Acre.

His efforts, in the early days of May, of blowing a breach in the walls, with the help of the guns which now were arriving, failed time and again. Now Napoleon resorted to a night attack. This also failed, however, as Djezzar had prepared in good time lanterns to light up the whole area. Another mine was exploded on 4 May, this time not under the corner tower as usual, but under the next one southward in the eastern walls. A breach was made, which could not be closed by the defenders, because of French gunfire. The walls between both towers were also partly destroyed. In the night of 4/5 May another mine was to have been exploded, to collapse the high outside wall of the moat and thus enable the French easy access to the now sizeable breach in the town wall itself. Napoleon was sure of success, but Djezzar's men managed to tunnel so quietly and quickly towards this mine, that the French did not become aware of their action, and the Turks burst into the French trenches in the nick of time, killed the men preparing the mine, and filled the trench next to the mine with earth covering the mine itself as well. Thus Napoleon's hopes of a decisive assault were again disappointed.

Napoleon planned to carry out his final general attack, with the help of all of his newly arrived cannon, on 9 May. However his proverbial luck certainly had deserted him during the siege of Acre. On 7 May his scouts on the nearby hill reported seeing a fleet of some 30 ships approaching from the west.[13] This was that part of the force being prepared at Rhodes for the invasion of Egypt, which had been ordered instead to come to the aid of Acre. It arrived too late to co-operate with Ahmed Pasha and the men of Samaria in a concerted attack against Napoleon, but in time to save Acre. Napoleon immediately decided that, instead of carrying out his attack on 9 May, he would bring it forward and attack immediately before the reinforcements could come ashore. But time was already getting very short indeed. The very arrival of this force showed that the main army from Rhodes could attack Egypt soon. Everything was now done by Napoleon in even greater haste than previously. Again there was no time for proper preparations. Napoleon seemed ordained in his last great attack on Acre to repeat the mistakes of his first attack. Again his assault was directed against the same area of the city wall and chiefly against the same corner tower. Again no diversionary effort was mounted, leaving the defenders free to concentrate all their forces in the correct area. Why did Napoleon for once not attack another part of the rather weak wall? Why not assault the two redoubts held by the Royal Marines beyond the wall and the moat? Why not try a diversion by night on a few improvised rafts against the sea gate, from where nobody would have expected the French? (The Austrians were to try this successfully in the siege of 1840, admittedly under very different conditions.) Napoleon seemed destined to ram his head bull-like again and again against the same section of the wall, in every single one of his attacks. If we want to find in the

Left: Napoleon in Cairo before embarking upon the expedition to Palestine.

Below: The French army halts at Syène on 2 February 1799 before advancing to El-Arish.

Napoleon inspects his troops as they advance from Egypt to Sinai.

Napoleon accepts the surrender of Jaffa, 6 March 1799. The uniforms represented here are those of a later date.

Baron Gros' painting of Napoleon visiting victims of the plague in the Armenian hospice at Jaffa. In fact, Napoleon only helped carry a corpse, but Baron Gros found that this scene made for a more dramatic picture.

Opposite: General Louis-Alexandre Berthier (1753–1815), Napoleon's chief of staff.

Right: Commodore Sir William Sidney Smith (1764–1840).

Below: General Jean Baptiste Kléber (1753–1800) commanded one of the four French divisions in the Holy Land. He succeeded Napoleon in the command of the French army in Egypt until assassinated on 14 June 1800.

Left: A trooper of the Dromedary Regiment. This unit was formed for raiding, scouting and to act as couriers. The men dismounted to fight. *(Courtesy of the John R. Elting Military Collection.)*

Below: Ottoman troops of the period. The man on the right is an Albanian infantryman.

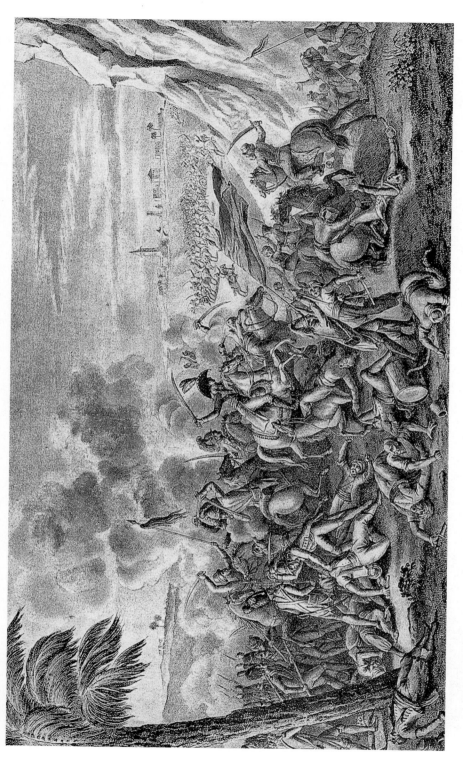

General Jean Andoche Junot (1771–1813) at the battle of Lubya, 8 April 1799. Napoleon suggested calling this 'the battle of Nazareth'.

A view of the battle of Lubya.

The battle of Mount Tabor, 16 April 1799. In the centre is one of the two French squares commanded by Kléber. In the background can be seen the Jezreel valley and Mount Gilboa.

A view of the battle of Mount Tabor.

1. *Corride*　2. *Deux Frères*　3 *Dangereux*　4. *Theseus*　5. Castle　6. Sea Gate　7. Port　8. English　9. Lighthouse　10, 11, 12, Gun-boats　13. *Marianne*　14. *Negress*　15. *Dame de France*　16. *Alliance*　17. *Tigre*　18. Bay of Acre　19. Mediterranean　20. Cultivated Valley　21, 22. Ruined Cisterns　23. Subterranean Aqueduct　24. Old Turkish Entrenchment　25. French Hospital　26. River Belus　27. Road to Jaffa　28. French Army Head-quarters　29. Lanusse　30. Regnier　31. Fresh Water Lake　32. French Reserve　33. Village　34. French Camp　35, 36. Parallels

British ships at anchor on either side of Acre. These ships provided supporting fire for the defenders throughout the siege.

Sir Sidney Smith
at the siege of Acre.

A British sailor, Daniel Bryan, burying a fallen French officer below the walls of Acre. A painting by J. B. Spilsbury.

Napoleon confers with his officers as another assault on Acre is launched.

A view of the fighting around Acre.

Kléber setting an example at the final assault on Acre, 10 May 1799.

Sir Sidney Smith and British staff officers meet a Turkish commander and aides after Napoleon's lifting of the siege of Acre. The British chief surgeon (and painter of this picture) J. B. Spilsbury, is on the right of the picture.

Napoleon, in early June 1799, retreating to Egypt after the failure of the siege of Acre.

A nineteenth-century illustration of Napoleon riding a dromedary in the desert.

young general preliminary symptoms of his later defeats in Russia, at Leipzig and at Waterloo – here, in front of Acre, they are all too evident.

Again everything was done hastily and without proper preparation. The attack started in the afternoon of 7 May, with a great barrage of gunfire, with the intention of penetrating the breach under cover of the night. Because of the shortness of time Napoleon had only three divisions in hand while Kléber's division, though recalled, had not yet reached Acre. The strong fire did destroy a sizeable part of the corner tower which had already been damaged in previous attacks. Lannes' division managed to enter the breach during the night and to hold out there, in spite of the heavy fire from the nearby walls and from one of the cannon which the Royal Marines had brought even further forward enabling them to shoot at the French at an angle of 90 degrees, killing and wounding many of them. According to Berthier they had 150 casualties, amongst them 17 officers.

In the morning of 8 May the defenders saw the French tricolour waving from the top of the corner tower. During that day they mounted three sallies, which were so effective that Napoleon was not able to reinforce those of Bon's men who held the breach. By 1600 hours, the French succeeded in creating, by their concentrated fire, a second breach in the wall, immediately southward of the tower which they held already. Thus a very wide breach was created through which the French of Lannes' division could attack 50 abreast. General Rambaud led the assaulting brigade, which penetrated into the town. The French entry into Acre could no longer be prevented. However a nasty surprise awaited them there. Beyond the north-eastern corner of the city walls, the ground was taken up by the gardens of Djezzar's palace. Here, on the advice of Colonel Phelipeaux – who had died in the meantime of sunstroke on 1 May – an interior wall had been erected, cutting through the open area of the gardens, but well concealed from the French, behind the city walls. The streets leading into this area were well barricaded. As Napoleon had always attacked the same spot, his old schoolmate did not have to strain his imagination as to where the next blow would fall. Djezzar used his court astrologer, who, with the help of chicken bones, interpreted the enemy's intentions. But even by this system he could not go wrong as long as Napoleon insisted on always attacking the same spot. Sir Sidney Smith[14] gives the credit for this scheme to old Djezzar: 'The Pasha's idea was not to defend the brink this time, but rather to let a certain number of the enemy in, and then close with them, according to the Turkish mode of war. The column thus mounted the breach unmolested and descended from the ramparts into the Pasha's garden, where, in a very few minutes, the bravest and most advanced among them lay headless corpses, the sabre, with the addition of a dagger in the other hand, proving more than a match for the bayonet.'

Thus when Lannes' men finally managed to force an entrance into the town, they found everything there ready for them. The elan of their assault was shaken on meeting these unexpected obstacles. The women of Acre encouraged the fighters by ear-splitting shrieks from the surrounding buildings. The English perceived the critical situation and Sir Sidney Smith personally led a relief force from his ships into the threatened part of the town. Hard hand to hand fighting took place in Acre during the afternoon of 8 May and the French were contained.

Berthier describes the fighting thus:[15] 'The fire from the buildings, from the barricades across the street, from Djezzar's palace, took those who descended from the breach into the town both from the front and the back, and those who were already in the town started to retreat, as they were unable to hold the town. They abandoned there two cannon and two mortars which they had got hold of inside the ramparts. The whole column inside the town was affected by the retrograde movement, General Lannes went forward in order to arrest it and get the column to move forward again. The Foot Scouts, who had been held in reserve, now scaled the breach. The men battled each other body to body, with the greatest bitterness, on both sides. But the enemy had again captured the crest of the breach. The effect of the first rush wore off; General Lannes was dangerously wounded, General Rambaud was killed there . . . The retreat became necessary, and the order was given.'

In the evening of that day the Turkish force from Rhodes, commanded by Hassan Bey, started to land. Its best unit, the Giftlic battalion, which had been trained on European lines, was denied admittance to Acre, as Djezzar would not agree, even at this critical moment, to their entry into his fortress. On the one hand he was involved in a life and death struggle with Napoleon, but on the other, he was suspicious of the intentions of any Turkish force not under his own control, believing that the Sultan would always be ready to trick him, if the occasion arose, trying to deprive him of his treasured independence. However Sir Sidney Smith persuaded him to let the Giftlic battalion pass through Acre on its way to attack the French. As its men had as yet no battle experience, they did not do too well in the evening of 8 May, but their attack on the French outside the walls did stop any further reinforcements reaching Lannes' men inside the town. In the meantime most of the French inside Acre had been overpowered and mowed down in the 'killing ground' Djezzar had prepared for them. One source[16] claims that 200 men managed to make a last stand in a mosque they had fortified, and in the end surrendered to Sir Sidney Smith, but most sources do not mention this incident.

However the breach in the town wall could not be closed and Napoleon decided to renew the attack on 10 May with fresh troops from Kléber's division, which had arrived before Acre the day before. Its men were in excellent spirit as a result of their three weeks rest in eastern Galilee. Impatient for the next day's assault they danced the farandole all evening.[17]

Again, however, the pressure of time did not allow proper preparations to be made and the actions of the various units involved were not sufficiently coordinated. Paymaster Peyrusse describes the action that followed thus:[18]

> 'Kléber's division was to begin the attack. Adjutant General Fouler commanded the vanguard. He was killed in the breach. This misfortune did not intimidate the 75th (Brigade); its men threw themselves into the city at the same time as Reynier's and Bon's divisions attacked the forces (from Rhodes) outside the walls. But the lack of coordination, or perhaps the efforts of the enemy resulted in discouraging those who had entered the city. Those not killed in action were either taken prisoner or assassinated, for they have not returned.'

The Giftlic battalion was used again in this battle to attack the French outside the city walls, and this time did so with greater bravery. The French were forced back to their own trenches, which the Turks proceeded to attack. General Murat, who so far, as cavalry commander, had not participated in the assaults on the city, now organized the French in the trenches to counterattack and drove the Turks back towards the breach. His aide-de-camp was badly wounded, but he himself was untouched though bullets passed through his jacket and his cravat.[19]

But Napoleon would still not give up. He used men of Kléber's division who had just arrived for the last assault of the siege. Peyrusse describes it as follows:[20]

> 'Surprised by so much disorder, we ceased fire. The troops rested for a while. All the men available were collected; the grenadiers of the 25th and carabineers of the 2nd arrived at that point and were ordered into the trenches. The ardour and courage of these fresh troops made the Commander-in-Chief believe that he could order a new assault. He wanted to be the first to scale the breach and it took a great deal of trouble to restrain him.'

According to the same witness the grenadiers threw themselves into the breach 'like madmen'. They had to step on the corpses of their fallen comrades to get there. However, once inside the town they encountered murderous fire from cannon now mounted in front of Djezzar's mosque. Further pieces of artillery were mounted elsewhere in the town and on the walls, and turned the open space of the gardens of Djezzar, into which the French were now penetrating for the third time, into a death trap. The defenders showed great flexibility in a most unusual situation. While a breached town was usually regarded as impossible to hold, they showed how such a situation could be actually turned to their benefit, by creating a killing ground inside the town in which they annihilated one French force after the other. Napoleon actually played into their hands by feeding his forces in piecemeal. After their successes Djezzar's men had now gained the experience and self confidence needed to carry through this difficult manoeuvre successfully. It is hard not to be struck by the way in which the defenders showed in these critical days a high degree of flexibility and of originality as against the inflexible and unoriginal way in which the assaults were handled. It was not by luck that Djezzar succeeded but by superior tactical ability in handling a novel and unusual situation. It was only rarely in his career that Napoleon was to meet so able a battle commander.

On the French side many of Napoleon's best soldiers and commanders were killed during the last day of the attack. General Bon was badly wounded, and because of his corpulent build and his refusal to be operated upon by Dr Larrey, he died later. Also the commander of the 25th brigade was killed and his successor wounded. The commander of the 9th brigade was wounded too. All Kléber's aides-de-camp became casualties and he himself was wounded, though only lightly. Berthier's adjutant was hit in the head, Murat's adjutant was wounded, and other headquarters officers also became casualties. The very need to use so many of them in the last assault indicates that the morale of the troops had been impaired and that they were required to give a much needed stiffening to the last assault.

Sir Sidney Smith claims that at the end the French grenadiers 'absolutely refused to mount the breach any more over the putrified bodies of their unburied companions, sacrificed in former attacks by Buonaparte's impatience and precipitation, which led him to commit such palpable errors as even seamen could take advantage of. He seemed to have no principle of action but that of pressing forward.'[21]

These last assaults showed only too clearly that any hope of capturing Acre had passed. Napoleon had tried time after time and had failed. His losses had mounted and his army could bear such losses no longer. The besieged had been reinforced and their morale had been strengthened by seeing the repeated defeats of their adversaries.

The opposite was true of morale on the French side. A further order to attack might have been met with open mutiny. When his soldiers saw Napoleon passing through the camp in the days immediately after, he was met with shouts of derision. His officers criticized (quite rightly) his handling of the attacks. Even his friend Murat told him to his face 'You have become the butcher of your soldiers.'[22]

Napoleon was left with no choice but to consider the best way to extricate his force and get it back to Egypt and how best to conceal the fact that he had been squarely defeated. Time, which had been in too short supply all through the campaign, had now run out completely. There was no possibility of making any further attempts to capture Acre. The invasion of Egypt by the main force collected in Rhodes could be expected any day now.

So as to get rid of his stock of ammunition, and best to conceal the fact of his defeat, Napoleon ordered a heavy bombardment, this time not of the walls, but of the town of Acre itself, during the days of 12 to 15 May and again 20 May. The damage done was considerable. Many of the inhabitants were killed and wounded. The most conspicuous building of the town (then as now), Djezzar's mosque, was badly damaged. Napoleon tried to explain his retreat by claiming that Acre had been destroyed anyway and there was no point in capturing a heap of rubble.[23] How successful he was with this excuse is best attested to by the fact that there are still historians who take it seriously.[24] If he had not brazenly lied his defeat away, it is difficult to see how, less than six months later, he could have carried out his successful coup d'etat in France. During his rule in France, Acre was obviously not a subject to be mentioned.

The siege had continued for 62 days, from 19 March to 21 May. No numbers have come down to us as to the losses of Djezzar's forces. Probably he did not know them exactly himself. But, undoubtedly, they were heavy, both in killed and in victims of the plague. Also the city of Acre was badly damaged. However Djezzar had most of it repaired quickly, and during the latter years of his life had it encircled with a second and much stronger line of walls. As early as 1801 western visitors no longer mention the damage done during the siege.[25]

The French also suffered heavily in killed, wounded and sick. Napoleon himself mentions only 500 killed and 1000 wounded in his report for all of his Holy Land campaign. However, nowadays the casualties are estimated at 1200 killed, and 2300 wounded and sick, which amounts to about one quarter of the total strength of the expeditionary force.[26] No wonder that with such a percentage of casualties, Napoleon had no choice but to retreat with all speed from Palestine. In spite of Napoleon's brilliant success at the battle of Mount Tabor, the defeat at Acre meant the failure of his whole Holy Land campaign. Thus it is important to try and analyse the reasons for his defeat before Acre. First of all the insufficient forces at his disposal are to blame and the absence of siege guns during most of the siege. The enemy by his timely preparations contributed to the French defeat, for instance by the deepening and strengthening of the moat, which defeated the first French assault and the preparation of an inner wall, which defeated the last assaults. The timely intervention of the British fleet was of crucial importance, not only in securing command of the sea, thus keeping the way open for supplies and relief, but also by capturing the French siege cannon, and by the activity of the Royal Marines ashore. A further factor was the continual lack of time, under which Napoleon was forced to act, and as a result of which he acted all too often rashly and without sufficient deliberation. However most crucial of all was perhaps Napoleon's disdain for the enemy in general and Djezzar in particular. Thus he did not trouble at all to disguise his actions, nor did he mount diversionary attacks, and furthermore he always attacked in exactly the same place. This is what enabled even Djezzar's court astrologer to interpret adequately Napoleon's intentions.[27] There is no escaping the conclusion that Napoleon himself was the main reason for the French defeat in front of Acre.

It is more difficult, perhaps, to establish who was the commander who vanquished him – a rare distinction, as Napoleon was not in the habit of being personally defeated, prior to his Russian campaign of 1812. Over the years historians have differed as to who really was the victor at Acre. This was usually judged on strictly national lines. Even the French cannot claim that Napoleon was victorious, and thus historians like Jomini and Bainville[28] have tended to see in his old schoolmate Phelipeaux the real victor. Englishmen are unanimous in the opinion that Sir Sidney Smith is the man who defeated Napoleon (for instance Rose and Markham).[29] Some Jewish historians (I. Ben-Zvi, M.D. Gaon, Sokolov, Y'ari-Polonski)[30] have tried to show that actually Haim Farhi was the real architect of victory. As there are so few Turkish and Bosnian historians only Djezzar seems to have been overlooked. But we believe that there can be little doubt that he was the real victor. If in his place there had been a run of the mill Ottoman pasha, neither English help, nor Phelipeaux's tactical flair, nor Haim Farhi's organizational ability could have saved Acre from swift capture by Napoleon.

15

THE RETREAT TO JAFFA

It was easier to decide on a withdrawal than to carry it out. There were now hundreds of wounded and sick and the question was, how to transport them? It would have been easiest to effect this by sea, however British seapower by now was too well known to be overlooked. It is possible that Sir Sidney Smith would have agreed to help, as his main mission was to stop Napoleon's advance against Turkey and India and this had now been achieved. However he and Napoleon had exchanged some highly uncomplimentary letters during the siege and had insulted each other in their public utterances.[1] Thus Napoleon was not prepared to approach him on this or any other subject. So, on 11 May Napoleon instructed Rear Admiral Perrée, whose flotilla was just then cruising near Jaffa, to sail to Tantura and to transport the worst cases among the wounded and sick to Egypt from there. At this stage naval commanders apparently did not regard themselves as coming fully under Napoleon's orders, and Perrée not only preferred not to approach too near to Sir Sidney Smith's force, but simply took off and returned to France. As we have previously seen that Captain Standelet acted in a very similar way, there obviously was something very wrong with the French navy. Apparently Perrée was not reprimanded for his conduct and even Napoleon in his memoirs has nothing but praise for him.[2] As a result of Perrée's withdrawal and Napoleon's refusal to deal with Sir Sidney Smith, a great deal of unnecessary agony was caused to the wounded and sick and many who could have been saved were to die.

Not all the sick were to be evacuated: Some of the plague cases were left behind. This incident is described by Private Millet, as follows:[3] 'The next day we were to leave and by a very cruel order we were to abandon the unlucky ones who had the plague. It pierced the heart of the army to have to leave our unfortunate brothers in arms at the mercy of the barbarian Arabs, who were to cut off their heads immediately when we had left. Some of these unfortunates came after us, beseeching us not to abandon them. But it was forbidden, under threat of severe punishment, to have any contact with them. This order, however severe, was perhaps necessary, as they might have communicated their terrible disease to the army and in order to save a few the army would have risked total destruction.' However, some of them survived, and we shall have occasion later to report the fate of one of them.

In order to prepare the withdrawal of his army, Napoleon decided on a limited attack against Samaria, so as to try and neutralize its forces, from which his expeditionary force would be most vulnerable to attack during the retreat. Lambert was put in charge of the 22nd and 25th demi-brigades and was given 50 men of the Dromedary Corps as well. With this force he carried out a raid into Samaria from 13 May onward, during which the local villages were looted and burned to the ground.

Napoleon ordered Junot at Nazareth to return to camp at Acre and to have his secondary units in Safet and Tiberias destroy those stores which could not be moved, and to evacuate Galilee. In Tiberias a heart rending scene was described by one of the French dragoon officers,[4] when the local population, consisting mostly of Jews, surrounded the French, who were preparing to leave, and implored them not to leave them to the tender mercies of Djezzar, who was sure to punish them for the friendly attitude they had shown the French. Also the small garrison from Shafr Amr and the other French outposts in Western Galilee were now withdrawn.

The various allies who had joined Napoleon's flag – Matuwellis, Christians, the family of Daher al-Umar, Mustafa Beshir and to a lesser degree, the Emir Bashir II and the Druses and Maronites – were now abandoned to Djezzar's revenge. One gesture was made by Napoleon (according to Beauchamp): he transferred some of his cannon to the Druses, promising 'to return one day'.[5] However when his nephew *did* return 61 years later, it was by sending an expeditionary force against these self same Druses.

Djezzar meted out the harshest treatment to the weakest, to the Christians and Jews. Without Sir Sidney Smith's intervention there might have taken place in Galilee a massacre of these minorities.[6] Bashir II went into exile for some time, before he was reinstated by Djezzar, after the Grand Vizier personally had interceded on his behalf.

Napoleon tried to mislead Djezzar and Sir Sidney Smith about his decision to withdraw, by his bombardment of Acre and by exploding mines beneath its walls. He tried thus to create the impression that the siege was going on and that another assault was imminent. He was so successful, that on 20 May the besieged mounted a major sally, which Reynier's division only barely succeeded in turning back, as most of the heavy guns and mortars and the rest of the ammunition had already been buried in the sands of the beaches.

In the meantime all preparations for the retreat were made in secret and it was carried out as quietly as possible on the night of 20/21 May. Immediately after it became dark, at 2000 hours, Lannes' division was the first to leave, in the direction of Haifa, carrying their wounded general at their head, in a litter.[7] They were followed by headquarters, the administrative personnel, the Foot Guides, the field artillery (the siege artillery was left behind), the engineers, Bon's division (still called so though commanded now by General Rampon)[8] and Reynier's division. The rear guard was composed of Kléber's division and of Murat's cavalry, who left at 2300 hours. All this time the defenders were shooting their guns off, as they were afraid of another French attack. After the whole army had passed, the bridges over the Na'aman and Kishon rivulets were blown up by the engineers so as to prevent any pursuit.

Only the next morning did the inhabitants of Acre discover that their long ordeal was over. They were overjoyed – until the last moment they had been afraid that their town could not hold out after all. Twenty-three guns were found abandoned, or buried in the dunes by the French, and were used four years later by Djezzar when he besieged the town of Jaffa.[9] Djezzar made no effort to pursue the French. From the moment that they had ceased to threaten his capital, they were of no interest to him. As a realist politician he imme-diately took up his old feuds with his adversaries within the Ottoman estab-lishment, at the point where he had been so rudely interrupted by that short statured Corsican adventurer.

In the meantime Napoleon faced the problem of evacuating his sick and wounded. When still at Acre (on 16 May) he had hinted to Dr Desgenettes[10] 'If I were in your place, I should put an end to the suffering of our plague patients and, at the same time, to the danger they represent for us, by giving them opium.' Napoleon claimed, that if he himself had the plague he would ask this to be done to him as a favour. Desgenettes, however, refused, saying 'As far as I am concerned, my duty is to preserve life.' Napoleon stressed that his duty was to keep the expeditionary force intact. However Napoleon was not eager to undertake such an action on his own responsibility and would have preferred to have it look as if the physician was following his own initiative. He never forgave Desgenettes for his refusal to help.

Thus Napoleon had to find other solutions to his problem. He divided the sick and wounded into three categories: those who could walk, those who could ride and litter cases. He ordered most of the horses, camels and asses of the army to be put at the disposal of the last two, except for those needed to transport the field guns, and those used by the officers. However the sick and wounded sometimes found that they had to make payments to stretcher bearers in order not to be left behind. The situation turned grave, especially after the army reached Haifa. It then became necessary to take along the sick and wounded who had been cared for by the Carmelite monks (who, for their trouble, were severely persecuted by Djezzar). The large number of these sick and wounded posed a severe problem. They were evacuated during the night from Mount Carmel and brought to Haifa. Some of the walking cases however hurried too much in the pitch darkness, took short cuts, stumbled over boulders, fell from the steep rocks and could not be located, though their cries could still be heard.

The others were concentrated in the main square of Haifa. Paymaster Peyrusse describes the scene that met the eyes of the army when it arrived there as follows: 'We had hoped that we should no longer have before our eyes the hideous sight of dead and dying men ... when, as we entered Haifa in the dark of night, we saw about a hundred sick and wounded who had been left in the middle of a large square. Those poor, desperate, people filled the air with their screams and their curses ... some were tearing off their bandages and rolled in the dust. This spectacle petrified the army. We stopped for a moment and men were designated in each company to carry these people in their arms to Tantura.'[11]

After a long and arduous march onwards to Tantura, they found 700 or 800 further sick and wounded who had been concentrated there for shipment to Egypt. In view of Rear Admiral Perrée's dereliction of duty, they had now to be transported by land. This was a really daunting challenge. The solution found by Napoleon was to leave behind all his remaining field guns. According to Berthier 22 cannon were thrown into the sea near Tantura and according to Richardot there were three 24-pounders among them. Modern archaeologists have recovered one of these cannon and also an iron cannon ball, lead musket balls and flintlock service muskets W33 as used by the French armies from 1777 to 1840.[12] The horses and camels thus released were all used for the transport of the sick and wounded. All officers were now ordered to give up their horses for the same purpose. Napoleon tried to set an example and walked part of the way. In order to make his point he struck one of his grooms when he offered him one of his horses.[13] As he never used to strike his servants, he thus made sure that his deed would be talked about throughout the army and he hoped that his example of not riding himself would be followed by the other officers. However it was not possible to enforce his orders during the chaotic conditions of a retreat. Some of the participants report that many of the officers did not obey and continued to ride. Bourienne reports that even those who did, tried to have their horses used for the wounded and not for the plague patients.[14]

As the journey continued, conditions became even more difficult – a burning sun in a season which in Palestine is already summer, lack of water, general tiredness. There were many cases when the litter bearers left their charges behind, on the roadside, even though they had been paid for their service. Bourienne claims the scene to have looked thus: 'A most intolerable thirst, the total lack of water, an excessive heat and a fatiguing march over burning sand hills, quite disheartened the men and made every generous sentiment give way to feelings of the grossest selfishness and most shocking indifference. I saw officers with their limbs amputated, thrown off the litters... I saw the amputated, the wounded, the infected ... deserted and left to themselves... The dying who, stretched on the roadside, implored assistance in a feeble voice, saying 'I am not infected – I am only wounded', and to convince those whom they addressed, they reopened their old wounds, or inflicted fresh ones on themselves. Still, nobody attended to them. "It is all over with him" was the observation applied to the unfortunate beings, while everyone pressed onward.'[15]

Some of them were despatched by the local inhabitants, who hated the French anyway but had now new accounts to settle. The French were systematically looting the nearby villages and, following a policy of scorched earth, were putting what remained behind to the torch. Miot describes the scene thus:[16]

'It was then that we started to put the villages and the houses to the torch. The inhabitants of that country had committed many acts of assassination; they had disturbed us during the siege of Jaffa and had attacked many of our convoys. We were more prudent than our enemy and wanted to make it impossible for them to follow us and to deprive them of the resources needed for an invasion of Egypt. Thus far from leaving them any stores, as, fortunately for us, they had done, we put the country into a state where it would be impossible for a long time to nourish troops with its products. The wind swept the flames nearly all the way to the mountains; they menaced the villages with frightful conflagrations and the ground covered with cinders resembled a vast altar with fumes arising from a just sacrifice in honour of the French heroes who had died in Syria.'

It can be doubted if the inhabitants shared these sentiments of the invaders of their country.

Bourienne elaborates further:[17]

'The march was illuminated by torches, lighted for the purpose of setting fire to the little towns, villages and hamlets which lay along the route, and the rich crops with which the land was then covered. The whole country was in a blaze... Those who were ordered to carry out this work of destruction seemed eager to spread desolation on every side, as if they could thereby avenge themselves for their reverses and find in such dreadful havoc an alleviation of their sufferings. We were constantly surrounded by plunderers, incendiaries and the dying.... The sun, which shone in a clear sky in all its brightness, was often darkened by our conflagrations. On our right lay the sea; on our left and behind us, the desert made by ourselves.'

The feeling of dejection was so strong in the army that even cases of suicide were reported. To complete this picture of a truly Dantesque hell, there were also enemy attacks. These were made not by Djezzar's men, but from the sea side, from where the retreating French were sniped at by English gun boats. Perhaps in order to put more distance between themselves and the British navy the French moved from the little Nahr-ez-Zerka (or Crocodile river) further inland. However the participants now missed the fresh sea breeze, which had cooled them so far.[18] On their other side they were attacked by the men from Samaria, who came down from their mountains into the coastal plain, in order to settle their scores with the hated French and were joined by the local villagers. It was thus impossible to linger, as all stragglers were liable to be killed. Bourienne reports that one of the 'Naplousians', as he spells it (actually there is no 'p' in Arabic, even though the original name was the Greek 'Neapolis') took a pot shot from quite nearby at Napoleon and missed his head by inches. He was captured and was to have been executed, but managed to escape.[19]

The next stop after Tantura was at Caesarea, again on the sea coast, where Napoleon and his staff enjoyed a swim.[20] The next day (23 May), when they moved away from the sea, the pressure of the attacks of the men from Samaria became specially noticeable. There was little food left now and thus the army had but little sleep that night, starting early so as to reach Jaffa again on 24 May, where ample stores awaited them.

According to Miot the greatest problem that day was the lack of sleep.[21]

'We were often forced to follow narrow paths; our horses would halt; we would stop for a few seconds only and would immediately fall asleep, and we slept even while marching. I fell twice from my horse and was forced to continue on foot so as to avoid the inconvenience of falling asleep. We would all have been ready to pay a high price for the favour of resting for a few hours; but the army had no supplies left and we had to reach Jaffa.'

16

THE POISONING OF THE
PLAGUE CASES[1]

When Napoleon departed from Jaffa on his way to Acre he had left there a garrison and his wounded, who were tended in the Greek Orthodox monastery, and the plague cases, who were looked after in the Armenian monastery next door. He had nominated a town council ('Diwan') in Jaffa, composed both of Muslims and of Christians, to run the civilian affairs of the town. As military commander he had left the Adjutant-General of his army, Grézieu, in Jaffa. This officer was so afraid of the plague that he tried not to have any contact with anybody so as to avoid contagion. However, in vain. He did catch the plague later and died after only one day.

During Napoleon's absence, the garrison of Jaffa tried to have the fortifications of the town rebuilt. With the help of the local inhabitants and some prisoners of war the streets were cleaned and the corpses of the slain buried.

About 200 (and according to other sources, 300) French plague cases remained in Jaffa. The man in charge of the administration of their hospital was the eminent physicist Etienne Louis Malus (later discoverer of the polarization of light), now a member of the French scientific mission. In his memoirs he tells us 'For ten days I went there assiduously and spent every morning in the loathsome stench of that cloaca, every corner of which was crowded with patients. It was only on the eleventh day that I noticed the symptoms of the plague. This was about the time that Adjutant General Grézieu died. Half of the garrison had already been stricken by then. About thirty men died every day ... About one man among twelve stricken survived ... The Plague was in every house of the town ... The monks of the Franciscan monastery quarantined themselves to avoid contagion. Almost all of them died.'[2]

How many of the plague cases survived? According to Malus' figures it would have been eight percent. But according to Desgenettes' notes it seems to have been many more, even though in Jaffa the plague had been especially virulent.[3] When Napoleon and his army returned to Jaffa, there were still about 200 plague cases left who had survived, which would indicate a far higher percentage of survival. Malus was one of them, and together with many others he was now evacuated by sea to Damietta. He, at least, fully recovered during the sea voyage. En route the French flotilla of seven ships met Sir Sidney Smith's squadron and did not hesitate to approach and ask for help with water and rations. The British were prepared to help, and took off the lighter cases (who might fight again) allowing only the really sick and badly wounded to continue.[4]

The physician who cared for the plague cases was a Turk, named Hadj Mustafa, who had been sent from Istanbul to look after the wounded in Jaffa and was taken prisoner when he stepped ashore. At Desgenettes' request he volunteered to look after the plague cases when the French left for Acre.

On 24 May the French army returned to Jaffa, after an absence of two and a half months. Because of the prevalence of the plague the French soldiers were not quartered in the town, and camped instead outside the walls, in the orchards and gardens which surrounded Jaffa. Because of their insufficient rations during their march, many of the soldiers ate their fill of the still unripe fruit, and Dr Desgenettes complained about the high incidence of diarrhoea among them as a result.

Most of the expeditionary force stayed at Jaffa for four days. However some groups left every day on their way to the south, so for instance, on 25 May did 300 walking wounded. Up to 27 May another 1300 sick and wounded left by the land route, partly on horses, partly on litters carried by Turkish prisoners, and the remainder walking. Some hundreds of the worst cases were sent by sea to Damietta. According to Dr Larrey these numbered 1200 men, but he reports that only 800 went by land. Because of lack of shipping not all the severe cases could be thus evacuated and some of the sick were left behind on the quay at Jaffa. These implored passers by to help them find a place on the boats, but in vain.[5]

The army brought with it many additional plague cases. They could first be seen lying among the tents in the camp, but were gradually either evacuated or transferred to the Armenian monastery. When all the others had gone, there still remained between 35 and 60 men (different sources mention different numbers). Rumours about their fate became public, when, in 1803, the same Robert Thomas Wilson, who had given wide publicity to the massacre of the prisoners at Jaffa, had this to say about the plague cases:[6]

'Buonaparte ... found an apothecary, who ... consented to become his agent, and to administer poison to the sick. At night opium was distributed in gratifying food, and wretched unsuspecting victims banqueted, and in a few hours five hundred and eighty soldiers, who had suffered so much for their country, perished thus miserably by the order of its idol. Is there a Frenchman whose blood does not chill with horror at the recital of such a fact? Surely the shades of these murdered unoffending people must be now hovering round the seat of government.'

This story did Napoleon's good name quite as much harm as the execution of the Duke of Enghien or the massacre of the prisoners in Jaffa. This connection of Napoleon with Jaffa, in which he spent so short a time, is most curious. It is as if the town itself had taken revenge on the man who had allowed the massacre of its inhabitants, by indelibly tarnishing his reputation.

However in the case of the poisoning of the plague cases it seems that the episode has been much exaggerated. The books and memoirs covering the Holy Land campaign can be divided – like all Napoleonic sources – into two groups: those written under the Bourbons with a strong anti-Napoleonic bias, and those which were published later. The more slanderous version is usually to be found in the first group, and should thus be treated with great caution. If we let ourselves be guided mainly by the versions of the second group, we get, more or less, the following picture: those 35 to 60 cases who were left behind in the Armenian monastery were too sick to be moved. They were all expected to die in a matter of hours or a day or two. Napoleon did not order them to be poisoned, but agreed (or initiated) that some poison be left with them (apparently opium) by the Turkish physician Hadj Mustafa,[7] and by the chief pharmacist of the expedition, Royer. Thus they could make use of it, if they so wished, in order not to fall alive into the hands of the enemy. Further Napoleon left in Jaffa a rear guard of 500 cavalrymen, after the rest of the army had left, to watch over the plague cases one more day. It was expected that this period would be sufficient for nearly all of them to die.

Napoleon gave his version of what had happened at some length to Dr O'Meara on St Helena:[8]

' "Previous to leaving Jaffa ... and after the greatest number of the sick and wounded had been embarked, it was reported to me that there were some men in the hospital so dangerously ill, as not to be able to be moved. I ordered immediately the chiefs of the medical staff to consult together upon what was best to be done, and to give me their opinion on this subject. Accordingly they met, and found that there were seven or eight men so dangerously ill, that they conceived it impossible for them to recover; and also that they could not exist twenty-six hours longer, that moreover, being afflicted with the plague, they would spread that complaint amongst all those who approached them. Some of them, who were conscious, perceiving that they were about to be abandoned, demanded with earnest entreaties to be put to death. Larrey was of the opinion that recovery was impossible, and that those poor fellows could not exist many hours; but as they might live long enough to be alive when the Turks entered, and experience the dreadful torments which they were accustomed to inflict upon their prisoners, he thought it would be an act of charity to comply with their desires, and accelerate their end by a few hours. Desgenettes did not approve of this, and replied that his profession was to cure the sick, and not to despatch them. Larrey came to me immediately afterwards, informed me of the circumstances, and of what Desgenettes had said; adding that perhaps Desgenettes was right." "But," continued Larrey, "those men cannot live for more than a few hours, twenty-four or thirty-six at the most, and if you will leave a rear-guard of cavalry, to stay and protect them from advanced parties, it will be sufficient." "Accordingly I ordered four or five hundred cavalry to remain behind, and not to quit the place until all were dead. They did remain and informed me that all had expired before they had left the town; but I have heard since that Sidney Smith found one or two alive when he entered it. That is the truth of the business. Wilson himself, I dare say, knows now that he was mistaken. Sidney Smith never asserted it. I have no doubt that this story of the poisoning originated in something said by Desgenettes, who was a windbag, which was afterwards misconceived or incorrectly repeated . . . Not that I think it would have been a crime, had opium been given to them; on the contrary, I think it would have been a virtue. To leave a few wretches, who could not recover, in order that they might be massacred by the Turks with the most dreadful tortures, as was their custom, would, I think, have been cruelty. Now would not any man under similar circumstances, who had his senses, have preferred dying easily a few hours sooner, rather than expire under the tortures of those barbarians? You have been amongst the Turks, and know what they are; I ask you now to place yourself in the situation of one of those sick men, and that you were asked which you would prefer, to be left to suffer tortures of those miscreants, or to have opium administered to you?" I replied, "Most undoubtedly I should prefer the latter." "Certainly, so would any man," answered Napoleon. "If my own son . . . were in a similar situation with those men, I would advise it to be done; and if so situated myself, I would insist upon it, if I had sense enough and strength enough to demand it. But, however, affairs were not so pressing as to prevent me from leaving a party to take care of them, which was done. If I had thought such a measure as that of giving opium necessary, I would have called a council of war, have stated the necessity of it, and have published it in the order of the day. It should have been no secret. Do you think that if I had been capable of secretly poisoning my soldiers . . . that my troops would have fought for me with an enthusiasm and affection without a parallel? No, no. I never should have done so a second time. Some would have shot me in passing." '

Basically the same story is given in Napoleon's memoirs[9] in a much more concise form. However here he adds that he ordered the physician who remained with Murat's 500 cavalrymen, to leave some opium with any of the sick who might still be alive when this rearguard had to leave, and to instruct them in its use.

A later traveller reports, that in the adjacent Greek Orthodox monastery sixteen to eighteen badly wounded patients were left behind, because they could not be moved.[10] According to his story their heads were cut off by the Nablussians when they entered Jaffa, after the French had left. If correct, this would prove Napoleon's concern not to have been unfounded. Most of the plague cases apparently did die of their illness, and only a few made use of the poison left to them. Sir Sidney Smith testifies that seven were still alive when his squadron arrived at Jaffa, after the French had left.[11] He states that the amount of poison had been insufficient, and this is borne out by Dr Larrey, who claims that there simply was no opium left with which to treat or poison anybody.[12] However Royer and Hadj Mustafa seem to have had access to limited amounts of opium of which Larrey apparently was not aware.[13] However it was apparently not very potent. Sir Sidney Smith claims that seven of the sick who had taken it vomited it up, and thus survived.[14] The Nablussians who occupied Jaffa for a short while before the arrival of the British, were apparently afraid of contagion and therefore did not harm them. According to Sir Sidney Smith these seven did survive, and recovered.[15] It seems thus that this episode has been much exaggerated and that it is difficult to blame Napoleon for it. Under the chaotic conditions of a retreat what alternative did he have?

In the meantime the expeditionary force busied itself with demolishing the same fortifications which it had only recently restored. Part of the walls were mined and blown up, and most of the towers were destroyed. Stores which could not be moved were put to the torch, as were some of the buildings in Jaffa.[16]

The French garrison consisted of men from different units, and General Vial, the last military commander of the city, was ordered by Napoleon to return them to their units, when the retreat recommenced. The final withdrawal took place on 28 May. Soon after the cavalry rearguard had left, Jaffa was occupied by the Nablussians, who started looting and murdering the population. However two days after the French had left, the British landed in the port, and with the help of their naval cannon evicted the Nablussians.

Jaffa was badly damaged by the French capture and occupation. Only about one quarter of its inhabitants remained behind. Two years later visitors report that the stench of unburied bodies was still to be felt in the air. Many of the inhabitants had been killed or injured, others had lost their property. The city looked unkempt and wretched for quite some time. The orchards surrounding it, which served as its main economic base, were also badly damaged. Jaffa was perhaps hurt worse than any other place; however all of the coastal plain suffered badly from the French invasion. But the French should perhaps not be judged too severely. In 1771 and 1775 two other, not much less damaging invasions from Egypt had preceded Napoleon's campaign, and in the years after 1799, Jaffa was besieged twice, and Acre three times. All these campaigns, raids and sieges can be equally regarded as results of the decline and disruption of the Ottoman Empire.[17] To the local inhabitants it did not matter much if the killing, looting and burning was done by the French, Egyptians or the Turks.

17

THE RETREAT TO EGYPT

The day before the French Army left Jaffa, it was attacked for the last time by Nablussians who were, however, repulsed by Murat's cavalry. They did not continue to follow the expeditionary force, as the distance from the mountains of Samaria was becoming too great. The Governor of Jerusalem was to have provided 2000 cavalrymen, to continue the pursuit,[1] but French sources mention nothing of their actually having made contact with them.

Here and there the French now experienced difficulties with local beduin, but the enemy pressure, in this second stage of the retreat, was incomparably less than in the first.

The sick and wounded were now carried by Turkish prisoners, which made things easier, too — at least for the French. The number of sick was now much reduced, because many had been evacuated from Jaffa by sea and others had left in separate parties, and still others had died during the first part of the withdrawal. This, too, made the second stage of the retreat easier to bear than the first. Furthermore, at first the French carried with them sufficient rations from the stores kept at Jaffa. But still this was a hard and difficult march, through the soft sand of the dunes; the weather was by now even hotter by day, while the cool nights were shorter.

Lannes' division served as vanguard, followed by Bon's division. Reynier's men made a detour to the east, passing through Ramle, in order to destroy the stores there. The cavalry covered the right flank of the withdrawing force, in the sand dunes near the sea shore. Farther south, however, all of the army followed more or less the same track. There were some difficulties in crossing the Nahr Rubin, where the bridge had been destroyed. From here they continued to Yebna, where Napoleon and most of the army spent the night. The next stage was to Isdud (nowadays the port of Ashdod). The French continued to burn down the nearby villages, to loot the cattle and to put the harvest to the torch.[2] These deeds seem particularly inexcusable as there was no point in a scorched earth policy, since they were no longer followed by any enemy force.

However, perhaps Napoleon hoped in this way to put obstacles in the way of any eventual invasion of Egypt. Perhaps, too, he hoped that in this way his men would find relief for their pent up frustration and disillusion. This was doubly important, as perhaps in none of his other campaigns was he personally so much the target of his men's disappointment and animosity. He was criticized quite openly and was met by cries of scorn and derision. As he was still only a general of the Republic, and not yet the all-powerful emperor, this is perhaps not surprising. Other generals of the revolutionary armies of France fared no better. The surprising thing here is that this defeated and discredited general, who was by now disliked by many of his men, was after little more than five months to take control of the destinies of France.

On nearing Gaza Dr Desgenettes remarks:[3] 'The paths which we had found so muddy in the month of Ventôse had become dry and cracked; we found only three wells, which were only three feet deep and from which it was very difficult to draw water for such a great number of men, as we were.'

On 30 May the expeditionary force reached Gaza. Here too the French garrison had suffered severely from the plague. From Desgenettes' notes we learn that from 7 to 18 March, 191 plague cases were admitted to the hospital, 98 were released, 76 remained and 17 died[4] – a very low rate of fatalities when compared with that at Jaffa. On Napoleon's return there were mostly convalescents left.

Bernoyer, the chief tailor of the expedition, was ordered to issue new uniforms to all the soldiers, so that they should resemble a victorious army on their entry into Cairo, and not a beaten one.[5] Their outward appearance was to back up Napoleon's version that his Holy Land campaign had been successful.

At Gaza the army was issued with water and rations for their march through the desert of Northern Sinai.

Some of the plague cases who were not able to go on, were left in Gaza, and hostages were taken from among the local notables as token that they would not be harmed.[6] These hostages were later held at Salahya within the borders of Egypt.

The garrison of Gaza now joined the army. Kléber, whose division formed the rear guard, had to ensure that the citadel of Gaza, which had only recently been restored and improved by the French, was blown up and thoroughly destroyed, and that the remaining stores were put to the torch.

On 31 May the army reached Khan Yunis.[7] Bernoyer reports how he met a friend there whom he had believed dead of the plague:[8]

'Entering my tent, I was very surprised to find Lallemand there: a few days earlier, struck down by the plague, he had been left behind at Acre. I myself had brought him to the hospital for plague cases with the sad prospect of never seeing him again. Imagine my surprise when I saw him alive! I thought I must be dreaming! But gathering my senses I expressed my joy at meeting him again, and asked him by the grace of what miracle he had been saved. He told me that on the evening (before Acre) when the poisoned soup was being distributed (to the plague cases) a friend had warned him not to touch it. Thus he left the deadly beverage in his bowl. Later in the night the news spread in the hospital wards that Bonaparte was leaving Acre with his army. All were seized by terror. In view of their horrible situation Lallemand regretted not having partaken of the beverage, which, by a painless death would have saved him from being massacred by barbarous enemies. He decided to search for the soup. The effort he made to find the bowl caused his body to tremble all over, he felt the plague bubes reopening and was seized by violent pain. As a result he fainted for a long time until daybreak. He was awakened by a confusion of noise throughout the hospital. The door of his room was noisily flung open: some Turks entered hurriedly, sabre in hand. He thought himself lost. But after observing their every movement attentively he was surprised to discover in their faces an expression of pity, of surprise and horror, at the spectacle of all the dying and the dead.

'The desolate picture caused them to raise their hands to heaven, demanding an explanation of such a catastrophe. They revived the spirits of those still alive by giving them water to drink. All those who had resisted the poisoned beverage were saved: more than forty had to thank the prompt help of the Turks for their lives. A commisar and a physician visited them: those who were well enough were given the choice either to enter the service of the Turks, or to be escorted to the nearest French outpost. Most chose to stay in the service of the Turks, and thus became our most redoubtable enemies. But Lallemand preferred to rejoin the French army. Thus I met him on my arrival.'

On 1 June the Army passed Rafa, thus leaving the Holy Land, and returning to what was then regarded as Africa. There were still some plague cases among the soldiers, who found progress in the desert so difficult that some of them asked their comrades to put an end to their misery by shooting them and their wish was reportedly met.[9] There were also however owners of horses who are reported to have offered them to the sick. Some of the plague stricken tried to follow the army at a slower pace, but were killed by the beduin.

Morale was low, and orders issued by the officers were not always carried out. When the men of the rear-guard were ordered by Kléber to fall in after a rest by the wayside, they refused to obey. The officers repeated the order, and nobody moved, and some of the men even cursed the officers. One of Kléber's

165

aides-de-camp advanced towards the men, but they stopped him with their bayonets. He returned to Kléber, who told him 'Leave them alone, let them give off steam, and curse us. It is the only relief they have, you must not take it away from them. Let us pretend we do not even notice their mutiny. They will come – you will see. Let us march ahead.' And indeed, after some time, the men got up and followed their general.[10]

The march through the desert to El-Arish was particularly hard and tiring and the heat was stifling.[11] The French reached El-Arish on 2 June, tired and hungry, and rested there for two days. In El-Arish they found plenty of water and stores from which they could draw rations for the onward march. El-Arish was not to be evacuated, like Jaffa or Gaza, since it formed part of Egypt and was needed for its defence. The fortress here was therefore not only not blown up, but strengthened against the day when it might be attacked by a Turkish army of invasion.[12] The garrison was reinforced. From now on this was no longer a hasty retreat from an enemy country, but a progress in a friendly one. Most of the army continued to Katia. It was so hot that quite a few of the horses died of heat exhaustion. The French found the temperature to be 33 degrees Réaumur and 45 degrees (41 and 56 degrees Celsius respectively) when the thermometer was brought in contact with the hot sand.

In the retreat from Acre some elements are to be found which reappear on a much vaster scale in the retreat from Moscow. Here too we hear about the collapse of morale and of military discipline. Some of the descriptions of the sights and horrors of retreat sound similar. But there are four main points of difference:

- The main problem in the retreat from Acre was the unbearable heat. In the retreat from Moscow it was of course the freezing cold.
- The light pressure of the Nablussians cannot be compared with the aggressive attacks of the Russians.
- The forces involved in Russia were incomparably vaster.
- The French army disintegrated as a result of the retreat from Moscow, while Napoleon succeeded in getting the expeditionary force out of Palestine in relatively good shape.

But in spite of these vast differences there seems to be a similar mood in both cases, as if this were the rehearsal of a play to be enacted a dozen years later.

Near the end of its journey the French army stopped at Katia, which had also served as its point of departure. From here Napoleon inspected the defences of the frontier and made arrangements for the defence of Egypt.[13] The

Palestinian Christians who had followed the French were not allowed to continue to Cairo, in order not to spread despondency by reporting the defeat in detail, and were left behind at Katia and Mas'udia. Kléber and his division were sent to Damietta, perhaps because of its notoriously low morale, which might have marred the 'victorious' entry into Cairo.

The army left Katia on 7 June and reached Salahya the next day. It advanced slowly, so that the soldiers would look healthy and well rested on arrival in Cairo, and not like a defeated rabble. Discipline was tightened again. Napoleon did his utmost to stage manage the entry into Cairo carefully. And indeed, when the expeditionary force re-entered the capital of Egypt on 14 June it once again looked like a well disciplined and powerful army, back from a successful campaign.[14] As a result the effect on the citizens of Cairo was just as hoped, and Napoleon did not have to cope with a revolution resulting from news about a disastrous defeat. In Egypt many of the French felt as if in their second home, and were glad to forget as quickly as possible the hardships, dangers, failures and horrors of the Holy Land campaign.

Kléber wrote 21 June 1799 to General Dugua:[15]

'We have committed in the Holy Land enormous sins and great stupidities; but it is necessary to let the curtain of the tabernacle fall on all this, and let us beware of ever raising it again for fear that the Almighty, in his wrath, will punish us for our temerity.'

18

THE CURTAIN FALLS

History did not stop in its tracks with the return of the expeditionary force. A month later the long expected Turkish invasion from Rhodes took place – and was utterly defeated only ten days later by Napoleon at Aboukir. A month after that Napoleon embarked for France and gained full control of her destinies on 9 November, only five months after his disastrous retreat from Acre.

The army he had led to Egypt was left cut off from home, but still managed to hold out for two more years. Napoleon handed its command over to Kléber, who was none too glad to have it. He believed that there was no alternative to a settlement with England, as a result of which Egypt would have to be evacuated. However when his protracted negotiations with Sir Sidney Smith on this subject failed – mainly because the English home government would not honour the terms worked out – Kléber renewed the war by completely defeating a Turkish army, which had in the meantime entered Egypt, in the outskirts of Cairo, at the battle of Heliopolis. The Turks were evicted from Egypt and Kléber arranged a settlement with the Mameluks, some of whom had fought the French so tenaciously throughout the Holy Land campaign. However, after he had been in charge for a year Kléber was assassinated by a fanatical Muslim from Jerusalem. He was followed in command by General Menou, who had embraced Islam, had taken the name of Abdallah and had married a local lady, thus showing his full support for Napoleon's colonial plans. He was however less capable as a general than Kléber and was not able to successfully oppose the new English–Turkish invasions, which put an end to French rule in Egypt, in 1801.

In the meantime the Middle East was fast becoming a backwater, as Napoleon's wars riveted the eyes of Europe first to his triumphal progress and later to his disastrous setbacks. In these wars Napoleon showed special consideration to those few senior commanders who had survived his Holy Land campaign: they had been together to hell and back. Three of them attained the rank of marshal: the chief of staff, Berthier; Murat, who continued as

Napoleon's main cavalry commander, and Lannes who was later created Duke of Montebello (and was killed in 1809 in the battle of Aspern). His widow, however, became the main confidante of Empress Marie Louise. Murat married Napoleon's sister, Caroline, was created King of Naples, and after his brother-in-law's final defeat at Waterloo, was executed in 1815, when trying to return to his kingdom. Junot did get a dukedom (Duke of Abrantes, but not of Nazareth), but failed to get his marshal's baton because of his defeat by the English in Portugal in 1808. He died in 1813, before the end of the Napoleonic epic.

General Reynier was not included in this glittering group as he made the fatal mistake of letting himself be decisively defeated by the British in the battle of Maida, in Calabria, in 1806. Still, perhaps because of the early promise he had shown at El-Arish, he was later reinstated, commanded a corps in the 1813 German campaign, and was captured by the enemy in the battle of Leipzig.

The artillery commander, General Dommartin, Napoleon's main antagonist among the generals, did not make it back home to France, and perished in Egypt, as the result of a local uprising.

Dr Larrey was created a baron by Napoleon and was still serving as chief surgeon at the battle of Waterloo, where Wellington ordered his soldiers not to shoot at him, while he was tending the wounded on the field of battle. He lived until 1842, in which year he was still sent on a mission of inspection of the medical services during the French occupation of Algiers.

Let us now turn to Napoleon himself. Was he able to derive any lessons from his Holy Land campaign? Military commanders, like most mortals, usually learn from mistakes. Napoleon's biographers have often tried to minimize his failures and defeats. However we cannot properly appreciate his later chain of victories without understanding that he, too, made mistakes to start with. Some of them were still committed on the limited stage of his native Corsica, where in the early years of the revolution he was deeply involved in the local struggle for power, and where all his efforts, military as well as political, ended in utter failure. When he appeared immediately afterwards on the much wider stage of France and Europe, he had these early experiences to draw on, and to learn from.

We have to assume that his defeat before Acre also taught him much. None of his biographers has described the inner misery he must have felt during his retreat. Nineteenth century historians saw him only too often as a larger-than-life figure, some as the greatest of French national heroes, others as an ogre and fiend and as an enemy of humanity; nearly all as a demi-god of war. It has been

169

the task of some of his biographers of the second half of the 20th century to reduce this figure to mortal size. We have thus to remember that even Napoleon the Great was, after all, only human and thus fallible. He too enjoyed success and abhorred failure. We have to see the general bringing back his forces from Acre to Egypt not as the figure of inhuman, or superhuman, hardness, immune to the feelings of mere mortals, that his biographers usually portrayed him to be. Actually this was a still young man who surely suffered greatly because of his failure. It was probably not at all easy for him to show the world that bold front which has been recorded by history. Deep inside he surely felt pangs of uncertainty, both as to his ability and to the luck which previously had not deserted him. The criticism of his friends and officers certainly hurt him, and it was even worse to be insulted to his face by his soldiers. He was very careful not to show the world the wounds to his spirit, but this does not mean that they healed quickly or easily. Even in the handling of the coup d'état of Brumaire 18 an uncertainty can be felt in his decisions and actions which stems perhaps from his recent defeat. However he was still young enough to learn and profit from his mistakes. For many years he was much less ready to underrate his adversaries, as he had underrated Djezzar. He learned to be much more thorough in his preparations and to leave much less to luck. In his future, much more famous campaigns, he was never as hasty and impatient as he had been in front of Acre. Pressure of events and of time could not get the same hold over him as they had there. If he was from now on a more mature and circumspect commander, Acre surely had its share in it. If we look at some of the most difficult moments of his military career, such as when he had already lost the crucial battle of Marengo, the purpose of which was not only to defeat the Austrians but to make his rule of France secure, he found the strength of soul not to panic, but to renew the battle and to turn it into one of his great victories. Or when in Eastern Europe in 1807 victory eluded him at Eylau, his character was strong enough not to give up, but to continue to campaign until he caught the Russians at a severe disadvantage which enabled him to crush them at Friedland. Perhaps his spirit was kept up at these, and similar moments, by the memory of how he had passed through much worse situations at Acre and after. The Napoleon of Marengo and of Friedland surely stood in debt to the lesson learned at Acre. Only when the chain of his victories became too long did he start to forget the lessons of his youth. In his last campaigns his mistakes were the same as before Acre: disdain of his adversaries, hubris, and an unreadiness to compromise. He had lost the power to control these traits in his character and hence his downfall.

What about his two main adversaries? Sir Sidney Smith's great hour was at the siege of Acre. Never again was he to stand in the limelight of history.

Djezzar, on the other hand, was to spend his last few years at the apogee of success. He subjected further territories to his rule, including all of Southern Palestine, and captured Jaffa after a long and hard siege. For the first time in his life he acted contrary to the express wishes of the Porte. But by now he felt himself powerful enough to force his will on his superiors, and the Sultan himself had no choice in the end but to accept the inevitable. Furthermore he bestowed on Djezzar the pashalik of Damascus and a short time before Djezzar's death in 1804 even that of Egypt. At least nominally Djezzar thus controlled a larger part of the Ottoman empire than any provincial governor before him.

However in actual fact he did not intervene in Egypt where different groups now fought for control: the followers of the Sultan, several groups of Mameluks, Albanian mercenaries who had mutinied after not being paid by the Sultan, and also units of the British army, who usually supported the Mameluks, though their government backed the Sultan. Hence the readiness to let Djezzar try to bring order out of this chaos. However the man who was to succeed in this task was a younger adventurer, who, like Djezzar, came from the Balkans: Muhammad Ali, who started out as second in command of the Albanian battalion and ended by ruling in Egypt, Palestine and Syria and threatening Istanbul itself.

Also in Lebanon a period of instability followed the French invasion, which was to continue much longer than that in Egypt. While some of the Christians and especially the Maronites, were strongly attracted to the French language and civilization, they were more and more detested by their Druse and Muslim neighbours. Thus Napoleon's campaign did much to strengthen the Maronite–Druse rivalry, which was to dominate Lebanon's history throughout the 19th century. The military intervention of Napoleon's nephew in 1860 was to decide it in favour of the Maronites, but not to resolve it, as events of our day prove.

Djezzar's Jewish secretary and banker, Haim Farhi, enjoyed a long period of power and prosperity during the governorship of Djezzar's successor Suleiman Pasha (1805–1818). However in 1820 he was put to death on the order of the next governor, whose appointment Farhi himself had obtained for him.

Looked at as part of the history of Palestine, Napoleon's campaign was but one of several campaigns, for which Egypt served as starting point – from those of Ali Bey and Muhammad Abu Dahab (The Father of Gold) in the 1770s and ending with those of Muhammad Ali and Ibrahim Pasha in the 1830s.

However regarded from another angle, Napoleon's campaign was to have results and historical importance beyond what could perhaps have been expected. This was the first western military intervention since the Crusades. It can be regarded as the first step of European colonialism in the Middle East, which, in due time, was to lead to a period of European control over all this area in the first half of the 20th century.

Some of Napoleon's ideas were to bear fruit many years later. Thus the ties between France and the Maronites became much more pronounced in the days of Napoleon III as a result of whose military expedition the near-independent district of the Lebanon controlled by the Maronites, was to be established. French became the language spoken by the Maronite upper class.

In Palestine, too, the 19th century was to be a period of French political, religious and cultural activity. Its outward signs were the numerous French convents, churches and hostelries, which were erected in many of her towns. From 1843 a French Consul in Jerusalem looked after the interests of France in the Holy Land, and competed with the consuls of England, Russia, Austria and Germany in the struggle for political and cultural influence. The main prop of French influence was the local Christian Catholic population, which grew in proportion to the growth of western influence. The restoration of the Patriarchate of Jerusalem by the Catholic church was a result of this development and was mainly French inspired, with a view to wresting the control of Catholic affairs in the Holy Land from the Franciscans, who were mostly Italians and Spaniards.

Another aspect of the renewed French interest in Palestine was the numerous pilgrims and travellers, who, throughout the 19th century, made her the goal of their pilgrimage. We shall mention here only a few of the more prominent among these visitors: the romantic writers Chateaubriand (in 1806) and Lamartine (in 1832), both of whom also served their country as foreign ministers; the sons of King Louis Philippe; the Belgian heir and later King Leopold II, who was the first Christian to be officially admitted to the Muslim holy district ('Haram Esharif') in Jerusalem; explorers and scholars such as de Saulcy, the Duc de Luynes, Guérin, Clermont-Ganneau and de Vogüé; famous writers such as Gustave Flaubert (1850) and Pierre Loti (1894); and early photographers such as Goupil Fesquet (1839) and August Salzmann (1850/1). But besides these, many thousands of less well known Frenchmen visited the Holy Land and its shrines.

Napoleon's campaign gave new impetus to the old French interest in the Levant, dating from the Crusades. Its outcome was to be French rule, as the mandatory power, in Syria and Lebanon, between the two world wars.

Also Napoleon's declaration concerning the establishment of a Jewish commonwealth, though overlooked by his contemporaries, was later accorded importance beyond its due, as it seemed to some to be the point of origin of modern Zionism. Thus it appeared to be the starting point of a development which would lead to the establishment of the state of Israel, 149 years after Napoleon's campaign.

19

HOW IMPORTANT IS NAPOLEON IN THE HISTORY OF THE HOLY LAND?

N apoleon reached first Egypt and then Palestine in a moment of dramatic change in the history of the Levant.

After the Crusades the Muslim inhabitants of that area were proud of their victory and felt superior to the Christians of Europe whom they had defeated. And indeed it cannot be denied that the European society of the 13th century was in many ways less advanced than that of the Muslim world, or for that matter Byzantium, or Chinese society in the late Song period.

However Europe forged ahead in the following centuries, and especially in the periods of the Renaissance and the Reformation. The great voyages of discovery strengthened Europe's position at the centre of world events.[1]

The Levant, on the other hand, became more and more a backwater, far removed from the great achievements of the social, scientific, intellectual and industrial revolutions of the 17th and 18th centuries. The Muslim inhabitants of the Middle East were as ignorant of these developments as if they had taken place on another planet.

Hence the enormous impact of Napoleon's arrival in Egypt. The French not only defeated the local armies, but brought with them new technologies and new modes of thought and of administration. In the three years of their occupation of Egypt (1798–1801) they opened the gates to the influx of European influences, so dominant in the 19th century history of Egypt.

It has usually been assumed that the same is true also for the history of the Holy Land, and that with Napoleon begins the European penetration there as well. But actually this is not the case. Napoleon's stay in Palestine was a short one, of only some three months. He never controlled the whole country, but only the coastal towns of Gaza, Jaffa and Haifa, and especially Western Galilee, from where he conducted his siege of Acre. Even the rest of Galilee he ruled barely more than a month, from the battle of Mount Tabor (16 April) to the withdrawal from Acre (21 May). Such districts as those of Jerusalem and

Nablus, were never penetrated by the French at all.

As a result, the immediate influence of Napoleon's campaign in Palestine was small. It certainly did not bring with it an immediate wave of European influence.

The local inhabitants regarded the Napoleonic campaign as just one of the numerous invasions starting mostly in Egypt, which swept through Palestine in the 70 years between 1770 and 1840. The fact that the others were mostly by local chieftains, while this one was of a completely different nature, did not strike the local inhabitants as such. Napoleon was not yet the great emperor of later years, but only a relatively little known young general. While he was very successful in Egypt, he made rather a mess of things in Palestine. Djezzar, for instance, was not impressed. Nor were his subjects.

As a result we find that Napoleon did not make much of an impression in the flow of history in the Holy Land. The same power struggle of the Kaiss and Yaman factions continued to dominate politics in the country and the same clash between local strongmen and the weak central government in Istanbul continued just as before. While Egypt developed as a direct result of the French invasion into a centrally ruled country under Muhammad Ali, in fact (though not in name) independent from Istanbul, nothing like this happened in Palestine.[2]

Actually only the conquest of the country by the Egyptians in 1831/2 and the rule of Muhammad Ali's stepson Ibrahim Pasha there until 1840, brought about the initial western penetration, which had been triggered in Egypt by Napoleon. But then Muhammad Ali himself can be regarded as an outcome of the French invasion of Egypt, which, it could be argued, thus reached Palestine at second hand, and 30 years late. But such an argument would stretch the simple facts rather too far.

And the simple fact was that Napoleon's importance in the history of the Holy Land was none too marked, at least immediately after the event. Later on, after the break-through in Palestine of European influence from the 1830s onward, Napoleon's 1799 campaign was regarded differently. The large number of French pilgrims and tourists to the Holy Land later in the 19th century reflect perhaps more, in their books, what was felt in France than what were the feelings in Palestine. France started to take an interest in the Holy Land, which had not been there earlier. Consuls were nominated (the first one in 1844), convents and hospitals were built, a Catholic Patriarch (initially a Frenchman) was nominated in Jerusalem. These and similar developments changed in time the character of the country itself.

Thus Napoleon's importance in the history of Palestine is very different when measured by the impact his campaign made actually in its own time, and the romanticized image of the great emperor in the Holy Land in his youth, as seen by later generations in Europe and especially in France.

This difference can be observed also in the historiography of the Holy Land campaign. Historians have usually treated the subject of 'Napoleon in the Holy Land' in too narrow a fashion. Too many outside factors on one hand, and local problems on the other, have to be taken into account to make this a subject easily encompassed. When the present author first approached it twenty years ago (the original Hebrew version of this book was finally published in 1984) he was surprised by how narrow and incomplete previous treatments had been. Let us hope now that historians will in future bring the same thoroughness and seriousness also to this, hitherto much neglected, period in Napoleon's life and career, as to his other campaigns.

If Napoleon's influence on the history of Palestine was but small, it can be claimed that the influence of the Holy Land campaign on Napoleon's life was very marked. His numerous mistakes in Palestine were not repeated in the great campaigns of his career, in the years 1800–1809. He had learned his lesson and absorbed its message. But in the ice-encrusted campaign in Russia in 1812 we seem to meet the young Bonaparte of the 1799 siege of sun-bleached Acre all over again.

Appendices:
Additional Quotations from Original Documents, Memoirs and Other Sources

Napoleonic campaigns are usually regarded and described on a very personal level. What did Napoleon do during the battle of Austerlitz and what, in that less fortunate one, of Waterloo?

But actually there is much more to a Napoleonic campaign than just Napoleon. Some 13,000 Frenchmen participated in the Holy Land campaign, each of whom had his own feelings, perceptions and experiences. Further, the logistical problems of such a campaign in the poor Middle East of 1799 were enormous. Relations with local inhabitants, national groups, strongmen etc. were involved and are of great interest today, in view of later developments.

While we have very little material about the campaigns of Alexander the Great, when his own person is not involved, we are much more fortunate in the case of Napoleon. Mountains of documents have survived. The problem is to locate and evaluate them. Here, again, we are lucky. About a century ago the French artillery officer C.E. de la Jonquière undertook this monumental task. He published five enormous volumes about Napoleon's 'Egyptian' campaign. Volume IV, of some 690 small printed quarto pages, encompasses his 'Syrian' campaign. It quotes many hundreds of documents of all types.

In these appendices we have tried to present some interesting documents. Our purpose was mainly to show some of the less publicized sides of this campaign.

Dromedary Riders

From the correspondence of François Bernoyer, Chef de l'Atelier d'Habillement de l'Armée d'Orient:

'September 1798

On 14 September, General Bonaparte summoned me to inform me that he was going to organize a company of dromedary riders for his courier service. He told me "I wish you to design me a model for their uniform, but I wish especially that it be entirely different from other French uniforms. Try to make it as original as that new form of cavalry." I promised to work on it immediately. Two days later, my model was ready: here is my conception:

Hat – turned down in front as a shield from the sun; turned up in back and crowned by a red panache of ostrich feathers.

Waistcoat – green cloth, cut *à la grecque* with gold Hungarian braid and cords (in yellow silk for privates). [Probably braided like a hussar dolman.]

Turkish sash – to hold pistols and a dagger.

Trousers – crimson, cut Mameluke style.

Short boots – Roman style.

Coat – scarlet, cut Polish style, with gold braid.

Cloak – green, *à la Crispin*. Gauntlets. [Crispin apparently meant a fairly short cloak.]

4 January 1799

Bonaparte reviewed the dromedary company, now ready for service. "The dromedaries were richly caparisoned, covered by a scarlet saddle-cloth, with fringes of several colours." '

At first, each dromedary carried two men, seated back-to-back, but this was soon changed.

El-Arish

1. From Captain of Engineers Sabatieri's report to General Caffarelli (9 February 1799):

'El Arish is a village constructed of bricks and stones. At its centre stands a fort, which appeared to me to be in a good state, and more than 30 feet long. We attacked it at 7.00 hours, but it has not yet capitulated. This resistance showed us how advantageous its position is; I do not think that much was needed to get it into a suitable state of defence ... I had the bad luck to be wounded at the very outset of the attack, which is the reason why I cannot give you full details of our position ... My wound is not considerable, a bullet has pierced my arm near the shoulder and then entered my right breast. The surgeon has not yet found the projectile.'[1]

2. Brigade Commander Sanson to General Caffarelli (13 February):

'I am writing to you in some haste a note in our position in El-Arish. I arrived here yesterday with 300 men, put under my command by General Kléber. I have attacked the cistern of Mesudiah, and had only one man wounded. I have reconnoitred today the citadel of El-Arish and it appears to be impossible to enter it, but by its main gate. We hold the houses in front of it ... The garrison is estimated at 600 men ... Gen Kléber is expected this evening ...

Sabatieri is badly wounded; nothing positive can be said as yet about the state he is in ...'[2]

(see No. 1 above).

3. Kléber to Napoleon, on his arriving at the Masudia cistern (14 February):

'I have arrived here about five hours ago ... The horses are exhausted and so are the camels. The enemy is estimated at 300 Mameluks, 100 further horsemen, 100 mounted Arabs and about 500 Albanians and other levies of Djezzar's. In the castle about 1000 infantry soldiers of different nationality are lodged and 50 to 60 mounted Mameluks.

The news from the enemy camp are that Abd. Pasha is disgraced; the cause is unknown ... I do not have to tell you, Citizen-General, that we suffer from the absence of food supplies ...'[3]

4. Lieutenant Colonel Richardot reports that Bonaparte was 'very dissatisfied' with the result of the first attack. His mood was improved by the success obtained in the night of 14–15 February. 'However he received General Reynier rather coolly, who, though ardent and calm in action, had a rather soft and even timid character, and appeared much affected by this cool reception.'[4]

5. General Reynier, as a result, sent a long letter of self-justification to Napoleon (17 February). Here are only some of the opening sentences:

'You have reproached me unexpectedly, Citizen-General, and I would like to explain how I have been treated in this expedition. I was given the weakest division, composed of those soldiers who were regarded as least good, but luckily, it was still found to be excellent. I was given the least agreeable tasks and if the others did not desire them, they were entrusted to me ... but my division is the best equipped in means of transport ... and so is my artillery, but it is poorest in the quality of personnel and equipment ...'[5]

6. General Dugua confirms: 'The division Reynier has been severely reduced by the pressing needs of the last fortnight. The soldiers have eaten the horses and camels of the officers.'[6]

7. Napoleon's offer of capitulation to the garrison of El-Arish (19 February):

'1. The fort of El Arish is handed over to the French troops at 4 hours after noon.

2. The garrison withdraws through the desert to Baghdad, and at least will not re-enter Egypt.

3. At 4 hours the agas will promise for themselves and their troops not to serve any further in Djezzar's army, and not to move towards Syria.

4. They will be granted a safe conduct and given a French tricolour flag with which they will march past.

5. They will leave all their supplies and possessions in the fort, and also all their horses.

They will supply 15 horses for the commander. The other horses will be faithfully handed over.'[7]

8. After the capitulation a relatively low estimate of the size of the garrison appears in the diary of Detroye:

'The besieged numbered only a little more than 1100 men, all armed with muskets, pistols etc. About 600 are North Africans, the others are Albanians or Egyptians or Greeks or Mameluks. The latter were disarmed. These troops resembled brigands more than soldiers. ... The North Africans, organized in their companies, took service in our army.'[8]

But according to an order of Chief of Staff Berthier of 22 February they were organized in four companies, three of which consisted of North Africans and one of Arnauts (Balkan Muslims).[9]

The Battle of Gaza

1. From the diary of Damas:

'We left, with a guide, picked from among the prisoners ... He made us march along a route usually taken by the Arabs for reaching Gaza, but which proved most difficult for the artillery ... We were to have reached that day the spring of Sheikh-Zawi, but our guide took another way and instead we camped in the desert at 9 hours in the evening.'[1]

2. General Kléber tells a similar story in a report to Napoleon, and adds: 'We returned part of the way, but luckily we captured a dozen camels, which both helped cool down our horses and to reach you during the night.'[2]

3. From the diary of Damas:

'We left Sheikh-Zawi at noon in order to reach Khan-Yunis. The Mameluks were supposed to intend to defend its fort. We arrived at 7 in the evening. The Commander in Chief had reached this place some hours earlier. But no defenders were found there.'[3]

4. Detroye gives in his journal the first impression on entering the Holy Land after the long journey in the desert (24 February):

'Leaving Khan-Yunis one finds pasturage and cultivated fields on the right hand side and sand dunes to the left. One enters here a completely cultivated country. We had to cross two river beds, which were dry. The first one was wider, while the second one (Wadi Gaza) had banks of some 6 to 10 feet in height.'[4]

5. Detroye and Malus claim that Gaza was plundered by the French (27 February). Detroye says in his journal: 'The town was devastated by [our] troops.'[5] Malus is more interesting, as he hints that here they got infected by the bubonic plague: 'In order to compensate for their hardships, the soldiers plundered the town and found here the germ of their later contagion, which from now on caused such ravages in the army.'[6]

6. Miot gives a description of Gaza:

'Gaza is to be found about half a league from the sea. It is inhabited by no more than 2000 souls and is composed of three villages. The fortress on a low hill divides the first of them from the two others. Some ruins of white marble, found in this town, show that it used to be a place of some luxury and opulence ... It used to be a port, which does not exist any longer ... The soil is very fertile and so light that it is difficult to find a stone in the plain. The well watered gardens produce excellent pomegranates and very good dates. The main branch of industry in the town is the production of cotton fabrics and of soap.'[7]

7. Napoleon's order to Berthier (26 February): 'The garrison of Gaza is composed of 50 men belonging to the Maltese Legion, 40 engineers, 40 artillerists.'[8]

8. Detroye's diary (28 February): 'Isdud is a small village on a hill from where one sees a magnificent cultivated plain, bordered in the west by the Mediterranean and in the east by the mountains ... It contains many villages.'[9] Nowadays Ashdod has one of the two largest harbours along the coast of Israel.

9. Detroye's diary (28 February):

'Ramle is three leagues from Jaffa and eight leagues from Jerusalem. It is situated in an immense plain, in the midst of a forest of olive trees ... There are two convents in Ramle, one Armenian and the other Catholic. They are housed in well kept buildings. When we entered, we found all the Christian women of the town assembled. They are very white, but use but few colours in their dress. Some of them are beautiful; they mostly do not use a veil. All of them, and also their children, showed great pleasure in meeting us.'[10]

The Capture of Jaffa

1. Kléber's division was the first to reach Jaffa, and its commander reported to Napoleon on 4 March:

'I took my place among the advance guard. Lying between the rivulets called by the natives Nahr el-Musrara [Ayyalon] and the larger, el-Audsha [Yarkon], the walls of Jaffa are about a league and a half distant. The infantry passed first and the water reached up to their thighs. The rivulet holds three or four feet of water, and its banks are very muddy. It will be necessary to construct some bridges near Jaffa, otherwise the army will be delayed, if the rain continues. The bivouac which we occupied offers some pasture for the horses ... Some mills are found near the banks, but the bridges were destroyed by the floods of last year.'[1]

2. Doguereau writes that:

'The front of the attack (on Jaffa) was in the strongest and highest elevated part of the town. The hills and the gardens there made it possible to approach to just 50 toises [100 metres] and decided the positioning of the artillery batteries and the place for the creation of the breach. Some care had to be taken in the choice of the right type of wood for the construction work; some houses which had been demolished produced the wood for the platforms. The men for the work did not arrive and one had to wait impatiently for the tools. They did not arrive till somebody approached the sappers or the divisional artillery.'[2]

3. In an Order of the Day for 4 March Napoleon complained:

'The Commander in Chief is unhappy about the troops' burning the straw and wood which has been obtained, when they break camp. These materials are scarce and would be utilised by the troops which come later. He recommends that all commanders prevent such useless destruction ... Signed Berthier.'[3]

4. From the journal of Detroye (4 March): 'During the day a spy was arrested, who has since been shot. A convoy of camels sent to Ramle in order to look for food, was attacked by Arabs [beduins] and some of the camels have been taken.'[4]

5. Napoleon's instructions to Chief of Staff Berthier in various matters of discipline (5 March):

'Adjutant-General Grézieu is to be put under arrest because he did not send his camels with the headquarter convoy and let them leave without order.

Artillery batallion commander Faure is to be arrested, because he sent a single worker to look for tools at the sappers' camp, without providing him with an escort.

The canteen manager of the horse guards and their musicians are to be put in prison, because they left their horses outside "the extension" (without guard) and from there they were taken by Arabs [beduins]. The loss is to be deducted from their pay . . .

The officer in charge of the cavalry detail is to be arrested, for not sending the camels of the cavalry of the food detail, with those of Kléber's division, and acquainted with the military orders stating that such a detail is not to be commanded by a sergeant but by an officer.   Aide de Camp Beaumont is to be arrested for visiting Ramle with eight dragoons, instead of marching with the convoy.

The surgeon of the ambulance service is to be put in prison, for being absent when he was needed.

The officer commanding a convoy is authorized to have lashes of a stick applied to servants and camel drivers who do not march in the rank reserved for them . . .'[5]

6. Doguereau's diary, on the progress in the placing of the artillery pieces (5 March):

'All night the work at the front of the planned assault continued, to place the two batteries for counter attacks and the break-in battery. The latter was 40 toises [about 80 metres] from the target, the other two about 150 toises [about 300 metres]. They could be employed only at night. We got very wet during a heavy downpour when we were thus occupied. Also two further batteries were placed on the right side, one of which was a 5-pounder mortar.'[6]

7. In order to make sure of the resupply of the Army, Berthier wrote to Daure (6 March):

'I advise you that I have given the order to the divisions Kléber, Bon and Lannes, that each should send you 40 camels, escorted by 60 infantry soldiers. These camels will report this morning in front of your tent. I have also given the same order for 40 camels to Headquarters. The convoy will leave at 9 hours, under the military direction of citizen Paultre, assistant at Headquarters. He will return to Ramle in order to look for food there . . . Please confirm.'[7]

8. Berthier wrote on 9 March to Dugua, that the French losses in the capture of Jaffa had amounted to 30 dead and 150 wounded.[8] In Detroye's diary 80 dead and 125 wounded are mentioned.

9. Detroye's diary reports on the appearance of bubonic plague (10 March):[9]
'In Bon's division a disease accompanied by bubos [boils] appeared widely from which the victim quickly died. The physicians assured us that this was not the plague . . .'

Again, on 11 March: 'This is a violent fever, accompanied by bubos, from which one dies promptly. Many soldiers have succumbed to it, and have died quickly. It is believed that the disease is the plague and this opinion is widely accepted, as four men whom it has attacked have died.'[10]

The Massacre of the Prisoners

1. In a letter to his generals Napoleon said that the garrison comprised 4000 men, 2000 of whom 'were killed in the town' and nearly 2000 more were executed 'yesterday and today'.[1] But in his report to the Directoire of 13 March Napoleon claimed '4000 of the troops of Djezzar have been executed, among them 800 artillerists.'[2]

2. Another version was published elsewhere:

'Among the 2500 prisoners were 8 to 900 men from the garrison of El Arish. The latter had sworn not to re-enter Syria during one year, and were sent towards Baghdad, but had thrown themselves into Jaffa. Thus they had violated their oath. They were executed. The other prisoners were sent back to Egypt, together with the trophies, flags etc.'[3]

4. Detroye's diary (in these extracts, Detroye has sometimes written 'Gaza' erroneously for 'Jaffa'):

[8 March]. 300 gunners from Constantinople, trained by French artillery specialists, had arrived in Jaffa two days ago. All the day was now utilised to distinguish between the inhabitants of the city and the Turks serving in Djezzar's troops and to execute the latter, except for these 300 gunners. It appears that the garrison was composed of 4000 to 5000 men.
[9 March]. They continued to shoot the Turks taken at Gaza. The Egyptians were spared, but refused to enlist in the [French] army.
[18 March]. 1041 Turks were shot, from the garrison of Gaza, who include the 300 gunners from Constantinople, who were trained by the French artillerists. This execution presented a terrible scene. For three days the men were reassembled, four battalions encircled them and led them to their death. They washed in a brook, after which they were deprived of their possessions and divided into several groups; these unfortunate men were packed together, one against the other, and thus received the bullets or were bayonetted.'[4]

During the assault more than 2000 Turks perished. Subsequently, 800 Turks were executed on 8 March, 600 on 9 March, and 1041 on 10 March.

5. From a letter of André Peyrusse to his mother (10 March):

'After three hours we had become the masters of the town ... About 3000 men laid down their arms, as a result of promises made to them in the name of the Commander in Chief, and were led into the camp.

'It is best to hide under a veil all the horrors of the capture of the town, the pillage, burning and killing by the soldiers of all they met; but how two or three days after the assault, when all passions had calmed down, how then in cold barbarity 3000 men were killed, who had delivered themselves into our hands in good faith, about this posterity should be informed ...

'About 3000 men had laid down their arms and were led to the camp. By the order of the Commander in Chief, the Egyptians, North Africans and Turks were separated. The North Africans were all led the day after to the sea shore, and two batallions commenced to shoot them. They had no other choice to save themselves but to throw themselves into the sea. They did not consider for long, but all started to swim. They were shot at and in an instant the sea was coloured by the blood and covered with bodies. Some were lucky enough to save themselves among the rocks, but soldiers were sent in small boats to hunt them down. Several detachments were left near the shore, and we in our perfidy enticed some of them to come near, only to massacre them too. This execution finished, we tried to persuade ourselves that it would not be renewed and the other prisoners would be spared. The Egyptians, numbering 800, were sent to Cairo, thus confirming our hopes. But they were deceived by our conduct towards 1200 Turkish gunners, who had for two days remained lying, without receiving any supplies, in front of the tent of the Commander in Chief. It was recommended not to waste any gunpowder on them, and they were subjected to the ferocity of the dagger and the blow of the bayonet ... This example showed our enemies that they could not count on French loyalty, and sooner or later the blood of these 3000 victims will come to haunt us ...'[5]

6. Paymaster Peyrusse had adventures of his own during his trip to join Napoleon with the war chest of the expedition:

'In the morning of 6 March we saw (near Ramle) a great gathering of Arabs and farmers; they had been told that the treasure of the army was there and all the villagers assembled to capture it. ... They emitted dreadful shouts, some of them were armed, the others were unarmed and had no resources except for their shouting. Some detachments were sent against them, but they were sufficiently prudent, to move out of their way.

General Bonaparte's carriage, which had crossed the whole desert, got stuck and thus the countrymen had time to reassemble. Three hours later they had covered the mountains. From a hill in front of us they tried to intimidate and stop us. Our convoy reunited, our troops took up a position for battle, the "charge" was sounded, and in a moment the human mass had disappeared.

185

They did not dare to oppose the first charge ... We continued on our way and reached Ramle without further incident.'[6]

The Battle of Kakoon and the Capture of Haifa

1. Napoleon to Rear Admiral Ganteaume (Jaffa, 9 March):

'You will give the order to Rear Admiral Perrée, that he will leave Alexandria with the three frigates *la Junon*, *l'Alceste* and *la Courageuse* and two smaller ships, without the enemy noticing, and will report to Jaffa where he will receive his new orders. If the wind will blow him towards Acre, he should find out if we are already there: it is probable that we shall have reached it by then ... On each of his frigates he will load a 24 cannon and a mortar, with 300 rounds. Each frigate will also carry a smithy, to prepare the roundshot properly. The shipping of these items should not delay the departure.

If he should think that he cannot come out without the enemy noticing, he should try to send to me at Jaffa two of his smaller vessels, such as the *Salamine* and the *l'Alerte*.

You will transmit this order by a marine officer, who will leave on board a local boat to Damietta and by tomorrow's mail to Cairo.

Bonaparte.'[1]

2. Napoleon to Adjutant General Grézieu (Jaffa, 13 March):

'Citizen, you will undertake the command of the provinces of Jaffa and Ramle. Your first task will be to place a cannon on each of the towers [of Jaffa], with the four heaviest ones towards the harbour, for its defence.

The sapper officer is to repair the city walls at the place of the breach. You will make sure that the gates can be easily closed. The two existing ones seem to me to be very close together, and thus it will be enough to leave one of them open.

The Greeks will supply the manpower for the hospital of the wounded.

The Catholics and Armenians will supply the manpower for the hospital of the sick [this included the plague cases]. You will form a governing body ('divan') of seven persons, composed of both Muslims and Christians ...

None of the ships in the port is to be allowed to leave, for whatever reason.

The commerce with Damietta and Egypt is to be encouraged as far as possible. You will end a proclamation to all villages demanding that the inhabitants stay peaceful. I shall instruct General Reynier to set up a divan also in Ramle.

A naval officer will remain here.

If you have very interesting news for me, and if the weather is good, you may forward them by land or sea.

186

If you are in contact with Egypt you are to pass on the news of the army to the Adjutant General Almeras in Damietta and to General Dugua in Cairo. Make sure that the stores are in a good state and are not pilfered. Make all efforts to obtain news.

Bonaparte'[2]

3. Berthier to General Reynier:

'The Commander in Chief orders you to evacuate all the sick from Ramle to Jaffa. You will also transfer all the grain stores which can be moved, but only one store of the barley will be transferred ... If the Christians of Ramle and Lydda need any arms, Adjutant General Grézieu, who commands at Jaffa and Ramle, is ordered to transfer them what they need ... Further you will take all necessary measures to make sure that the city will not be pillaged during your absence. After having effected these operations, you will move to Jaffa with your division and will join the move of the army to Acre.'[3]

The Siege of Acre: The Early Stage

1. From a letter of André Peyrusse to his mother (21 March):

'On the 29th, at noon, we had taken up our new positions, about 1500 toises [3000 metres] from the town. A battalion of the 18th was ordered to move closer to the town. The enemy made a strong sally, but he did not resist our bayonets for long, and returned hastily within his fortifications. The besieged threw some bombs at us, with very unfortunate results.'[1]

2. Doguerau describes the arrival before Acre (n.d.):

'We arrived near the swamp and crossed it in the customary places. Our horses were in the water nearly up to their bellies in the deepest spots. We passed together with the cavalry and the scouts and stopped on a hill which dominates the town at a distance of some 7 or 800 toises [1400–1600 metres]. It is there that Djezzar has started the work of fortification ... Later arrived the infantry and also the divisions crossed the swamp. The enemy artillery fired a few shots at us, which did not produce a great effect. At first sight the place did not look impressive, without a proper ditch, which should not hold us up for eight days.'[2]

3. Peyrusse to his mother (2 April):

'Our camp resembles a great fair; wine, alcohol, figs, flat bread, raisins, butter etc – all in abundance, at a price, but while campaigning one does not calculate prices ... Fifty sheikhs of villages have arrived to ask us to protect them. All the Syrians hate Djezzar. This pasha, aged 70, is a monster of cruelty ... He has noses and ears cut off, the thighs cut, the eyes torn out ... Everyone eagerly awaits his downfall.'[3]

4. Sanitary instructions by Dr Desgenettes, the chief physician (21 March):

'The army is advised that it is very important for its health to wash frequently the feet, the hands and the face with fresh water, or with tepid water, into which some vinegar or alcohol has been put.

It is important on a warm day to drink a great quantity of water, and is prudent to rinse the mouth beforehand and to soak the hands in the water.

The army should reject with suspicion the clothing and underwear of the Turks, because its previous owners were dirty and often sick, without any understanding of their health.

The sickness which now frightens so many people needs the restoring of perspiration which has stopped. This can be achieved by ablutions or washings of the body, by the administration of emetics, especially if there is a tendency to vomit, and by supporting, in all cases, their vigour by a drink made up of coffee, quinine and lemon.'[4]

This malady, so diplomatically left without a name, was the plague.

5. In order to combat the spread of the plague, various instructions on hygiene were issued in an order of the day of 23 March. Among the instructions of how to set up army camps: 'It is especially ordered that the latrines should be placed 40 feet behind the last tents of the camps. The pits should be emptied every 24 hours.' In other theatres of war the time was set at 48 hours.[5]

6. Napoleon to Adjutant General Grézieu (5 April):

'I send back to you the ship which has arrived this morning from Jaffa, in order to advise you of our requirements.

Eight days ago a battalion was sent to Jaffa with transport, in order to fetch pieces [cannon] of size 4, and munitions. We expect it to return tomorrow.

Rear Admiral Ganteaume has sent an officer four days ago on a ship to Damietta. I assume that he will land at Jaffa. He was sent to Damietta in order to have all the munitions at Damietta sent to Jaffa. Mostly, we need size 12 and size 8 roundshot, high explosives and bombs, for the mortars in Jaffa, and infantry cartridges. Only when they arrive shall we be able to attack and capture Acre.'[6]

7. Napoleon to Adjutant General Alméras (5 April):

'You are to send by barque ['djerma'] or by any other vessel, all the size 12 or 8 roundshot, the shells, and infantry cartridges which you have at your disposition in Damietta ...

We have sufficient equipment ... The Metuwalis, the Maronites and the Druse are on our side. Damascus only awaits the news that Acre has fallen, in order to send us its keys.'[7]

8. Napoleon to Adjutant General Alméras (14 April):

'I have sent you two ships ... so that you will know our needs in artillery. The cannon-balls which the enemy has passed on to us, together with those which you have sent to us from Jaffa, have made it possible for us to attack in three or four days. We have dug a mine which extents 30 feet underground and is only 18 feet from the ramparts, and at the front of the (planned) attack one undermining was already nearing the far side of the ditch; thus it is probable that, when you read this letter, we shall already have taken Acre, by assault.

All the country is entirely submissive and devoted to us. One army sent from Damascus has been completely beaten; General Junot with 300 men has beaten 3 to 4000 cavalry soldiers, killing or wounding 500–600 men, and taking 5 flags. This was a brilliant feat of arms...'[8]

French Rule in Galilee

1. Napoleon's letter of investiture of Sheikh Abbas-el-Daher as governor of Tiberias (19 March):

'I have chosen the Sheikh Abbas-el-Daher, son of Omar-Daher, in consideration of his personal merit, and out of the conviction that he is, like his father, an enemy of wrongdoing and a benefactor of the people, to command in all of Tiberias, and to achieve a position of power like that of his father. I order therefore the sheikhs and people of Tiberias to recognize the Sheikh Abbas-el-Daher as their sheikh.'[1]

2. The [Druse] emir Beshir of central Lebanon received personal letters from Napoleon (20 and 21 March):

'I am anxious to let you have all the news, because you will find it agreeable, as our victories have annihilated the tyranny of a ferocious man [Djezzar] who had done wrong to the brave nation of the Druses and to all humanity.

My intention is to make the Druse nation independent, to lighten the tribute they are paying, and to give them the port of Beyrouth and other towns which they need for their ... commerce.

I desire that as soon as possible you come to visit me here at Acre, or send your representative to do so, so that we can make all the necessary arrangements for the defeat of our common enemies.

You can proclaim in all the villages of the Druse nation, that all the supplies of meat and wine etc. will be paid in full.

[21 March] To the Sheikh Mustapha Beshir, who is commendable because of his talent and his credit, he, who has suffered the persecution of Ahmed-Pasha (Djezzar), who has held him prisoner for seven years in his fortress, whom I nominate commander of Safet and of the Bridge of the Daughters of Jacob.

All the sheikhs and the inhabitants are ordered to give him full help to stop the Muslims, the troops of Djezzar and others, who oppose our orders.

It is suggested to him, not to humiliate the fellahs and to repel courageously all those who will enter the territory of the pashalik of Acre.'[2]

3. In a general order Napoleon spelled out his policy towards the Druse population who were concentrated in southern Lebanon and in northern Galilee:

'20 March. The Commander in Chief advises the army that the villages around Acre are inhabited by the Druse, a people friendly to France and enemies of Djezzar, who eagerly supply provisions for the Army, which has armed them for our side. Therefore all the persons and property in all the villages of these parts are to be scrupulously respected; he orders the arrest of all plunderers, who will be shot.

The Commander in Chief orders especially the commander of the cavalry to take all the steps needed to prevent looting. The general commanding the cavalry will be held responsible for any looting that is not suppressed.

The success of the Army and its well being depend on the good order and discipline which we show towards a people who love us, who lived in these parts before we arrived, and who are the enemies of our enemies...'[3]

4. Berthier to Murat (22 March):

'The Commander in Chief orders General Murat to leave the camp with 300 horses and one cannon in order to move to the village of Shafr-Amr, where he will protect the removal of camels and grain belonging to Djezzar. General Murat should add to this force all the armed inhabitants of Shafr-Amr and together repulse the Nablussians...'[4]

5. Bonaparte to Berthier (23 March):

'You will give the order, Citizen-General, that the 50 men whom General Murat has left in the village of Shafr-Amr will stay there, till they receive new commands. They are to patrol in order to secure the roads there; and if there is news that Arabs [meaning beduin] or other thieves menace the peace of Nazareth, they should warn me and take those steps to help which are within their means...'[5]

6. Berthier reports in his memoirs that Djezzar, too, was active in much the same area:

> 'Djezzar sent his emissaries to Nablus, Tyrus, Damascus and Aleppo. He gave them a great deal of money in order to get all the Muslims to rise, arm and fight the infidels.
>
> He advised them that the French were only a handful of men, that they lacked artillery, that they were faced by strong English forces and that it would be sufficient if they would just show themselves, to finish off Bonaparte and his army.
>
> This appeal had its effect. From the local Christians we heard about gatherings of troops in Damascus and about the establishment of stores in the citadel of Tiberias, which was occupied by the Moroccans.'[6]

7. Napoleon had many letters written to local notables, among them the following to the Mufti of Damascus, Murad-Rade (27 March):

> 'I am in front of Acre, which in a few days will be in my hands. I want you to tell the ulemas, the sheriffs and the main sheikhs of Damascus, and also the janissaries, that it is not my intention to do anything which is contrary to the religion, the customs and inclinations of the people of the country.' Further he promised to protect the yearly caravan to Mecca, and to protect the inhabitants of Damascus, with the same goodwill as those of Cairo.[7]

8. Berthier mentions in his memoirs General Vial's occupation of Tyre in southern Lebanon:

> 'General Vial left early on the 14th [Germinal, i.e. 3 April], in order to make himself master of Tyre. He arrived after eleven hours of marching, by a route which is not feasible for artillery. He passed the White Cape [Nakurah] at the height of the mountains and rested in the castle held previously by the Metuwalis, and destroyed fifty years ago by Djezzar. After passing the White Cape and entering the plain, he came upon ruins of one castle and two temples.
>
> On the approach of General Vial and his troops, the inhabitants of Tyre were preparing to escape. They were, however, reassured. They were promised payment and protection if they would renounce their hostile intentions. They returned to their town; Turks and Christians were treated equally. General Vial left a garrison of 200 Metuwalis in Tyre, and returned on the 16th Germinal [5 April] to the camp at Acre.'[8]

The Battle of Mount Tabor

1. In Desgenettes' memoirs (III, p. 237):

191

'In Nazareth there was a remarkable effect after the victory. The Catholic monks opened their vast convent both for the use of headquarters and as a hospital for both the wounded and the sick. Our victories were celebrated both by public prayers and the singing of a solemn Te Deum. At a christening General Bonaparte served as godfather and Mme Verdier as godmother. An officer of the 14th Dragoons, who was sick and felt his end nearing, demanded to end his days with the consolations and ceremonies of religion . . . Another sick soldier who was pressed by the fathers to prepare himself by receiving extreme unction, was advised by his comrades "Do not offend these nice monks, who have taken good care of you. After all, what are you risking?" '[1]

2. Napoleon had a letter written to the sheikh of Nablus (17 April):

'After the letter which he had written to you from Jaffa, the Commander in Chief Bonaparte, had thought that you would be sufficiently wise, to stay quiet, and not to expose your country to the horrors of war . . . As General Bonaparte is lenient and forgiving, and as he knows that till now you are enemies of Djezzar, he wants to content himself with the lesson he has taught you yesterday, and not carry fire and atrocities into your villages . . .'[2]

3. General Kléber's report to Napoleon (20 April):

'I left on 18 April for Tiberias, where I found General Murat, who left the next day on his way back to Acre. He will give you a report on the approximate state of the stores which are to be found in Tiberias.

After the hasty retreat of our enemies to the Jordan I have taken provisionally, if you have not ordered otherwise, the following dispositions:

General Junot with most of his brigade will camp in Tiberias: he will send 100 men to Safet and a further 100 to the Bridge of Jacob's Daughters; 100 foot soldiers, 25 horses and one 3-pounder cannon to the Jessrs-el-Madjami (south of Lake Genezareth). He was ordered to keep up contact with his various outposts, and I left him the necessary cavalry for this purpose. In addition a cannon was left in Tiberias. All the units of the brigade will draw their food supplies from Tiberias. I recommended to him to send emissaries to Damascus in order to report any news.

The brigade commander Venoux, with three companies of grenadiers, of the 25th, will reach Nazareth this morning, to take up there the post of watching the plain of Jenin. I gave him a unit of 20 dragoons for [carrying] correspondence and scouting . . .

Two battalions of the 75th and about 50 horses occupy the camp beneath Mount Tabor and form the reserve of the corps. I have established my headquarters there. There are water and trees in this camp, but all the plain from Nazareth to the Jordan is deserted and all the inhabitants have left their villages . . .

As to Sheikh Abbas Daher, he presented to me, on my arrival at Tiberias, the patent you have granted him, to serve as head of that province. I have passed him on to General Junot. As he commands much respect and consideration among his people, he will find it simple to ensure order and obedience. This sheikh has written circulars in order to get the inhabitants to return to their homes and to submit to French domination. He expects complete success.'[3]

4. General Kléber to Napoleon (1 May):

'General Junot has pointed out to me that Safet cannot nourish his troop and there are not sufficient means of transport for so long a distance for him to get his supplies from Tiberias. I have to withdraw him from that place [Tiberias] and establish him at Lubiah with a small advance guard at the Height of Hattin. He will leave 100 men at the citadel of Safet. It is true that the Bridge of Jacob will thus not be under observation. But the waters of the Jordan are so low and cannot be regarded any longer as a barrier, and instead its place is taken by the mountains between us and the enemy . . .

All reports confirm that the enemy has received considerable reinforcements from Damascus . . . Their first corps is in Kuneitra, seven leagues from the Jacob bridge. The inhabitants are so frightened that they estimate its members from 60,000 to 100,000 men.'[4]

5. General Kléber to Napoleon (4 May):

'No other engineer-geographer has arrived here, except for citizen Jacotin, who has continued this morning to Nazareth, to map its environment, and also that of the Plain of Esdraelon, where the battle of 16 April took place. He will return via Mount Tabor, in order to get an impression of the whole area, and will then visit Sadjera, where the combat of the 16th April took place, and afterwards will visit Lubia, where Gen. Junot fought the enemy on April 13th. Then he will descend to Hattin in order to visit Tiberias and map the course of the Jordan as far as Madjami.'[5]

Jacotin is still famous for his maps of Egypt, Sinai and Galilee.

The Siege of Acre: High Hopes and Ultimate Failure

1. Report by Rear Admiral Perée to the Minister of the Marine (n.d.):

'According to the order received from Rear Admiral Ganteaume on the 29th Ventôse, which reached me on the 13th Germinal, to take aboard three cannons of 24, their munitions and all the equipment needed for them, and to embark for Jaffa, where I should receive my latest instructions, I left the harbour of

Alexandria on the 19th Germinal of the year VII, with a flotilla consisting of the frigates *la Junon*, *l'Alceste*, *la Courageuse*, gunboats and the barges *la Salamine* and *l'Alerte*.

One vessel and one frigate, which usually blockade this port, had moved near to Abukir, which obliged me to steer northward ...

On the 20th Germinal I retook from the English the gunboat *la Foudre*, which was sailing in these waters ... The contrary winds and the windless intervals delayed my arrival at Jaffa to the 26th. I landed my boat in order to collect the messages; at noon General Ganteaume's letters were delivered, which instructed me to unload the three cannons of 24, which I had brought from Alexandria and four 18 from the *Junon*, with munitions for 200 shot for the cannons of 18 and 1000 shot for the cannons of 12 ... I also sent, in accordance with these orders, my armed dinghy loaded with powder, to the port of Tantura. At 1.00 am, having finished my unloading, I hoisted sail.'[1]

2. Berthier to Adjutant General Boyer (18 April):

'You are instructed to leave today at midnight with 100 men, taken from the two divisions [Lannes and Reynier, which had remained near Acre], 20 gunners, 12 sappers and 50 cavalrymen, to escort the horses and camels the general of artillery has sent to Jaffa, in order to fetch the artillery which has arrived there. You are to leave 80 infantrymen of the escort in Haifa and 120 in Tantura, and take in Haifa and in Tantura all the men of the 22nd Light, which are there, and who make up more than 300 men. This batallion, together with the dragoons, gunners and sappers, will be the escort of this convoy; the sappers are to be utilized in repairing the road where necessary, so as to help the passage of the artillery.'[2]

3. Order of the Day (19 April):

'Generals Reynier and Lannes are to order the cleaning up of the camps of their divisions [outside Acre]. The chief physician of the army has found that there exists danger of infection. The latrines are to be moved back, and so are the dead animals, which should be buried with greater tidiness. The health of the troops necessitates greater surveillance of these measures, as it is difficult to change the site of the camps before the fall of Acre ...

The General in Chief instructs the many soldiers to sell the silver vessels found in their baggage, which were taken at the Baths of Mount Tabor, and authorises the paymaster to pay the soldiers their value according to their weight.

The General in Chief exhorts the generals and commanders of corps to make the greatest efforts possible to recruit among the local population and especially among the inhabitants of the mountains of Safet and Nazareth. They are to take young men of 18 to 25 years.'[3]

4. Napoleon to General Headquarters in Paris:

'The commander of the English cruiser before Acre, behaved like a barbarian in putting French prisoners taken near Haifa on board a ship which had been infected by the plague ... The besieged had two volunteers beheaded. The responsibility for this act is attributed to the English commander. This conduct contrasts very much with the honourable way in which English soldiers and officers who have been taken prisoner are treated.

The English help to defend and supply Acre, in spite of the awful conduct of Djezzar, who had 200 Christians strangled and thrown into the sea, with their arms bound. Among them was the secretary of a French consul. The responsibility rests here, too, with the same officer [Sir Sidney Smith], as the pasha is completely dependent on him...

I suggest that you order the different commanders along the coast to desist from any communication with the English fleet, which cruises in these seas.'[4]

5. Among the French files of the Archives de la Guerre one document has survived that includes several testimonials to Sir Sidney Smith's good treatment of French prisoners of war.[5]

6. Several groups of beduin, around Mount Carmel, endangered the communications of the Army. Berthier ordered an operation against them (19 April):

'General Leturq is instructed to leave on the 25th [Germinal] with 100 horses and 200 men, who will be delivered to him by the brigade Destainville, commanded by the formidable Detroye ... There he is to join citizen Farinières in the area where the camp of the beduin sheikhs is to be found, and to be joined by 50 men from Shafr Amr. The General-in-Chief relies on the prudence of General Leturq in the execution of this operation.'

Berthier also reports the result of this operation:

'Adjutant General Leturq left on the 19th April with a unit of 300 men, surprised the beduins in their camp and killed about sixty of them, taking some 800 of their beef cattle, which helped to nourish the Army.'[6]

7. Berthier writes in his memoirs on the death of General Caffarelli, the commander of the sappers: 'A bullet broke his arm and he did not recover from its amputation. Caffarelli took with him to his tomb general regrets. The nation lost in him one of its most glorious defenders ...'[7] Caffarelli had lost one leg in a previous campaign. He died on 27 April. His remains were recovered by modern archaeologists and sent to France for reburial.

8. From a letter of Paymaster André Peyrusse to his mother (12 May):

'... In the evening, at 6 hours, the breach became feasible. The Commander in Chief ordered the assault. Lannes' division attacked. They threw themselves with vivacity into the breach. 2 or 300 brave men launched themselves into that place. It would have been ours if a coward had not spread terror by shouting that we were surrounded. The enemy launched himself in mass at the breach. Those who were outside attacked our posts at the same time and in the general turmoil the brave men who were in the town could not hold out and were all either wounded or killed. Brigadier Rambeaud was killed and General Lannes dangerously wounded in his head.'[8]

Was it a 'coward' or an enemy ruse? Some historians claimed later that there were English soldiers, or even Sir Sidney Smith himself, who called out in French. Jonquière (IV, p. 482) regards this as unlikely.

9. Chief physician Desgenettes reports in his memoirs on the state of the plague hospital:

'Near the end of the siege we no longer had any nurses, they were either sick or dead. Those left belonged to those discarded by society: most of them were foreigners, had been condemned for crimes, had escaped from the prisons of Genoa, Civita-Vecchia or Malta; they stayed in the hospital only for the money which they stole from the sick.'[9]

The Retreat to Jaffa

1. Extract from the session of the Marine Council, on board the frigate *la Junon* (16 May):

'The General had ordered Rear Admiral Ganteaume to come to Tantura, to fetch 400 wounded in order to transport them to Damietta and to Alexandria, and afterwards to set sail for Europe.

The members of the Council voiced their opinions.

Considering that the two enemy vessels hoisting the English flag had made a sweep in the vicinity of Tantura on 14 May, where they had anchored the *l'Alceste* and one frigate and two barges along the coast; this made it impossible to carry out the orders received.

As to General Ganteaume's dispatch of 11 May, the general disregarded the fact that the flotilla had encountered superior enemy forces on the 24th.

As the flotilla found itself without water and supplies, and without any means to obtain them, deprived also of a considerable amount of weapons and munitions, which had been transferred to the land forces, it was no longer in any condition to offer a prolonged and honourable resistance ...

We declare unanimously that under these circumstances the wisest course, and the one most in the interest of the Republic, is to set sail for Europe and to gain there a suitable port.

Signed by the members of the Council:

Vidal, lieutenant with *Courageuse*
Beville, lieutenant with *Salamine*
Priguy, lieutenant with *l'Alceste*
Martin, lieutenant with *la Junon*
Laudry, captain of the *Salamine*
Demay captain of the *l'Alceste*
Pourquier captain of the *la Junon*
Poulain, adjutant of the flotilla
Barré, captain of the *l'Alceste*
Trullet, captain of the *Courageuse*

After the declaration of the Council, and with my opinion conforming with theirs, that it was impossible to fetch the wounded, and to remain for an extended period at that coast...

I believe that the security of the flotilla under my command necessitates the setting of sail for Europe.

Rear Admiral, commanding the flotilla, Perrée'[1]

2. Letter by Berthier, addressed to Djezzar, to be delivered under flag of truce (13 May):

'The General in Chief has ordered me to propose a suspension of hostile activity, in order to bury the corpses which are lying unburied along the trenches.

He desires, too, to arrange for an exchange of prisoners. He has in his power a group from the garrison of Jaffa, the general Abd-Allah, and especially the gunners who were part of the convoy which arrived three days ago at Acre, coming from Constantinople. He has also a great number of soldiers of the army who had come from Damascus...'[2]

3. Berthier to Commander Farinières (13 May):

'Citizen Farinières is ordered to leave the North Africans and to rejoin Kléber's division. The fortress of Shafr Amr is to be returned to the local leader and to be defended by the inhabitants. If he feels secure among them the General in Chief wishes him to stay in Shafr Amr; otherwise he is authorised to return to headquarters.'[3]

4. Napoleon's report to the Divan of Cairo (16 May):

'Finally I can advise you now of my departure from Syria to Cairo, where I shall arrive promptly. I shall leave in three days and arrive in fifteen. I shall bring with me many prisoners and some flags.

I have razed the palace of Djezzar and the fortifications of Acre and have bombarded the town in such a manner that no stone is left in its place. All the inhabitants have evacuated the town and taken to the sea. Djezzar is wounded and has retired with his men into a fort on the sea shore. He is badly wounded.

Of the 30 vessels loaded with troops, which went to his aid, 3 have been sunk by my ships, 4 have been seized by my frigates, with the artillery which they carried, the rest are in a very poor condition and entirely destroyed...'[4]

5. Berthier to General Junot (17 May):

'The General in Chief orders you to burn down all the mills near the Jordan, to sell, give away or burn all the wheat, oats etc which remain in the stores of Tiberias and to destroy the cannon, which are to be found in the fortress.

General Junot is ordered to take up his position on 19 May at Safurieh and from there to return to Haifa, with the women, the baggage, the lame, who are with him, and also the infantry and cavalry. He should not forget to withdraw the 38 men of the 2nd from Nazareth, together with all other Frenchmen or people employed by us...

General Junot should order Daher's two sons to come tomorrow morning to headquarters, for a meeting with the General in Chief.'[5]

6. Berthier to General Junot (18 May):

'Order General Junot to collect all the inhabitants of Nazareth, who want to come with us; after which they should come tomorrow in the night around the Valley of Obellin, so as to cover the camp all the time and to collect all the inhabitants of Shafr Amr who will want to come with us.'[6]

7. Paymaster Peyrusse to his mother (24 June):

'We followed the sea shore nearly all the time. We visited Athlit, otherwise called "Port of the Pilgrims", built by the Crusaders. The ruins there are still superb and the walls have retained their majesty...

At 3 hours noon we arrived at Tantura. This is a tumbledown group of old cottages on the sea shore, which forms a very nice port here. This was to be the basis for our evacuation to Damietta. We expected all of us to be evacuated. But we found still 700 to 800 wounded and plague cases, some twenty cannon and 1200 bombs, but not a boat to transport all that. There was no point in reflection. All the pieces were buried and the bombs thrown into the sea. The food was incinerated. All the army's horses and asses were requisitioned. The sick were sent away, except for a dozen, and the army left.'[7]

8. Berthier to General Dommartin (21 May):

'The General in Chief wants to inform you, Citizen-General, that we have a problem: the existence of about 600 wounded, who can only be moved by transport animals. This forces all of us to make a special effort, but only till Jaffa. The General in Chief expects you therefore to furnish at least 80 mules, which are not engaged in the moving of war materials. He orders that these animals are to be conducted by mule drivers, who are to be attached to your camp, under the supervision of an assistant from your headquarters, who will be charged with bringing them at 10.30 hours in the evening to the tent of the Adjutant-General Boyer, which is situated next to the tent of the Commander in Chief. This assistant will supervise the preservation of the animals which belong to your division and will stay with them till Jaffa. Adjutant-General Boyer conducts the 600 wounded while being escorted by a battalion from the 69th. You see, General, how this measure, which is fatiguing for the divisions, is indispensible for those who were our brothers in arms, but are now wounded. As to stretcher cases, your people will carry their charges till Jaffa. They will follow your division.'[8]

Other commanders of units received near-identical orders, but with different numbers of mules and men (the sappers, for instance, had to supply 25 asses or horses, the brigade Sanson, 50 men).

9. The cavalryman Pierre Millet, in his book of memoirs:

'All those who had horses were dismounted, also those from headquarters and others. The Commander in Chief himself kept only one horse and gave the others up, for the transport of the wounded.

The next day we were to leave, and by a very cruel order had to abandon the poor plague cases. It pierced the heart of the army, that we had to leave our unfortunate brothers in arms at the mercy of barbarous Arabs, who cut off their heads once we had left. Many of these unfortunate ones followed us, crying not to abandon them. But we were forbidden to have any communication with them, otherwise we would be severely punished. This hard order was perhaps necessary, because they might have communicated their terrible disease to us, and in order to save a few, the army might have perished altogether.'[9]

Other sources give different descriptions of what happened and did not happen to the plague cases.

10. The map maker Jacotin reports from Tantura (n.d.):

'Two pieces of the 24 cannons were buried in the ground and 18 others were thrown into the sea. Their wooden parts were burned. Many bombs and bullets were buried too, as there were no means of transport.

Many plague cases were left.

At 10 hours the troops set out. They arrived at 4 at the ruins of ancient Caesarea. We camped in that town. This town is not large. It is possible to jump over its walls. We could see beside the sea a large number of columns, which come from the first villa built there by Augustus.'[10]

11.   The retreating French were continually harassed by the armed inhabitants of Nablus. Niello Sargy reports:

'The General in Chief had them pursued by the cavalry of General Murat, with strict orders to shoot all those who were carrying arms. They were attacked with some success. At the same time numerous units of infantry spread out through the villages and took away the animals, chased out or massacred the inhabitants, and put the buildings to the torch. The country between Acre and Jaffa became a picture of devastation.'[11]

Jaffa and the Plague

1. Desgenettes, in his memoirs: 'The Army arrived before Jaffa after seven hours of marching, using the western route, along the sea coast, which it did not leave, until crossing the river Audja [Yarkon].'[1]

2. Doguereau in his diary:

'We had to leave many of our pieces of property, because our camels were wounded and unable to carry their loads any further ... We left the country going up in flames. At 9 hours we reached a village built of stone. Not a single inhabitant remained behind. The torch was put to anything that might burn. We soon reached the sea coast beyond the moving dunes, and met a convoy carrying food for the rear guard. This path, covered with dead horses, showed the difficulties met there by the artillery when passing. We finally saw the minarets of Jaffa and passed a considerable stream, where a bridge of boats had been constructed. At 2 hours we arrived in Jaffa.'[2]

3. Berthier noted in his book of memoirs: 'The time [in Jaffa] was used to punish the villages in the vicinity which had misbehaved.'[3]

4. André Peyrusse in a letter to his mother:

'The barges were prepared and armed as well as was possible. 300 of the 2000 wounded and sick in Jaffa's hospitals were embarked. All of them were captured by the English. Those less sick were guarded on board, the rest were landed at Damietta.'[4]

The Retreat to Egypt

1. Berthier to the Adjutant General Boyer (24 May):

'Adjutant General Boyer is ordered to leave the next day at half past midnight with 300 of the wounded who can march. This is to be arranged with citizen Larrey (the surgeon-in-chief). He is to assemble these 300 men at 11 hours in the evening at a place he will indicate, and he is to supply them with food for 3 days.

On arrival at Gaza, Adjutant General Boyer is to take a further 300 wounded who can march and is to add them to the 300 from Jaffa. At Gaza he will acquire the food strictly necessary for the journey to El Arish . . .

Adjutant General Boyer is to leave Gaza as soon as possible with two battalions of the 69th and the 600 walking wounded, in order to reach Salhiah, where he will stay with one battalion of the 69th and all the wounded. General Lannes [who was wounded himself] and his other officers will continue to Cairo with the other battalion of the 69th.

Adjutant General Boyer might receive at Salhiah a direct order from General Dugua . . . which he will carry out.

When passing through El Arish and Katia, he will leave behind those wounded and sick who are too tired to continue their march . . .'[1]

2. Napoleon to Berthier (24 May): 'Adjutant General Boyer is to take with him the Turkish flags. They are to be displayed as trophies of war and victory, at all villages through which he will pass.'[2]

NOTES

For full titles see Bibliography. Throughout these Notes, 'Napoleon, II' refers to Napoleon, *Der Ägyptisch–Syrische Feldzug*, Vol. II.

Chapter 1: The Curtain Rises

1. Charles-Roux François, *Les Origines de l'Expédition d'Egypte* (Paris, 1901)

Chapter 2: The Holy Land in 1799

1. Amnon Cohen, *Palestine in the 18th Century* (Jerusalem, 1973)
2. Uriel Hed, *Daher el-Umar* (Hebrew) (Jerusalem, 1942)
3. Al-Amir Haidar Ahmad Al-Shihābi, *Tarīkh Ahmad bāsha al-Jazzār* (Arabic) (Beirut, 1955)
4. V. Clarke, p. 10
5. Ādel Mannā, 'The Sijil'

Chapter 3: Napoleon's Plans and Preparations

1. Bernoyer, p. 152f.
2. Ibid., p. 134f.
3. Raguse, *Voyage*, III, p. 70f.
4. F. Markham, *Napoleon* (New York, 1966), p. 55f.
5. David G. Chandler, *The Campaigns of Napoleon* (New York, 1966), p. 234
6. Napoleon, *Der Ägyptisch–Syrische Feldzug*, II, p. 17f.
7. 22nd Pluviôse, an VII [10 February 1799], *Correspondance de Napoleon Ier*, No. 3952
8. Thiry, p. 299, quoting an unsigned and undated GHQ note
9. Herold, p. 264
10. Jonquière, IV, p. 581 (note 2)

Chapter 4: El-Arish

1. Gichon, *El Arish*
   Jonquière, IV, pp. 151–206
   Doguereau, pp. 137–53
2. Miot 1814, p. 124f.
3. Napoleon, II, p. 94
4. Ibid., p. 34
5. Larrey, *Mémoires*, I, p. 281f.

Chapter 5: The Battle of Gaza

1. Napoleon, II, p. 39f.
   Miot 1804, p. 122
2. Doguereau, p. 214f.
   Desgenettes, *Histoire Médicale*, p. 44
3. 'Journal de Detroye', in Jonquière, IV, p. 217
   Bernoyer, p. 140
   Napoleon, II, p. 42
4. Napoleon, II, p. 43
5. Damas, in Jonquière, IV, p. 216f.
   Detroye, in Jonquière, IV, p. 217f.
   Doguereau, p. 218
   Bernoyer, p. 141
6. Napoleon, II, p. 44f.
7. Richardson, in Larrey, p. 60f.
8. Napoleon, II, p. 45
9. Bernoyer, p. 142
10. Jonquière, IV, p. 221
11. Napoleon, II, p. 45f.
12. Miot 1804, p. 223
13. 23rd Ventôse an VII [13 March 1799], in F.M. Kircheisen, *Briefe Napoleons des Ersten*, I (Stuttgart, 1910), p. 177
14. Jonquière, IV, p. 282
15. Bernoyer, p. 144
16. The traditional burial place of St George, England's patron saint.
17. In the Bibliothèque de Carcassone, quoted by Jonquière, IV, p. 275f.
18. Bourienne, I, p. 178

Chapter 6: The Capture of Jaffa

1. Jonquière, IV, pp. 241–87
   Berthier, pp. 61–4
   Doguereau, pp. 170–82
   Cesari
   Gichon, *Jaffa*
2. Napoleon, II, p. 49f.
3. Detroye, in Jonquière, IV, p. 248
4. Jonquière IV, p. 248
5. Napoleon, II, p. 52f.
6. Miot 1814, p. 137
   Journal du Capitaine François, I, p. 279f.
   Gichon, *Jaffa*, p. 118
7. *Journal du Capitaine François*, I, p. 279
8. Ibid., p. 280
9. Miot 1814, pp. 137–40
10. Bernoyer, p. 145
11. Malus, p. 135f.
12. Richardson, in Larrey, p. 62
13. Jonquière, IV, p. 262

Chapter 7: The Massacre of the Prisoners

1. Robert Thomas Wilson, *History of the British Expedition to Egypt*, (London, 1803), p. 74f.
2. Miot 1814, pp. 145–7
3. Bourienne, I, pp. 179–82
4. Clarke, IV, pp. 439–41
5. Ibid., p. 440, note 1
6. Barry E. O'Meara, *Napoleon in Exile, or a Voice from St Helena*, I (London 1822), pp. 328–30
7. Napoleon, II, p. 54
8. Bernoyer, p. 145f.
9. Jonquière, IV, pp. 265–72, 588f.
   Richardot, *Relation*, p. 20

Doguereau, p. 178
Desgenettes, p. 46
10. Detroye, in Jonquière, IV, p. 270
11. Bernoyer, p. 148
12. Jabarti, p. 169 (dated 9 July 1799)
    Napoleon, II, p. 54
13. Bernoyer, p. 148
14. Desgenettes, p. 87
15. Ibid., p. 50

Chapter 8: The Battle of Kakoon and the Capture of Jaffa

1. Nimr, I, pp. 216–23
2. Jonquière, IV, pp. 289–91
3. Dar, in *Teva Va'aretz* 24/1
4. Jonquière, IV, p. 648f.; see also Delesalle
5. Jonquière, IV, p. 290
6. Ibid., p. 282
7. Ibid., pp. 295–8
   Napoleon, II, p. 61f.
   Bernoyer, p. 149
   Doguereau, p. 186f.
   Nimr, I, p. 220f.
   Gichon, in *Carta Atlas: History of Eretz Israel* (Hebrew) (Jerusalem, 1974), map 153
8. Bourienne, I, p. 183
9. Jonquière, IV, p. 346, note 1
10. Ibid., p. 280. When the French Army reached Katia on its retreat to Egypt in early June 1799, it met Menou there on his way to take up his appointment (Jonquière, IV, p. 606).
11. Napoleon, II, p. 63
    Bernoyer, p. 150f.
    Jonquière, IV, pp. 298–301
12. Napoleon, II, p. 63
13. Sidney Smith, I
14. Jonquière, IV, pp. 301–3

Chapter 9: The Siege of Acre: The Early Stage

1. Napoleon, II, pp. 66–86
   Jonquière, IV, pp. 304–54
   Bernoyer, pp. 151–66
   Richardot, *Relation*, pp. 22–48
   Berthier, pp. 67–96
   Sidney Smith, I, pp. 270–312
   Miot 1814, pp. 153–66
   Desgenettes, pp. 54, 87f., 90–4
   Doguereau pp. 197–208
   Anon, *The Siege of Acre* (London, 1801)
   Gichon, *Siege of Accho*
   Gichon, 'First Assault'
   Watson, pp. 17–35
   Alderson, pp. 26–38
   N. Schur, *History of Acre*
2. Jonquière, IV, p. 308
3. One toise = six feet
4. D. A. Bingham, (ed.) *A selection of the Letters of Napoleon*, I (London, 1884), p. 449f.
5. Nahman of Breslau, p. 491f.
6. Napoleon, II, p. 111
7. N. Schur, *History of Acre*
8. Miot 1804, p. 224
9. Ibid., p. 152
10. Jonquière, IV, p. 336
11. Miot 1804, p. 163. According to Bernoyer (p. 154) he shouted 'You are cowards! I shall defend myself singlehandedly!' As few of the French attacking party could speak Arabic or Turkish, it is to be assumed that both versions are inexact. If his real words were known, they might well prove to be unprintable.

Chapter 10: French Rule in Galilee

1. Napoleon, II, pp. 69–74
   Jonquière, IV, pp. 355–74

  Miot 1814, pp. 166–73
  Berthier, pp. 77–80
  Gichon, *Western Galilee*
2. Nimr, I, p. 221f.
3. Gichon, *Western Galilee*, pp. 153–64
4. Miot 1804, p. 225
5. Jonquière, IV, p. 320f.
6. Wachsman and Raveh, 'Underwater Work'
7. Napoleon, II, p. 70f.
8. Jonquière, IV, p. 364
   Napoleon, II, p. 71f.
9. Miot 1814, pp. 168–71
10. Jonquière, IV, pp. 355–61
    Miot 1814, pp. 165–72
11. Napoleon, II, p. 72f.
12. Pierre Millet, p. 93f.
13. Engineer Favier, in Jonquière, IV, p. 362
14. Jonquière, IV, p. 362f.
15. Order of 2 April, signed by Berthier, in Jonquière, IV, p. 363f.
16. Napoleon, II, p. 73
17. Jonquière, IV, p. 464f., and see also p. 489
18. Kircheisen, *Briefe Napoleons des Ersten*, I (Stuttgart, 1910), p. 181
19. Napoleon, II, p. 74

Chapter 11: The Offensive of the Pasha of Damascus

1. Jonquière, IV, pp. 378–414
   Napoleon, II, pp. 90–3
   Miot 1814, pp. 172–9
   N. Schur, *History of Safet*
   N. Schur, *Mount Tabor*, p. 38f.
2. Anon, *Journal d'un Dragon d'Egypte (14e Dragons)* (Paris, 1899)
3. Letter dated 8 April from Nazareth, in Jonquière, IV, p. 380f.
4. According to the report of a spy sent out by Lambert, in Jonquière, IV, p. 379
5. Jonquière, IV, p. 379
6. Ibid., p. 402f.

7. Miot 1814, pp. 172–9
   N. Schur, *History of Safet*
8. Miot 1814, p. 179

Chapter 12: The Battle of Mount Tabor

1. Napoleon, II, pp. 93–9
   Jonquière, IV, pp. 414–29, 436f., 501f., 589
   Berthier, pp. 81–4
   Paultre, p. 37f.
   Raguse, *Voyage*, III, p. 16f.
   Delorme, *Voyage en Orient* (Limoges, 1843), pp. 147–50
   Klärer: *Kléber*, pp. 292–6
   Watson, p. 27f.
   N. Schur, *Tabor*, pp. 38–44
2. Jonquière, IV, pp. 395–7
3. Klärer: *Kléber*, p. 292f.
4. Napoleon, II, p. 93f.
5. Karl Paultre, another officer and map maker, tells us (p. x), that during most of the campaign he was retained by General Kléber to prepare maps of the areas through which they were passing; if, however, his 'New map of Syria' which is attached to his volume, is any indication, Kléber did not get much help from him.
6. Napoleon, II, p. 97f.
7. Millet, p. 104f.
8. Napoleon, II, p. 99
9. Ibid.
10. Nimr, I, p. 221f.
11. Napoleon, II, p. 100f.
12. Jonquière, IV, p. 426
13. La Vallette, I, p. 312

Chapter 13: Napoleon and the Jews of Palestine

1. Napoleon, II, p. 73f.
   Gelber, pp. 263–86
   Guedalla, *Napoleon and Palestine*

Toledano, pp. 109–14

Godechot

Ya'ari-Poleskin

2. Nahum Sokolow, *History of Zionism*, I (London, 1919), p. 72f.

3. Toledano pp. 109–11

4. M. Werte, in a paper read to the second World Congress on Jewish Studies (Jerusalem, 1957)

   Mahler, *History of Israel Vol. IV: Later Generations* (Hebrew) (Merhavia, 1956), p. 202f.

   M. Eliav, *Eretz Israel in the 19th Century* (Hebrew) (Jerusalem, 1978), p. 38f.

   B. Mevorach, *Napoleon utkufato*, (Hebrew) (Jerusalem, 1968), p. 15

5. Napoleon, II, p. 74

6. Schwarz, p. 374

7. Ibid., p. 373f.

8. J.L. Burckhardt, *Travels in Syria and the Holy Land* (London, 1822), p. 317

Chapter 14: The Siege of Acre: High Hopes and Ultimate Failure

1. Napoleon, II, pp. 103–20

   Jonquière, IV, pp. 438–545

   Berthier, pp. 81–96

   Anon, *The Siege of Acre* (London, 1801)

   N. Schur, *History of Acre*

2. Bernoyer, p. 152f.

3. Miot 1804, p. 226f.

4. Desgenettes, p. 83

5. Ibid., p. 68

6. Miot 1804, p. 193

7. Anon, *Vie du Général Maria Joseph Maximilien Caffarelli du Falga* (Paris, 1801), pp. 79–83

8. E. Schiller: 'How Caffarelli's tomb was found', (Hebrew) in *Kardom* 24/25 (Jerusalem, 1983), p. 177f.

9. Doguereau, pp. 197–208

10. Miot 1814, p. 210f.

11. Bernoyer, p. 156

12. Jonquière, IV, p. 453

13. Alderson, p. 32
    Bernoyer, p. 161
14. Anon, *The Siege of Acre* (London, 1801)
15. Berthier, p. 93
16. Bernoyer, p. 161
17. Thiry, p. 368f.
18. Jonquière, IV, p. 496
19. Miot 1804, p. 209
20. Jonquière, IV, p. 496
21. Anon, *The Siege of Acre* (London, 1801)
22. Bernoyer, p. 163
23. Napoleon, II, pp. 114–19
24. Thiry, p. 371f.
25. N. Schur, *History of Acre*
26. David G. Chandler, *The Campaigns of Napoleon*, (New York, 1966), p. 241f.
27. J.B. Spilsbury, *Picturesque Scenery in the Holy Land and Syria, delineated during the campaigns of 1799 and 1800 (London, 1819)*, p. 5f.
28. Jomini, *Life of Napoleon*, I (H.W. Hallek, ed.) (New York, 1864), p. 229; J. Bainville, *Napoleon: Livre de Poche* (Paris, n.d.), p. 102
29. J.H. Rose, *The Life of Napoleon*, I (London, 1912), p. 209ff.; F. Markham. *Napoleon* (London, 1966), p. 5f.
30. Y. Ben Zvi, *Eretz Israel under Ottoman Rule* (Hebrew) (Jerusalem, 1955), p. 320ff.
    M.D. Ga'on, *Yehudei Hamizrah be'Eretz Israel*, II (Hebrew) (Jerusalem, 1938), p. 571
    Sokolow, *History of Zionism*, I, p. 70

Chapter 15: The Retreat to Jaffa

1. It has even been reported that Sir Sidney Smith challenged Napoleon to a duel (denied in *The Life and Correspondence of Admiral Sir William Sidney Smith*, I, p. 291). Napoleon's famous answer 'I'll accept, if they will send Marlborough' was apparently invented by Reybaud (*Histoire de l'Expédition*, III, p. 396). See also Jonquière IV, p. 442.
2. Napoleon, II, p. 103ff.
3. Millet, p. 126
4. Anon, *Journal d'un Dragon d'Egypte* (Paris, 1899)

5. Beauchamp, *Mémoires Secretes*
6. Burckhardt, p. 316f., p. 340

   M. Russell, *Palestine, or the Holy Land, from the Earliest Period to the Present Time* (London, 1854), p. 338, claims that after the French withdrawal, Djezzar 'Had resolved to massacre all the believers in Moses and Jesus Christ, who might be found in any part of his dominions, and had actually sent orders to Nazareth and Jerusalem to accomplish his barbarous design. But Sir Sidney Smith, on being apprized of his intention, conveyed to him the assurance, that if a single Christian's head should fall, he would bombard Acre, and set it on fire.'
7. Miot 1804, p. 221
8. Jonquière IV, p. 595 (1). General Bon died when the retreating French had reached Atlit on the coast, between Haifa and Tantura.
9. N. Schur, *History of Jaffa*
10. Napoleon, II, p. 122
    Desgenettes, p. 245f.
11. Letter to his mother dated 24 June, quoted in Jonquière IV, p. 548
12. Wachsman and Raveh
13. Bourienne, I, p. 192f. Napoleon tells it differently, see Napoleon, II, p. 120f.
14. Bourienne, I. p. 193
15. Ibid., p. 192
16. Miot 1804, p. 133f.
17. Bourienne, I. p. 192
18. Desgenettes, p. 95
19. Bourienne, I, p. 193
20. Napoleon, II, p. 121
21. Miot 1804, p. 233

Chapter 16: The Poisoning of the Plague Cases

1. Napoleon, II, p. viif., p. 122f.
   Desgenettes, p. 245f.
   Jonquière, IV, pp. 574–83
   Galli, p. 135f.
   Miot 1804, p. 218
   Bernoyer, p. 180f.
   Martin, p. 315

François, p. 335

Roussilon, p. 608

Richardot, *Relation*, p. 53

A.M. Jahn, *Reise von Mainz nach Aegypten, Jerusalem und Constantinopel*, III (Mainz, 1826/7), p. 322

William Whitman, *Travels in Turkey, Asia Minor, and across the desert into Egypt during the years 1799, 1800 and 1801* ... (London, 1803), p. 128

Bourienne, I, pp. 194–7

Irby and Mangles, *Travels through Nubia, Palestine and Syria* (London, 1823), p. 186

Watson, p. 31

N. Schur, *History of Jaffa*

P. Triaire, *Napoleon et Larrey* (Tours, 1902), p. 117

Cadet de Gassicourt, *Voyage en Autriche, en Moravie et en Bavière* (Paris, 1818), pp. 386–96

Raguse, *Mémoires*, II (Paris, 1857), p. 12

2. Malus, pp. 140–3
3. Desgenettes, pp. 72, 75
4. Sidney Smith, I, p. 311f
5. Doguereau, in Jonquière IV, p. 580
6. Wilson, *History of the British Expedition to Egypt* (London, 1803), p. 76f.
7. Jonquière, IV, p. 285f.
8. O'Meara, *Napoleon in Exile*, I, pp. 330–3
9. Napoleon, II, p. 121f.
10. Ambrose Firmin Didot, *Notes d'un Voyage Fait dans le Levant en 1816 et 1817* (Paris, 1826), p. 219f.
11. Sidney Smith, I, p. 313
12. Triaire, p. 117
13. Cadet de Gassicourt, pp. 386–96
14. Sidney Smith, I, p. 313
15. Ibid., p. 313
16. Jonquière, IV, p. 583
17. N. Schur, *History of Jaffa*

Chapter 17: The Retreat to Egypt

1. Ādel Mannā, 'The Sijil'
2. Jonquière, IV, pp. 583–87

Napoleon, II, p. 123
Miot 1804, p. 239
Desgenettes, p. 99
3. Desgenettes, p. 99
4. Ibid., p. 63f., p. 68
5. Bernoyer, p. 177
6. Millet, p. 130
Jonquière, IV, p. 593
7. Jonquière, IV, p. 595f.
8. Bernoyer, p. 180f. I have seen no other reports mentioning the poisoned soup given to the plague cases at Acre.
9. Jonquière, IV, p. 596
10. Richardot, *Nouveaux Mémoires* p. 178
11. Jonquière, IV, p. 596
12. Ibid., p. 597f.
13. Napoleon, II, p. 123
Jonquière, IV, p. 603
14. Jonquière, IV, pp. 623–7
Roussilon, p. 609
Doguereau, p. 289
15. Jonquière, IV, p. 634

Chapter 19: How Important was Napoleon in the History of the Holy Land?

1. N. Schur, *The Relevant History of Mankind* (Brighton, 1997)
2. N. Schur, *History of the Land of Israel* (Tel Aviv, 1998)

Appendix: El-Arish

1. Jonquière, IV (Paris, n.d.), pp. 163, 164
2. Ibid., p. 164
3. Ibid., pp. 165, 166
4. Richardot, *Mémoires* (Paris, 1848), pp. 110, 111
5. Jonquière, IV, p. 186
6. Ibid., p. 187
7. Ibid., p. 198
8. Ibid., p. 202
9. Ibid., p. 203

Appendix: The Battle of Gaza

1. Jonquière, IV, p. 211
2. Ibid., p. 212
3. Ibid., pp. 215, 216
4. Ibid., p. 217
5. Ibid., p. 220
6. Ibid., p. 221
7. Miot, pp. 130, 131
8. Jonquière, IV, p. 228
9. Ibid., p. 236
10. Ibid., p. 237

Appendix: The Capture of Jaffa

1. Jonquière, IV, p. 242
2. Ibid., p. 249
3. Ibid., p. 250
4. Ibid., p. 250
5. Ibid., pp. 250, 251
6. Ibid., p. 252
7. Ibid., p. 253
8. Ibid., p. 262
9. Ibid., p. 264
10. Ibid., p. 284

Appendix: The Massacre of the Prisoners

1. *Correspondance de Napoleon Ier*, Nos 4019, 4021, 4024, quoted in Jonquière, IV, p. 267
2. Jonquière, IV, p. 267
3. Another version was published in Napoleon's *Les Campagnes d'Egypte et de Syrie*, II, p. 49
4. Jonquière, IV, pp. 269, 270
5. Ibid., pp. 271, 272.
6. Ibid., pp. 275, 276

Appendix: The Battle of Kakoon and the Capture of Haifa

1. Jonquière, IV, p. 277
2. Ibid., pp. 281, 282
3. Ibid., pp. 292, 293

Appendix: The Siege of Acre: The Early Stage

1. Jonquière, IV, p. 306
2. Ibid., p. 307
3. Ibid., p. 315
4. Ibid., pp. 319, 320
5. Ibid., p. 329
6. Ibid., pp. 369, 370
7. Ibid., p. 371
8. Ibid., p. 391

Appendix: French Rule in Galilee

1. Jonquière, IV, p. 313
2. Ibid., pp. 313, 314
3. Ibid., p. 314
4. Ibid., p. 324
5. Ibid., p. 328
6. Berthier, p. 71, quoted in Jonquière, IV, p. 355
7. Jonquière, IV, p. 356
8. Ibid., p. 364

Appendix: Battle of Mount Tabor

1. Jonquière, IV, p. 425
2. Ibid., p. 425
3. Ibid., pp. 426–8
4. Ibid., pp. 488, 489
5. Ibid., p. 484

Appendix: The Siege of Acre: High Hopes and Ultimate Failure

1. Jonquière, IV, pp. 429, 430
2. Ibid., p. 434
3. Ibid., pp. 439, 440
4. Ibid., p. 440
5. Ibid., p. 441
6. Ibid., p. 442
7. Ibid., p. 417
8. Ibid., p. 482
9. Desgenettes, I, p. 86

Appendix: The Retreat to Jaffa

1. Jonquière, IV, pp. 540, 541
2. Ibid., p. 515
3. Ibid., p. 516
4. Ibid., p. 525
5. Ibid., p. 535
6. Ibid., p. 537
7. Ibid., p. 549
8. Ibid., p. 551
9. Millet, p. 126
10. Jonquière, IV, p. 555
11. Sargy, p. 293

Appendix: Jaffa and the Plague

1. Jonquière, IV, p. 559
2. Ibid., pp. 559, 560
3. Berthier, quoted in Desgenettes, I, p. 91
4. J. Derogy and H. Carmel, *Bonaparte en Terre Sainte* (Paris, 1992) p. 442

Appendix: The Retreat to Egypt

1. Jonquière, IV, pp. 560, 561
2. Ibid., p. 561

BIBLIOGRAPHY

Sources

Anon, *Journal d'un Dragon d'Egypte (14e Dragons): Notes recuillies par le Ct M.* (Paris, 1899)

Anon, *The Siege of Acre, or Descriptive Collections relative to the Late Scene of Contests in Syria* (London, 1801) (including letters by Sir Sidney Smith)

Anon, *Les Français en Egypte, ou Souvenirs des Campagnes d'Egypte et de Syrie par un Officier de l'expédition (Recueillis par J.J.E. Roy)* (Tours, 1868)

Beauchamp, *Mémoires secrètes et inéditées pour servis à l'histoire contemporaine* (Paris, 1825)

Beauharnais, Eugène de, *Mémoires et Correspondance Politique et Militaire*, I (A. du Casse, ed.) (Paris, 1858)

Berthier, Louis-Alexandre, *Relation des campagnes du général Bonaparte en Egypte et Syrie* (Paris, an VIII/1800)

Bernoyer, François, *Avec Bonaparte en Egypte et en Syrie 1798–1800* (Christian Tortel, ed.), (Abbeville, 1976)

Bertrand, Henri-Gratien, *Cahiers de Sainte-Hélène*, 3 vols, (Paul Fleuriot de Langle, ed.), (Paris, 1949–59)

Bourienne, Louis-Antoine Fauvelet de, *Memoirs of Napoleon Bonaparte* Vol. I (London, 1836)

Burckhardt, John Lewis, *Travels in Syria and the Holy Land* (London, 1822)

Clarke, E.D., *Travels in Various Countries of Europe, Asia and Africa*, Vols IV, V (London, 1817)

Desgenettes, R., *Histoire Médicale de l'Armée d'Orient* (Paris, 1835)

Delesalle, Augustin, *Cent Heures d'Agonie, ou Relations des Aventures d'A. D. . . . fait Prisonnier par les Arabes en Syrie* (Paris, an IX/1801)

Doguereau, Jean-Pierre, 'Journal de l'Expédition d'Egypte', in C. de la Jonquière (ed.), *L'Expédition en Egypte 1798–1801*, Vol. IV (Paris, 1904)

François, C., *Journal du Capitaine F., dit le Dromedaire d'Egypte* (Paris, 1903)

Galli, H. *Journal d'un Officier de l'Armèe d'Egypte* (Paris, 1883)

Jabarti, 'Abd al-Rahman al, *Journal d'un Notable du Caire durant l'Expédition Française, 1798–1801* (Jean Tulard, ed.) (Paris, 1979)

Jonquière, C. de la, *L'Expédition en Egypte 1798–1801*, 5 vols (Paris, 1899–1907)

Larrey, Dominique-Jean, *Mémoires de Chirurgie Militaire et Campagnes*, 4 vols (Paris, 1812–17)

La Vallette, Antoine Marie-Chamans, Comte, *Mémoires et Souvenirs* (Paris, 1905)

Malus, Etienne-Louis, *L'Agenda de Malus* (Paris, 1892)

Mangerel, Maxime *Le Capitaine Gerbaud* (Paris, 1910)

Martin, P.D., *Histoire de l'Expédition Française en Egypte*, 2 vols (Paris, 1815)

Millet, P.-J.-S., *Le Chasseur P.M.: Souvenirs de la Campagne d'Egypte, 1798–1801*, (Paris, 1903)

Miot, J. *Mémoires pour Servis à l'Histoire des Expéditions en Egypte et en Syrie* (Paris, 1804; Paris, 1814)

Nahman of Breslau, Rabbi, 'Masa'ot', in A. Ya'ari, *Masa'ot Eretz Jisrael* (Hebrew) (Tel Aviv, 1946)

Napoleon I, *Correspondance de Napoleon Ier*, 32 vols (Paris 1858–70)

Napoleon I, *Correspondance Inéditée, Officielle et Confidentielle de Napoleon Bonaparte*, Vols V–VII (Paris, 1819–20)

Napoleon, *Der Ägyptisch–Syrische Feldzug*, Vol. II (R. Conrad, ed.) (Stuttgart, 1911)

Nicolas Turc, *Chronique d'Egypte 1798–1804* (Gaston Wist, ed.) (Cairo, 1950)

Paultre, Karl, *Kurze Geographische Nachrichten von Syrien* (Weimar, 1804)

Raguse, Duc de, *Voyage en Hongarie, en Transylvanie . . . en Palestine et en Egypte*, 5 vols (Bruxelles, 1841)

Raguse, Duc de, *Mémoires*, Vols I, II (Paris, 1857)

Richardot, Charles, *Relation de la Campagne de Syrie, specialment des Sieges de Jaffa et de Saint Jean d'Acre* (Paris, 1859)

Richardot, Charles, *Nouveaux Mémoires sur l'Armée Française en Egypte et en Syrie* (Paris, 1848)

Roussilon, Vigo, 'Mémoires Militaires', in *Revue de Deux Mondes* (1 August 1890)

Sargey, Niello, *Mémoires sur l'Expédition d'Egypte* (Paris, n.d.)

Savary, A.-J.-M.-R., Duc de Rovigo *Mémoires*, 8 vols (Paris, 1828)

Smith, Sir Sidney, *Life and Correspondence*, 2 vols (John Barrow, ed.) (London, 1848)

Later Works

Alderson, Lieutenant Colonel R.C., *Notes on Acre and some of the Coast Defences of Syria* (Professional Papers of the Royal Engineers, Quarto Series VI, 1843)

Cesari, C., *Napoleone in Siria: La Presa di Giaffa nel 1799* (Roma, 1912)

Cohen, Amnon, *Palestine in the 18th Century: Patterns of Government and Administration* (Hebrew) (Jerusalem, 1973)

Dar, S., 'When were the Forests of the Country Destroyed?', in *Teva Va'aretz* 24/1 (Hebrew) (1982)

'D.A.S.', *Campagna del Gen. Bonaparte in Egitto, 1800* (n.d.)

Deblérain, Henri, *Histoire de la Nation Egyptienne*, Vol. V (Paris, 1931)

Gichon, Mordechai, 'The Conquest of Jaffa by Napoleon', in *Eretz-Israel: Historical, Archeological and Geographical Studies*, Vol. X (Hebrew) (Jerusalem, 1971)

Gichon, Mordechai, 'Napoleon in Western Galilee in the Spring of 1799', in *Western Galilee and the Coast of Galilee* (Hebrew) (Jerusalem, 1965)

Gichon, Mordechai, 'Napoleon Lost the Battle of Acre at El Arish', in *Et-Mol*, I (Hebrew) (April 1975)

Gichon, Mordechai, 'The Sands of El Arish and Mount Tabor', in *Ma'arechot* 160 (Hebrew) (July, 1964)

Gichon, Mordechai, 'Napoleon's Siege of Accho', in *Western Galilee and the Coast of Galilee* (Hebrew) (Jerusalem, 1965)

Gichon, Mordechai, 'Faulty Intelligence', *Military Review* (1962)

Gichon, Mordechai, 'Acre 28th March 1799: Napoleon's First Assault', in *The Army Quarterly* (October 1964)

Gelber, N.M., *Napoleon and Eretz Israel*, Dinaburg Volume (Hebrew) (Jerusalem, 1949)

Godechot, J., *Les Juifs et la Révolution Française* (Paris, 1976)

Guedalla, Philip, *Napoleon and Palestine* (London, 1925)

Guitry, Commandant, *L'Armée de Bonaparte en Egypte* (Paris, 1897)

Herold, Christopher, *Bonaparte in Egypt* (London, 1962)

Kircheisen, Friedrich, *Napoleon im Lande der Pyramiden und seine Nachfolger* (Munich, 1918)

Klärer, N., *Leben und Thaten des Jean Baptist Kléber* (Dresden, 1900)

Kobler, F.: *Napoleon and the Jews* (Tel Aviv, 1975)

Mackesy, Piers, *British Victory in Egypt, 1801* (London and New York, 1995)

Mannā, Ādel, 'The Sijil as a source for the study of Palestine during the

Ottoman Period, with special reference to the French Invasion'. Paper read at Congress at Haifa University (December, 1979)

Nimr, Ihsanal, *Ta'arich Djabal Nablus wa al-Balka*, 4 vols (Arabic) (Nablus, 1975)

Schur, Nathan, 'Napoleon's battles in the Vicinity of Mount Tabor', in *Kardom* 20 (Hebrew) (Jerusalem, May 1982)

Schur, Nathan, *History of Safet* (Hebrew) (Tel Aviv, 1983)

Schur, Nathan, *Napoleon's Holy Land Campaign* (Hebrew) (Tel Aviv, 1984)

Schwarz, Joseph, *A Descriptive Geography and Brief Historical Sketch of Palestine* (Isaac Leeser, ed.) (Philadelphia, 1950)

Thiry, Baron Jean, *Bonaparte en Egypte* (Paris, 1973)

Toledano, Ya'aqov Moshe, 'Napoleon's Declaration and Letters of Rabbi Aharon Halevy from Jerusalem', *Luah Jerushlaim* (Hebrew) (1944)

Wachsman, S. and K. Raveh, 'Underwater Work carried out by the Israel Department of Antiquities' in *The International Journal of Nautical Archeology and Underwater Exploration*, 9/3 (1980)

Watson, Sir C.M., 'Bonaparte's Expedition to Palestine in 1799', in *Palestine Exploration Fund, Quarterly Statements* (London, January 1917)

Wilson, Sir Robert Thomas, *History of the British Expedition to Egypt* (London, 1803)

Ya'ari, Avraham, *Masa'ot Eretz Israel* (Hebrew) (Tel Aviv, 1946)

Ya'ari-Poleskin, *Napoleon Bonaparte ve'Eretz Jisrael* (Hebrew) (Tel Aviv, n.d.)

INDEX